MOTHER FOLLY

Cultural Memory
in
the
Present

Mieke Bal and Hent de Vries, Editors

MOTHER FOLLY

A Tale

Françoise Davoine

Translated by Judith G. Miller

STANFORD UNIVERSITY PRESS

STANFORD, CALIFORNIA

Stanford University Press
Stanford, California

Printed in the United States of America on acid-free, archival-quality paper

Library of Congress Cataloging-in-Publication Data

Davoine, Françoise, author.
 [Mère folle. English]
 Mother folly : a tale / Françoise Davoine ; translated by Judith G. Miller.
 pages cm — (Cultural memory in the present)
 "Originally published in French in 1998 under the title Mère folle."
 Includes bibliographical references.
 ISBN 978-0-8047-8277-7 (cloth : alk. paper) —
 ISBN 978-0-8047-8278-4 (pbk. : alk. paper)
 I. Miller, Judith Graves, translator. II. Title. III. Series: Cultural memory in the present.
 PQ2664.A9463M4713 2014
 843'.914—dc23
2014004713
 ISBN 978-0-8047-9223-3 (electronic)
 ISBN 978-0-8047-9224-0 (electronic with video clips)

Typeset by Bruce Lundquist in 11/13.5 Adobe Garamond

To Jeanne, Batiste, Émile, and Kaléa

Contents

x *Contents*

PART III: BIG HISTORY AND LITTLE HISTORY

Author's Note for the American Edition

Mother Folly was inspired by the seminar "Madness and Social Ties," which I have been teaching with Jean-Max Gaudillière for many years at the École des Hautes Études en Sciences Sociales in Paris, France.

At the end of the book the reader will find references to works consulted that enabled my research. I wish to thank here the participants of the seminar, staff at the psychiatric hospital, and my patients. I am very grateful to them all.

I also wish to thank heartfully: Mieke Bal, Cathy Caruth, Emily-Jane Cohen, Siri Hustvedt, Dyani Gaudillière, Jean-Max Gaudillière, Valérie Waldkerdine, and Judith Miller, my daring translator, who made Mother Folly's dream to discover the New World come true.

Françoise Davoine

Preface

Mieke Bal

Françoise Davoine, author of many books—some with her partner Jean-Max Gaudillière—is an inspired writer of what I call, after Freud, "theoretical fiction." In her primary incarnation, she is a French psychoanalyst specializing in the analytical treatment of traumatized people. Her work in this area is world-famous because the world keeps producing so much trauma that its treatment continues to be urgently needed. And Davoine's work in this area is impressively successful. This is especially remarkable if we consider Freud's own conviction that the trauma-generated psychosis—for reasons I will explain, I call it "madness"—cannot be analyzed. The key issue in this debate is the possibility of "psychotic" patients to perform the necessary transference.

Davoine's success is due to her empathic, respectful, and at the same time, down-to-earth approach, but also to her great theoretical mind. For she is not only an effective clinical psychoanalyst but also, as her many books and lectures demonstrate, a very strong theorist, both independent of any school and profoundly knowledgeable about many: Freud, Lacan, the British school, American approaches to psychoanalysis, and aboriginal modes of healing; as well as philosophy, history, classics, sociology, and historical and modern literature. She integrates the collective wisdom and knowledge of these varied sources and disciplines, to develop and articulate, neither eclectically nor with orthodoxy, her unique theory of the psychoanalytic treatment of the mad. Thanks to her open and equality-based approach she demonstrates that the mad are capable of transference after all.

But she is much more than a high-level scholar and clinical practitioner. Two more features are relevant here. Her ongoing seminar "Madness and Society" at the École de Hautes Études en Sciences Sociales in Paris, which she has been teaching for many years with Jean-Max Gaudillière, attracts a consistently large group of active participants, many also practicing in

Davoine's vein. Its popularity is due to the fact that, as a third element of her intellectual profile, she is also an extremely engaging teacher. This is partly related to the fact—a fourth of this author's traits—that she is also a born storyteller. Whether it is about "cases" or about events in her own life, about History or about small events, Davoine's stories are moving, as riveting and as suspenseful as a first-rate murder mystery. Murder is, incidentally, frequently part of her stories; she is deeply invested in understanding and responding to the way violence generates madness.

This book exhibits all four of these traits. What's more, all four are indispensable to achieving the book's ambitious goal, which is to articulate a theory that takes psychoanalysis out of its orthodoxies and makes it what it was always meant to be: a truly *social* science. And it does so by way of dialogic feeling: argumentation, saying, demonstration, showing, and affective engagement. The result is a book comparable to no other. At once an explanation of a theoretical thesis and a development of a great number of documented case studies, a gripping story and a picture book, a learned treatise and a humorous tale, this book can be read in different ways and for different ends. In my own experience, it bears many re-readings. One look at the opening page says it all: theoretical, narrative, humorous, tragic; the beginning grips readers, whatever their intellectual interests.

The story is positioned in time: "All Saints' Day was hovering." That makes "today," the present of the story, the Day of the Dead. And indeed, the author has just learned that one of her patients has died. This death sets the story as well as the first-person narrator's crisis in motion. The narrator immediately begins her self-interrogation: "Was I a monster? Just before leaving home, I'd almost killed a clumsy insect—mechanically, without feeling—on the simple pretext it had no business being in my house." Between the huge event of the death of a patient and the automatic gesture of killing—but only "almost"—an insect, Davoine establishes a similarity-in-difference that sets the tone for the entire book.

The encounter with that insect, not coincidentally that mythical *social* insect, a bee, opens a barrage of associations that lead in a variety of directions. We traverse psychoanalytic theory, sociology, personal reflection on the use or ab-use of professional behavior. We also go to classical Greek—for example, the meaning of "therapist" as "buddy," a social function that, since the AIDS crisis, has gained in visibility. And all this is broached in a tone that meanders between playful and serious, while the profound and pertinent thoughts that announce the theoretical thrust of the book are understandable, concrete, and affectively appealing for everyone. Erasmus' Folly is introduced—the source for the book's title—and the equality between the "I" and the bee prefigures the theoretical position of equality between patient and analyst that is the foundation of the theoretical and clinical approach to psychoanalysis. All this on the first page.

In this preface I can only touch upon a few elements of this rich book. Given my own intellectual and creative engagement with the book, which inspired me to make a film, I limit myself to its narrative and verbal images, hoping to show these are not simply frivolous. On the contrary, they are the building blocks of its complex but limpidly exposed intellectual, theoretical, and clinical point.

STORYBOOK

This intricate and integrative mode of writing makes it impossible to distinguish the many levels on which this book operates or, to use a more adequate term, performs. One of many possible summaries of the story goes like this. The narrator—let's call her Françoise, to distinguish her from Davoine the author—has just learned of the death by overdose of one of her psychotic patients. Discouraged, she enters a deep crisis. The story is the development of that crisis, although with Davoine's non-melodramatic mode of writing, this crisis is not an explicit topic as much as it is the motor of the narrative. She is tempted to abandon her job at the psychiatric hospital. While pondering this decision in the hospital's courtyard, she takes a book on the Middle Ages out of her bag.

Then, the enigmatic figure of Mother Folly appears—as if out of the book—as its embodied *interpretant*. And so the story begins to unfold. Mother Folly is depressed because the Fools do not obey her anymore. Their traditions have been destroyed. She sits down in silence, in melancholy. This depressed state turns Mother Folly into a patient of sorts. (In the film *A Long History of Madness* that Michelle Williams Gamaker and I made on the basis of this book, on which more below, this depression and its ending in political combat is shaped with a wink to iconography: she takes the pose of Dürer's famous engraving *Melencolia I*; when she recovers, she becomes, or performs, the Statue of Liberty.)

A discussion ensues from this encounter, in which a deadpan Françoise remains situated in the present without being astonished by the confrontation with another historical time, and responds as if discussing with colleagues or patients. Absolute equality is the basis of both narrative and intellectual persuasion. It is this ability to remain her professional self while engaging with other times and their discourses that is her primary strength, as a writer, as an analyst—and, as it happens, also as an actress.

Throughout the story an ontological uncertainty about madness reigns between *enactment, being,* and *being-perceived.* Since playing the fool is the Fool's profession, this quest takes a specifically theatrical form. Parallel to the confrontation between the psychoanalyst and her severely traumatized ("mad") patients, this encounter enacts a second confrontation with which the first is intertwined. This first encounter sets the contemporary world up against medieval fools, agents and performers of late-medieval political theater. That this is theater, and political to boot, is crucial for the serious function of the fools in the book. Most of the time, these two worlds mingle. That is a major point of the book, a philosophy of time interwoven with a philosophy of the permeability of "madness" and "sanity." This creates a risk of anarchy but also an opportunity to mitigate the frontier that casts the mad as a different species, outside of our social view. The ontological uncertainty of madness runs through the entire story and is, indeed, a major theoretical point the book makes. The intermediate spaces of the courtyard and the treatment room in the hospital, the corridors and the analyst's office, contribute narratively to these ambiguities.

The inextricable intertwinement of theoretical and narrative articulation becomes visible, and thus demonstrates the way the literary and scholarly modes of writing strengthen each other. The medium of space, performative as it is, shapes each appearance differently. In this way, the ontology of personhood embedded in the idea of madness is questioned. What is at stake in this playful enactment is the notion of the individual subject itself. And since the book proposes a theory of a *social* psychoanalysis, where the small histories of the patients converge with the tragedies of History, this questioning is in tune with the book's theoretical thrust.

In the case of the narrator, her boundaries—in time, space, and identity—melt down. The relevance of this undermining of individuality becomes clear when she becomes capable of identifying not only with her patients, in whose adventures she begins to participate, but also with her former self. The autobiographical slant of the narrative becomes multi-layered, and is not in the least hampered by the evidently fictional elements.

Two patients from the past stroll through Françoise's world when she least expects it, like specters. These are Sissi—Davoine's first failure of twenty years ago—and the timeless elfin Ariste (Aristaeus), who dies at the beginning only to resurface regularly throughout the book when she evokes his hovering presence as an "inspector" (or as Françoise's bruised super-ego), as a source of gossip, and as a memory. These two phantom patients constantly confront Françoise with the difficulty of her work and the danger, indeed likelihood, of failure. Ariste becomes Françoise's *specter*, in the combined philosophical and sociological-political sense Derrida has put forward; his death a sacrifice to earn insight into the importance of identification; a kind of gift.

The issue of transference is key to Davoine's theoretical disagreement with Freud, and her insistence that analysis can help the mad to heal. She converses with the historical scientist Schrödinger as if they had been long-term friends. The dialogic form, so appropriate for philosophizing, not only borrowed from Socrates but also from her own earlier book *Wittgenstein's Folly* (published in English in 2009), is eminently suitable for the staging of opinions and doubts, moments of hope and of despair, illusion and discouragement, reasoning and passion.

Françoise gains a capacity to practice immersion in the deliriums of her patients, in order to become a fraternal equal to them. Only through such an "extreme identification" (my term, not hers) will she be able to carve for them a space in between wherein the "catastrophic regions" already evoked on the opening page, and which generated their madness, can be confronted. Throughout the story, the narrator has been doing precisely that: becoming an equal to the "fools" and the "mad."

Nodding to the rules of classical tragedy, all this action is set in a single day. Between the trial and the Carnival, Françoise's day is not over. She goes on to treat Herlat, a homeless patient who turns up at her doorstep when she returns from the trial-like encounter with the Fools. After that, she pays an overdue visit to the grave of her former teacher, the sister of her father's Resistance friend, Monsieur Louis, as well as to that of the latter's "mad aunt" who also haunts Françoise's childhood memories. Temporal turbulence reigns in this book as strongly as spatial swirling.

Theoretical considerations, which initially occur only in the mind of the narrator, will be taken over and continued, alternately initiated, by Fools, colleagues, or patients. Case histories, sometimes elliptical but always both clear and based on actual session notes, provide these considerations with an empirical basis, while the patients becomes theorists or "buddies" of the theorist. The book thus produces *theory*: a theory of madness as bound up with historical catastrophe; of psychoanalysis as an emphatically social science and practice; of the individual subject as fatally but also, helpfully porous, inseparable from other subjects; of images and their capacity of speech; of speech as imaged and imaginative; of space as a medium that facilitates sociality. And last but not least, of theory itself as (the product of) a collective process.

Davoine's entire project is a battle against the individualism that keeps the Mad impermeable to psychoanalysis and cuts them off from society. *Mother Folly* depicts her own crisis and the voyage of discovery that leads to her insight. It is a kind of *Bildungsroman* or travel story; what the Spanish created in the tradition of the picaresque novel. Through the intensely engaging writing, the book persuades readers both intellectually and affectively. It is, as I indicated above, strongly performative.

It is widely known that the concept of performativity has been taken up in philosophy and cultural studies, primarily under the influence of Judith Butler. Butler emphasizes that it is not the exceptional speech act but routine, reiterated speech acts that determine who one is. Treating people consistently as "mad"—refusing to take them seriously, responding to their mad utterances with disbelief, instead of using the opportunity fiction provides in exemplary manner to ask "What if . . . ?"—actually contributes to madness. But the habits of reiteration are also open to (slow) change. Through inhabiting a routine, one can change it from within. Narrative is eminently suitable to shape such subtle and dynamic transformations. And reading a narrative can be an exciting process of getting to know alternative possibilities. There lies its social relevance; its performativity.

PICTURE BOOK

This performativity is also significant for images, including images that, according to our ontological distinctions, do not materially exist. Davoine's book is also strongly visual. This has had enormous consequences for me as a cultural theorist, critic, and filmmaker with a keen interest in visual culture.

When I first read this book, for "purely academic" reasons—at the time, I was writing a book on a video artist who stages war trauma—I was astounded by its visuality. While I was reading, images whirled through my head. I could never detach those images from the theory and the narrative. But they were images—as in dreams. At that time, my colleague Michelle Williams Gamaker and I were looking for inspiration for our first fiction film. Thus far, we had made social documentaries, and we felt compelled to turn a page and try our hand at fiction while maintaining our commitment to the social side of things. That it became this book—for all intents and purposes a rather academic book, after all—that formed the basis of our film was the last thing I would have expected. And yet, it was a perfect match. How this happened demonstrates the power of visuality in writing. One of *Mother Folly*'s strengths is that it is a picture book as much as a storybook: you *see* what you read. Not coincidentally, "seeing" is a long-standing metaphor for understanding. In addition to affect, perception contributes to knowledge, and the etymology of "theory" leads back to "seeing through." As one of the innumerable fringe benefits of reading this book, I learned more about how this seeing and/as knowing, and this understanding and/as affect, operate from it than from any of the academic word-image studies I have read.

First, an author wrote a book in which she described images that came out of her own readings. Second, my colleague Michelle and I read that book, and images—the same ones? different ones?—arose from our reading of Françoise's readings. Except for the image on this book's cover, a detail from Pieter Breughel the Elder's painting *Dulle Griet* (*Mad Meg*, 1562), which represent women driven mad by war, there were no images in the material sense involved in the book. The cover image gelled with the epigraph from Musil—"War is born, like crime, from the little incivilities that unthinking men enact every day"—also about war but on the micro level, the bee's level, so to speak, to form a word-image hypothesis: this book is about war, its madness, and the madness it generates, and we will see what that looks like; it is about the routine, the small things, from which war and subsequent madness emerge. Unthinkingly, every day.

The book itself contains no visual illustrations. Nor does it need them. For these written images were so strong that after seeing them with my mind's eye, I had to make them, not as or "after-images," although chronologically they came later, but as "inter-images" that were *interpretants* of the images evoked but not presented.

To explain how this book achieves its exceptional effectiveness as, among other things, a book of theory, I use the term *interpretant* in the sense in which American philosopher Charles Sanders Peirce theorized the sign: thus images can be signs even if they are not materially extant. Peirce begins his definition of the sign with a perceptible object. The question posed by this object—"What does it mean?"—cannot be answered by revealing something inherent in the object. Instead, the cultural group in which the object circulates works the meaning out in a practice that yields a second, further-developed object. That second object, or sign, is the *interpretant*, a new sign developed on the basis of, and evoked by, the attempt to understand the first sign. In this way, interpretation is both ongoing and social.

Objects, hence also images, are active participants in the performance of analysis in that they enable reflection and speculation; they can contradict projections and wrong-headed interpretations (if the analyst lets them), and thus constitute a theoretical object with philosophical relevance, whether materially embodied or not. Reflecting "from within," in my case as filmmaker, on how these processes work is itself an activity steeped in a larger cultural context.

A good example of this interpretive process that allows collective theorizing to happen is the figure who gives this book its title. The figure of Folly emerges from a historical tradition, but traditions are never "pure" and homogeneous. Ours has at least three genealogies.

1. She is the leader of the late-medieval political theater the French call *sotties*, an anachronistic interpretation of which appears in the book. The story is actually structured quite precisely like a *sottie*. That theater frequently took the form of a mock trial, in which political abuse was exposed and tyrants undressed at the end, so that their true colors, the yellow and green of folly, became visible. This figure becomes the title character of the book; readers see her throughout.

2. She is inspired, secondly, by the speaker of Desiderius Erasmus' *In Praise of Folly*, a text in which the personification of Folly speaks in the first person, as announced in Erasmus' text: "An oration, of feigned matter, spoken by Folly in her own person." This aspect of the figure is already mentioned on the book's opening page. Readers hear this voice throughout.

3. When she has been driven mad by the violence of war, the figure shows up as Brueghel's Dulle Griet/Mad Meg. This incarnation of the figure is on the cover of the French edition of the book. The theme of war this Brueghel figure embodies is insidiously present across the entire book.

Between words and images, the formation of *interpretants* can be seen as a version of intertextuality. The invocation of Erasmus' Folly thus brings in more than the citation alone. We are sensitized to the importance of her voice and address, by words like these, again from the beginning of Erasmus' text:

> But if you ask me why I appear before you in this strange dress, be pleased to lend me your ears, and I'll tell you; not those ears, I mean, you carry to church, but abroad with you, such as you are wont to prick up to jugglers, fools, and buffoons.*

Like Davoine, Erasmus masterfully introduces the main issues with his opening words. Contrasting "church" with going "abroad," meaning the opening of oneself up to the unknown, the strange, the mad, is the most productive way of learning from Folly. Incidentally, it is also about hearing, address, and listening as the essence of sociality. This suits the audiovisual medium of video perfectly.

Following the book, not to the letter (church) but to the spirit (abroad), our film, *A Long History of Madness* (or in French, *Histoires de fous*), stages a praise of Folly through a praise of anachronism. The two, it appears, go together in their attempts to break through the boundaries of a narrow, and constantly narrowed, genealogical, evolutionist "reason," and instead appeal to openness, to what grammar calls the "second person," while searching for wisdom and knowledge in unorthodox ways. Many of the choices made for an audio-visualization of a book, especially a theoretical one, are necessarily "deviations" or "betrayals." But from making this film, we learned what really matters in *Mother Folly*, namely, not to be literal with regard to loyalty (church) but to be bold and inventive (abroad), like this extraordinary book itself.

From conception, to script, to actual filming and editing, we made *Histoire de fous* (A Long History of Madness) in close collaboration with the author. The images she "saw," or had in mind, when she wrote her book are inevitably very different from the ones that ended up in the film. There are several layers of interpretation and imagination between the one and the other. This complexity is compounded by the fact that the author plays herself. But only *after* the images had circulated, and we had transformed them, did they come back to the author—from the outside, so to speak—who, in playing her role, transformed them again. This is why the film images can only be "*inter*-images," with several temporal and visual layers separating the "original" from the images in the film. This process of collective work has a dynamic that fits the theory Davoine puts forth here.

* Desiderius Erasmus, *The Praise of Folly*, trans. John Wilson (Rockville, MD: Arc Manor, 2008), 9–10.

A SENSE OF AN ENDING

All this is also in line with a specific conception of the fundamental inter-temporality of images, which makes "ending" impossible. Even a material painting has once existed in the artist's mind, before it was realized on canvas as something quite different. And that material painting subsequently keeps changing in each act of viewing projected upon it, with the time, place, and social circumstance of its subsequent "life" as a work of art. To that, there can be no ending.

For an image, in this sense, will always be in the process of "becoming." The mad people Davoine calls upon in this book know this. They deploy forms that are never definitive but always coherent with the compulsion to *show what cannot be said*—to make visible what the silence imposed on them—denial, forgetting, taboo—has made inexpressible. But in their wisdom, the mad know this silence cannot "disappear it"—to render this verb active-objective and release it from its more usual fatalism. They make images that, unendingly, *move*; this was yet another reason why this book lent itself to a moving-image medium.

Both Davoine as author and Françoise as character have learned this survival of the past from their mad companions, to whom she/they serve(s) as *therapôn*, buddy, dialogic double—and vice versa. To show is ultimately the mission of the book, and thus the mission the book assigns to the film: to show, audiovisually, the transformable realities in which the past can recuperate its place—that place it had refused to give up anyway. For example, in the film, when Sissi, Françoise's first patient who interrupted her treatment, appears and behaves regally, this is not simply a mad arrogation of movie-star allure inspired by her namesake made glamorous by Romy Schneider in *Mayerling*. Instead, she reclaims the dignity that had been taken from her. Visualizing this self-dignification by means of stylish costumes and hairdo was our way of enabling this allegedly mad person to become a source of unexpected wisdom to which her elegance and beauty constituted a form of access, while still showing her wounds in the form of facial expression and mode of speaking. Thus the character and her inter-locutor, the analyst, become each other's doubles, a doubling that in turn enabled a restoration of the broken social connection. This then is healing as becoming whole again. It requires a reversal of time, so that the past can participate in the present. The sense of an ending, as a result, consists not of an end but of a change in feeling; a lightness of being against the heaviness of the social rejection that preceded.

Each new phase of such becoming-lighter is informed by a later moment that retrospectively glosses an earlier one. That becoming, and the mad reversal of time that makes it possible, also holds for the collective work of author and subjects, filmmakers and actors—the work consisting of multiple images, the body of images called "*Mère folle*," inflected by what "my work," as a reader, filmmaker, and critic of the resulting images, adds to and changes in that corpus on the basis of what was already there but needed showing. Obviously, this book with its many allusions and quotations, its staged encounters between antiquity, the Middle Ages, the twentieth century, and a dozen disciplines, poses a great challenge for translation. Judith G. Miller did a masterful job, turning its literary qualities into genuine American literature, just as visual as the original.

Showing is also what scholarly writing and fiction have in common. I have mentioned that Davoine's book hovers between fiction and theory. I consider it a "theoretical fiction," the term Freud uses frequently, for example, to explain the genre of *Totem and Taboo*, his 1913 story of the primitive band of revolting sons killing and eating the tyrannical father. Sometimes, Freud's story intimates, it takes fiction or other forms of imaginative thought to understand something for which reason is too simple. Like Freud, Davoine has theoretical points to make and uses speculation and fiction to develop, articulate, and make them. But unlike Freud's primary tool of *plot*, Davoine's points are primarily made through *images*. The plot itself serves rather to *frame* the images. In this way, looking back at my first reading of it, it seems to me that the book already harbored a film; indeed, asked for one.

Ending this preface, then, is the hardest part, because there is no ending. Davoine does not like to use the word "cure," and even less "cured," to denote a finite state. To do so would entail belief in a strong boundary between "mad" and "sane" people. She does not believe in such a boundary. On the contrary, it is the facile but false assumption of such a distinction that continues to isolate the mad. By refusing to acknowledge the responsibility of society—a society that condones rape, abuse, and war—for the continuous generation of trauma and its aftermath, "we" the collective that stigmatizes madness make it impossible for the mad to be, and feel, acknowledged as "one of us." Their stories must be believed, even if distorted by the thick layers of pastness that constitute their madness, confusing generations and subjects. We must co-inhabit their "catastrophe zones" as Davoine calls them, open them up for cohabitation and also for exit. If there is an end to madness, it is not as cured but as socially integrated. "Healing," rather, is what can take place. No end but a partial transformation.

In this preface, as in all publications about this book and its cinematic partner that I have written thus far, I have consistently spoken of "madness" and "the mad." This is due to another refusal of boundaries in Davoine's conception. A great impulse of the book is a polemic against pharmaceutical treatments, which tend to be based on the wisdom of the widely consulted American *Diagnostic and Statistical Manual of Mental Disorders*, currently in its fifth edition. On the basis of its classifications, patients are frequently diagnosed, which boxes them in into a specific kind of illness. This diagnosis comes with a prognosis, which is in turn pursued by means of pharmaceutical medication. In protest against this "fixating" mode of dealing with mental disorders, and heeding the preferences of patients themselves, we prefer to use the ludicrous but nicely vague and ambiguous term "madness" to anything that reeks of classification. Out of the box, as they say.

Moreover, in English, as the title of this book indicates, there was a choice to make. The French "*folle*" covers both madness and folly. English does not allow this ambiguity. Too bad; I'd have liked the sense of "angry" in "mad" to remain present. The choice of "folly," which resonates with Erasmus' text but also with the tradition of the *sottie* and such festive variations as Carnival, wrenches the word and the event, the people and the tradition, out of any classificatory isolation, and makes the turbulence Davoine has staged the subject of the book. In that turbulence, the reader is called upon to participate. He or she is asked to listen, and instead of questioning, to go with the flow towards an adventure that makes the best of what "social" means: the tendency of groups and persons to develop links and live in communities and to form transient but vital groups, living together in becoming, in cheerful not fearful difference.

MOTHER FOLLY

PART I

BUFFOONERY OR POLITICAL THEATRE

1

The Entrance

APICULTURE

All Saints' Day was hovering.

And here's the conundrum I faced. Like every Monday for the last twenty years I found myself reluctantly driving to the psychiatric hospital where I worked. Yet I would always leave wanting to return again the following week. And that day, while my car waited in front of the iron gates, I was less inclined than ever to be carried inside. I'd just learned that one of my patients had died.

Was I a monster? Just before leaving home, I'd almost killed a clumsy insect—mechanically, without feeling—on the simple pretext it had no business being in my house. Looking closer, I saw a bee, who managed to get back to her feet after having messed up her landing and tumbled about. She was unable to fly away and she didn't touch the jellied biscuit she'd targeted. She just let me watch. I thought I could read in the prisms of her eyes: "What's the use?"

What's the use of these comings and goings required by the queen, these countless flying hours, these ceaseless transferences, especially in the blooming months when a worker's life won't last more than six weeks? And on this autumn day, what's the use of this completely unseasonal morning outing?

I had no idea how to answer and, in the same tone, upped the ante: "What's the use of my work as an analyst in a psychiatric hospital? Why should I work in a clinic; who's forcing me to do it? Who can explain the wasps' nest I've been plunging into for nearly twenty years without anyone making me do so? I go there of my own free will. Did *she* know why? Let me tell you what I really think: They are right, those doctors with their shock treatments and tranquillizers. Psychoanalysis has lost its edge. It takes too much time, leaves itself open to too many questions, ends in brick walls, exhausting transferences, lame results, without locating the slightest nectar to nourish the queen.

Maybe, indeed, folly *is* our queen, and analysts and patients her worker bees and knights errant. This is Erasmus's Folly, the one who speaks like a woman: 'I know no one who knows me better than myself.' The words of a sovereign, but what kind of knowing are we talking about?"

The insect shot me a cross-eyed glance. What's the use of knowing oneself, she must have thought, when there are so many collective problems? Psychoanalysis is just excessive individualism.

I took that prejudice to task: "That's a completely unfounded rumor! Folly tries to create a social bond in order to escape winter's hibernation. What looks like a session with a shrink reveals a concentrated and busy society. There's no need to number in the thousands like you! Our work goes so much farther than the limits of the self that it exposes society's fissures. I paid the price to learn this through many sessions of crazy-making transference. The analyst often finds herself taking the place of a monster or a tyrant, or becoming the cause of horrors going back farther than her own birth: the First World War, the Second World War, the Hundred Years War. Are you surprised by all this? I bet like lots of others you don't realize how folly shows us the zones of social catastrophe. Yesterday, today, tomorrow, it's all the same to folly. Time gets confused, it stops, even reverses itself. . . . But what could you know about folly's time or ours," I whispered, "You're just a bee . . ."

To conclude, I wanted to take her down a notch. Missing its landing, my lecture flew off on its own wings: "You pride yourself on being a social insect, so be it. But in the matter of sociology, folly also has a lot to say. For example, to survive in case of danger she becomes a plural body, sometimes even becoming a thing. If you want to see what I mean, go visit those people who persist in speaking to patients in the obscurity of their own institutions. Some of them will remain objective, as if they personified science. Others will tell you that once back home, they find themselves exhausted and don't know who they are. They've paid with their person in building and rebuilding the frame of each session, in defending it from outside attacks, in reaping the harvest of the unconscious, in inventing language games when the unconscious grows mute, and especially in finding dream food for subjects undergoing birth."

The bee raised her eyes to Heaven.

"You think I'm idealizing the profession and you're right. As is true of the hive's darkness, the secrets of analysis don't really eliminate pillaging hatreds, deadly rivalries, massacres of colleagues or suicide attacks against those who relentlessly hunt honey. But year after year, as I've said, all those hours spent talking culminate in a new social bond. At least in theory . . . because, today, you see, I'm not sure I believe anymore . . ."

I wanted to share my doubts with her. But as she was acting like a dumb animal, I had to explain: "The social bond has to be stitched back together when it gets torn on society's death zones. Folly entreats her agents to fix things up or to take off in a swarm. A lot of people get lost in the effort. They wander without rhyme or reason and end up being hospitalized. Sometimes an analyst travels with them, moving between dream and reality. And believe me, more than one person has recovered because they encountered someone to talk to in the midst of their hell."

The bee looked incredulous; she didn't like the word hell: wasn't her society a model of harmony and democracy, with a monarch whom Diogenes praised as needing no arms to rule?

"Your honeyed words are pure propaganda," I grumbled. "Your queen has a stinger and she uses it. Of course it's true she saves it for running through her rivals during a putsch. Drop the official line and let's face facts: for example, the Varroa epidemic that threatened to exterminate every last one of you in every corner of Europe, the civil wars, the summary executions of so-called useless males during the slow period before autumn. What do you do then about the Name of the Father? And what if your queen, who guarantees your survival and the language that unites you, disappears by accident? It's a calamity, isn't it? Doesn't the orphaned hive turn into a kind of hell, left to chance and certain death?"

WAR VETS

"Institutionalized people know best about zones of catastrophe, whose importance can impact not just a beehive, but also generations of human beings, their homelands, their jobs, and the way they speak. Thrown by necessity or by chance into those zones, regions where no one wants to go, such people try to survive by living negatively, offering as little as possible of themselves to the devastation threatening them. But, inexplicably, even if shut up and gagged, they can't stop themselves from showing what shouldn't be shown and putting their fingers on what shouldn't be touched. Just like yesterday's Royal Fool, they're the Jesters of contemporary society.

You don't know a catastrophe zone? Ask your Slovenian friends, whose runways were real works of art. Are you trying to tell me war didn't drive them crazy? I bet you some of them are inventing a language right now to capture their experience. Unless their poets have all disappeared . . . in which case nobody, not even History, will believe them.

Sometimes the land of death has the last word. I didn't know what to say to hold on to that patient who just died. He wasn't Slovenian, but from Lorraine, where in the past a huge number of ordinary people from his own family died a violent death and where generations after them also died violently. He told me his grandparents and all their grandchildren were deported during the First World War. Some of them never returned from the concentration camp. It was apparently called 'Holtzminden.'

You say, 'delusional'? As you see, he probably had his wars mixed up. But what does any of it matter now? It's all in the past, disappeared, effaced, and he's just a disappeared person from the hospital, at one with what he used to call his nothingness."

The unmoving bee was paying attention.

"I can't tell you much more than that. Since public welfare is measured by statistics, nobody cares about the so-called handful of people deported in 1914. In terms of the millions killed in the trenches, they're insignificant.

You want me to stop these old vets' tales? Don't twist the stinger in the wound. It's all my fault, I know. I didn't figure out how to play my role in the theatre I called our sessions. I sat in my comfortable chair and watched history go by as though it had nothing to do with me. I know what you're thinking. I should have jumped on the stage and given the reply. I shouldn't have cared about historical truth. I didn't know the right gestures to save him. . . . And what gestures might those be?"

THE SHIP OF FOOLS

"You should go ask that question of somebody who really knows. Fly to Basel, to the city of Erasmus, Paracelsus, and Sebastian Brandt, the author of *The Ship of Fools*. It's best to go during Carnival. Go see the psychoanalyst Gaetano Benedetti. He knows how to decrypt the hermetic language of madness, a little like Von Frisch did in order to understand your bee's dance. I don't know how your Nobel Prize winner proceeded. But Benedetti's method is to join the dancing in order to be with the patient in the catastrophe zone he haunts.

He dares speak to him about his own musings and even his dreams, betting they will register and resonate secretly with the traces of negative existence that absorb the patient. Of course the patient can't express this. Benedetti trusts the movements that pull him into the music of this particular ship of fools. It's a moment when the therapeutic unconscious can resonate with the patient's, like a double. I'm afraid I'm incapable of such a manoeuver."

The bee grew impatient; I could guess her objections.

"There's no witchcraft in any of this. When you return to the hive, the other bees have to decode your gestures so your dance doesn't appear to be a useless, even exasperating and dangerous spectacle, something they want to stop as soon as it starts. Preferably by a blow to the head, which you would have received a few minutes ago if I hadn't stopped myself in time.

Well, if no one listens and engages with it, madness pushes you to the limits; it takes a shot of some kind of 'trankillizer' to calm you down. Benedetti wants the analyst to become the pole of otherness that no one else dares inhabit. He resists panicking when he's hit by it and he can articulate his position in the danger zone. From there, much like the way your eggs hatch, analysis can offer the promise of a new bond."

I thought I heard my agitated companion buzz, "Analyst!" while she obstinately repeated her figure eights on the table. I tried to interpret what was happening: "Is this Möbius' strip, Lorenz's attractor? Don't get so excited; what you're doing is all Greek to me. You don't like the word 'analyst'? OK. So what about *annaliste*? A specialist of all those facts wiped out of the annals of history? Or what about *histrion*—the medieval name for minstrels who performed history through gestures?"

The bee continued her dance without comment.

"And what about 'therapist'? From *therapon* or 'caretaker' in the ancient Greek of your ancestors, the bees of Mount Hymettos; a ritual double like Patroclus for Achilles, Pylades for Orestes, August, the red-nosed clown, for the white one. . . . But I—I didn't even know how to be Sancho Panza for my patient."

Still turning and twisting, my therapist wasn't listening to me. Maybe she was trying to show me the path to melliferous flowers? I was in great need. All this talking was making me dizzy. Dire straits, indeed.

"It's worthless to talk, forget everything I said. This morning I believe in nothing. What's the use? The man who died was called Aristaeus—you know, like the god of beekeepers and cheese-makers. Did I kill him? Just who killed him?"

The bee's only response was to take off towards the heavens. Maybe she was returning to the neighboring hives in the apiary of the Luxembourg Garden. For over a century, her sisters had been teaching the ageless art of apiculture to countless veiled men and women.

FIRST ASYLUM

A hoary monk officiated at the school. He interpreted what was happening, swinging a smoker instead of a censer, to smoke out the bees. As soon as springtime came round, I'd stop by to watch his cabalistic gestures, mesmerized by the echoes of my youth. I could see myself dressed like a fencer, wire mask over my face, armed with only a smoker that I kept brandishing next to my grandfather, who was gathering the honey combs barehanded. My memory told me he was barefaced as well, going to battle with only the smoke from his pipe to keep a riot from happening.

One day my grandfather disappeared. Maybe he was hiding behind the veils in an enclosure, off limits to the public? It was a mystery! So I went on my way, always looking for signs of him: the monk's bushy beard resembling the beard of the Head Doctor who'd welcomed me to his hospital when I'd just begun practicing. That was in the north of France, some twenty years ago. The clues stopped there.

"You're getting warm," I should have told myself when I let myself be tickled by that psychiatrist's beard. (And an analyst to boot!) What pushed me to want to work in his ward? The carelessness of youth, the fire and smoke of beginnings? Why did I insist and follow him here, when he decided to move closer to Paris?

In front of me the sinister gates were still closed. What was the guard doing? At least the first hospital had enticing cast-iron ones we could open ourselves. Twenty years already? What had made me want to enter this place come hell or high water? Even in those days, analysts were leaving hospitals in droves. I should have listened to their good advice. They told me that analysis was incompatible with restraint.

And Sissi, the patient I left behind when I changed hospitals, the one who thought she was Empress of Austria. Was she still institutionalized? My ears were ringing with the goodbye she chose to throw at me: "Shit on you, Davoine. You're stupid. You're a cretin. She's crazy! A nurse! A nurse! May Day!"

It was all too much. I'd had it. I swore I'd never again cross the threshold where Aristaeus had just died for good.

TORTURES

Last night the Head Doctor told me it was certainly an overdose. He announced over the phone that they'd found him outdoors in the early morning, face down, a few meters from the unit where he'd been demanding every day for the last ten years, in the name of God, his driver's license, registration card, and identity papers.

I hung up without saying a word. Among the staff, we'd soon be proclaiming in our quarters: "A hopeless psychotic." In the corridors, the patients would protest with fervor: "the best among us." Incapable of saying no, of refusing the slightest favor asked of him by his fellows in misfortune, Aristaeus had nonetheless managed to push back with all his might against several different therapies. Maybe it had something to do with his great soul; no one could match it.

Starting to deliver his eulogy in my head, I suddenly saw his face when he approached me for the first time in one of the corridors of the hospital: "They're torturing me, please do something, it's horrible, they're killing me little by little."

I took this at face value. Each week he talked to me of infinitesimal massacres, made apparent by the way he threw himself against doors, bracing himself to keep the torturers, predators, and poachers from entering.

I had asked him: "Who are these people? Where are they coming from? From outside or inside?"

"From outside and from inside, from outside inside, your question is idiotic."

This morning I saw too late he was demonstrating an invasion, the violation of a territory. And I'd taken myself out of that space. I thought he was the only one concerned. I didn't recognize his efforts not only to fight the monsters swarming in his hospital bed—all those snakes, rats, hornets—but also to show me a dangerous zone I didn't want to see. I should have understood by the dread in his eyes that he was trying to make me grasp the shape of a world starting to disappear, both for him and for me.

The resident who was following his case, keen on René Thom's theory of catastrophes, told me it was a "general catastrophe" from which we'd

probably all be effaced. And there would be no trace of us because the outside and the inside would no longer be differentiated. I hadn't understood
what he'd said nor gathered the slightest hint of how I could think about
it. All during this time, Aristaeus had kept saying: "Don't you see they're
trying to kill us?"

Who was this "us" he was talking about? "Of course not," I spat back
like a coward (and as an aside): "My work is to banish madness, not end
up its prey." Yet I was the prey of my own stupidity; I understood nothing
of his riddles.

He would say: "You're like all those totalitarians who think that ghosts
work for them." And then he'd hum: *Of the past let's make a clean slate.* . . .
And he'd ask me about what the slate was hiding.

Snakes, rats, hornets, and many other unnamable things squirmed there.
Was he hallucinating? Was it the unburied corpses of those people who had
disappeared in the deportations that haunted his imagination? I didn't dare
put myself there. Faced with my neutrality, he fell into the chasms of horror
I thought I'd neutralized. That's where my blindness led us.

Yet he seemed to get better and better. The disgusting beasts had given
way to a couple of caged birds placed in his room, meant to be a prelude
to opening his own cage. His leaving was right on the horizon, but always
out of grasp, like the horizon—not enough money, no lodging, no luck,
no family he could count on.

"My family doesn't give a damn." That's all anamnesis could get from
him. The only thing that came back like a ghost from time to time in
our conversation was the enigmatic Holtzminden. "A splendid resort for
mothers and especially grandmothers deported in 1914," he'd ironize again.

"And where is that?"

"Near Poland maybe . . ."

"We're not going to see the light at the end of the tunnel any time
soon," he told me one Monday, looking up the tunnel of my sleeve. He
couldn't find a trick card, a rabbit, a duck, the least little bit of magic that
would let him keep on playing. Mastering the game, he decided: "That's it.
I'll see you later, at the clinic, after I've been released for good."

I'd been had once again. Since then, he'd given me cursory hellos and
goodbyes when we passed each other. Except once, not so long ago, he'd
asked for a French literature textbook from the tenth grade, the last time
he'd been good at school. It covered the Middle Ages through the Sixteenth Century and featured a buffoon on the cover. I'd picked up the

book as soon as I could, but kept on forgetting to give it to him. Last Monday when I got home from the hospital, I'd put it in my bag so as not to forget. Too late.

SPRING WATERS

Aristaeus had kept his word. Hardly out of our world for good, he came back to see me last night in a dream. He was leading a cohort of buffoons. The jesters were all seated around a table, but I was on a low chair: I couldn't rise to their height. They wanted me to talk. To say what? That I'd killed him? I protested to the jury: why not accuse the isolation cell where he'd been recently locked up in his piss and shit after having raided, with a few rowdy and rougher others, a doctor's medicinal spirits? Should I be condemned for treason? For having collaborated out of exhaustion with the usual refrain: too late, too difficult, too crazy? For not having stayed by his side?

In my dream, he didn't listen to my whining and demanded his inheritance. A spring-fed plot he'd inherited somewhere up north at his father's death. Where was that? A mystery. Was it a mythical terrain, like Holtzminden? My disbelief was not lost on him: "Madmen are very convenient when it comes to inheritance. They don't count. I see you don't believe me. You're not worth much either."

How did he know? "You're really not worth much!" my grandmother used to say to keep me in my place. He added, as she did: "We were doing just fine all by ourselves; we had plenty of our own."

All his own had evaporated a long time ago. From giving up on his own, he'd even opened the cage with the one surviving bird in it. (What was the use of keeping it, if the other was gone?) Me, too, I'd allowed myself to stop being the other. So he'd followed the path of the bird, free, he said, to return to his forefathers' country, even if he knew that the morning's autumnal cold would carry his soul off to the land of eternal springs.

"Help me find my spring-fed plot," he insisted in my dream. "It's urgent."

I woke up with a start from this very telling dream. I couldn't question his demand. But how was I to find a land of springs?

INSIDE AND OUTSIDE

The electric open sesame of the gate finally did its job. My car slowly made its way towards the hospital. I recognized from a distance one of my ward's patients, as usual silent and bent over. His pathetic silhouette seemed to yearn towards an impossible freedom. He gestured for me to enter. Closer in, I knew I must stop commiserating. His usually pale and pope-like face swelled red from laughter. I wondered what this serious man found so funny: seeing me return to my psychotherapy work? I lost my bearings. I saw him outside and me inside. From outside the asylum, psychoanalysis and psychiatry look like a zoo, where we normal folks circle behind bars.

"Life rages out there," Sissi, the Empress, would say to me twenty years ago in my old hospital, pointing to the street with her imperious finger. "How can you live in it?" An avalanche of remorsefulness chased away that long-forgotten vision. By way of consoling myself, I attempted some theory. Wittgenstein exclaims in his *Notes on Private Experience,* "Inside and outside! It is as if now we have an insight of something which before we had only seen from the outside." I'd let myself be seduced again by an image of interiority that always trapped me. I'd imagined Sissi and then Aristaeus haunted by internal torturers of which the rest of us were mere projections. But they never stopped telling me there was always an outside on the inside, a public domain in the privacy of their family, and especially in our own rapport.

"It's the war that drove me crazy," Sissi would say without further details. "Don't you see we're at war?" Aristaeus would sing from *La Marseillaise,* as if they'd communicated with each other from hospital to hospital: *There's still blood watering the furrows.* It's now obvious to me that the furies, those goddesses of revenge, were screaming through them, demanding their tribute of human sacrifice to make up for ancient crimes. I'd been hoodwinked. Was Sissi, that great Empress, that great curser, even among us anymore? I needed to know right away.

Basta! Don't think about it anymore, walk towards the door of the ward. Stumbling along, I couldn't stop pleading my case before the court set up by my dream's jesters. OK, I was a monster, no doubt of that. But in my defense—and many nurses reported it—Aristaeus had often "thrown himself around like a bear, roared, climbed on the furniture, acted like an ape, and alarmed the night watch."

When I asked him about the weirdness of his behavior, he always answered that his monsters were political. It was his right to act the wild man, he'd say, another one of his enigmatic proclamations that left me hanging, like the bird in his cage.

IN BUFFOONERY ALL IS MADNESS

"For he was a right fool, ready to play and perform—farcical singing or rhetorical poetry; he burned to expose through any allegorical means." Where did that refrain come from? Maybe I'd seen it in the French book Aristaeus had asked for. In the section on the Renaissance, in the chapter entitled "Buffoonery or Political Theatre," I'd read that this particular literary genre had first appeared in the second half of the Fifteenth Century and reached its height in the Sixteenth. Its extraordinary success wasn't without connection to the chaos of the Hundred Years' War. Jesters were recruited from circles of intellectual protest and organized themselves in joyous fraternities throughout the north and center of France. There were the Enfants Sans Souci in Paris, the Infanterie Dijonnaise, and the Conards de Rouen. . . . They mounted and performed farcical sketches, and some of the authors are still known to us: Clément Marot or Pierre Gringoire, whom Hugo made famous in *The Hunchback of Notre Dame*. On the trestle tables set up in public squares, in the Basoche or Law schools or in the colleges of the Latin Quarter to which they belonged, they ended their pre-show come-ons with the phrase: "In buffoonery all is folly." They shielded the virulence of their satire beneath the immunity of the fool's cap.

All of a sudden I wanted to read huge bits of this book, hoping, I guess, to find Aristaeus there on his own turf, at the origins of the oral tradition, at the confluence of my own foolishness. So I sat down on a bench in the honor court, my feet on the lawn, facing a bed of purple and yellow chrysanthemums, and once more put off going to work. In the garden's center, a statue of Mercury pointed the way to the exit to a swooning Beauty. Nobody was around. A ray of autumn sun sheltered me. I opened my book.

2

The Honor Court

More *ingenium* than *fatum*

In those days, according to the book's introduction, when the long Middle Ages stretched into the Renaissance, people were eager to learn from madness: they thought of it more as a stroke of genius (from the Latin *ingenium* or "engine," "intelligence," "talent") than as fate or doom.

"Whore's son, heretical pox, you're being had by a bunch of hypocrites. Let me pass! I'm the King."

I raised my head to the screaming. Not far from where I sat, somewhat beyond the archway that led to the courtyard, I saw a young man threatening to beat his elder. I supposed that his father was bringing him back after a leave. The father wasn't putting up with any of this: "Take your stinking hands off my clothes, you crazy fool, or you won't like what happens to you."

The younger one bellowed again, even before the other touched him: "Help! See how this nasty piece of work hits me. I might as well be a punching ball."

Somewhat cowardly, I kept to myself, counting on some white-bloused nurse to come put a stop to the fight. Instead of the hoped-for help, I heard the same refrain as a few minutes ago: "For he was a right fool, that *dervé*, ready to play and perform—farcical singing or rhetorical poetry: he burned to expose through any allegorical means."

Those lyrics again. Where the devil did they come from and what did they mean?

Farcical singing? I searched in the book's glossary: a highly technical style of buffoonery, where a piling up of words is meant to produce a feeling of euphoria. And a *dervé*? The name for a fool in the language of Picardy, like the fool in Adam de la Halle's Thirteenth-Century *The Play of*

Folly and Foliage, a musical from Arras, a northern market town. It was inspired by the Feast of Fools, that time out of time, that feast for the feast-less, a re-establishing of the Realm of Childhood.

The mystery grew thicker. What if the fool were Aristaeus, returning from one of his usual escapades to that northern town where a supposed relative was meant to host him. (The relative always alerted the hospital.) Two nurses were regularly sent to fetch him back and each time he was more disoriented. To straighten himself out, he'd launch into a delirious pile-up of words resulting in the euphoria he tried to share with me. How could I not have attempted to transcribe his fantastic word games? I had nothing on him, not the least trace of our sessions, not a single word.

The refrain started up again, somewhere beyond the archway to where Mercury, the god of travelers, doctors, and thieves, was still pointing. Around the now calm younger man, I could make out a small group from which a ferocious woman stood out. She was a crazy one all right—huge, gangling, toothless, disheveled, and she stormed into the grassy corner where I'd taken shelter. I jumped. She stopped. Then deciding it was safe, she signaled the others to follow her. They parked themselves under the arch, on the threshold of the honor court. I wasn't feeling at all too well. Hunkering down on my bench, I pretended to lose myself in my book.

"You, over there . . ."

Raising my eyes, I saw her dead in front of me. She grabbed the book from my hands.

"You listen when Folly speaks to you!"

My God, she thought she was Erasmus's Folly, the one who pretends to speak like a woman, as if we women needed that foul-mouthed motor to speak in our place! Luckily, she wasn't expecting any praise but only a simple piece of information: "Is this the right place for folly?"

"You couldn't dream of a better place for fools than this one," I readily answered.

Without warning, she let out an enormous shout and headed in the other direction. I nearly fell off my bench. I was sure an armada of nurses would finally take her in hand. Is anybody there? Anybody at all? *Elck*? *Niemand*? "Do I need to yell it in Picard, in High German, in Flemish," I grumbled to myself, "while that other nutcase manages to rile up her troupe?"

"Come along, my fools, my buffoons, my jesters, come along! Winning fools, noisy fools, glorious fools, real fools, fools of fools, break it all down, explode this place, run faster than the wind."

I was getting ready to hide under my seat. But nothing happened. Lowering her arms, she sat down on the bench in front of me, her head in her hands. That pose seemed to move the others. Some of them crossed the invisible line that separated us. One fellow got up enough courage to come sit next to me. His clothes were torn; his face was worn. I asked him if he wanted to be hospitalized. He looked at me without understanding, leafed through the book that Folly had thrown on the ground, shook his head, shut it and opined: "Another book. To stuff the heads of children with pure nonsense and make their crazy mothers and idiot fathers obsess over grades. You like such things? I bet you're dying to write one."

"How could you guess?"

"So you're crazy?"

"No, not me, I mean, not here. Here is where I work, normally . . ."

"Working or not, I bet you're ready to make any sacrifice to be published. You're ready to add, change, eliminate, abandon, reshape, consult, keep your manuscript for nine years in a drawer; and you never think about lack of sleep, your passing youth, failing eyesight, bad health, lack of pleasure, as long as some mucky-muck who really doesn't give a damn approves your work. Even better, as long as someone envies you. Here's my diagnosis, you're suffering from an advanced case of Writers' Folly. You have the word of Erasmus. Check it out!"

"And just who do you think you are to speak to me like this?" I hurled back, impressed all the same. His features resembled more than just a little Holbein's portrait of the Prince of the Humanists. But he shattered my illusions: "Fool Number One, even crazier than you are! Come along now, all of you, so I can introduce you."

The others stepped forward. He counted on his fingers: Fool Number Two, Fool Number Three, Fool Number Four, and so on.

"Don't they have names?"

"What's the point? We're all fools, no need for any other identity. Just like the Binche Carnival in Belgium where all the men are 'Gilles,' just like Morgestraich Night in Basel, where all the men are 'Larva' or 'Ghost'— just like the old days in Rome when all the Christians called themselves Christ to provoke their persecutors at the Coliseum. Before they tried to put an end to us at the Basel Council of 1468, we were known as the children of the Feast of Fools, the Feast of the Innocents. . . . It's impossible to kill us off. If you go to Basel on Morgestraich Night, you'll see us there, haunting the city."

"So we're talking about an underground!"

"And also about what's on the ground, for instance in Ecclesiastes, which tells us that 'fools' numbers are infinite.'"

I pitied his melancholy: "You don't seem to be doing so well. Please don't worry; someone will be here soon. What about the others? Homeless like yourself?"

He stared at me, open-eyed. I tried to explain: "You know, living in the streets, living precariously . . ."

"Are you kidding? We'd love to be in the streets, on the squares, in the crossroads, but they threw us out."

"Who did that? The cops?"

"No! François I."

Stunned, I tried to act normal, discoursing on injustice, on the privilege of the rich and other things of that nature. He didn't listen; he was too busy persuading his friends to come forward.

OUTSIDE SENSE

"Are they shy?"

"No, they're pouting. Humiliated, get it?"

"Because of that harpy who's mistreating them?"

"You mean Mother Folly? You must be joking. She's just as sad as they are. Can't you see? And if someday you end up writing this story—and you won't be able to stop yourself from doing it—I ask you now to use the words 'outside sense' instead of 'non-sense.' Then people will see we're talking about what's on the outside instead of the inside."

"Thank you for this lesson in semantics. Here's something you should know yourself. Maybe it's not my business, but you shouldn't hang around. It's a lot worse inside. Everybody runs himself ragged trying to make sure all the institutionalized have a project, make some progress, but nobody really gives a damn."

"Maybe Nobody is so busy thinking about other things that Everybody is of no interest to him."

"What other things?"

"The end of the world, for example. Apocalypse is on everyone's mind at this point in the millennium."

"Probably, and everyone thinks about it too much. From the time people get up in the morning, it's what they chew on. Even the patients know this isn't any way to live!"

"'Patient,' what an awful word! 'Fool' is sweeter and kinder, or what about 'buffoon,' 'jester,' 'joker,' 'clown,' your choice! And don't think for a minute that a fool's life is easy. Take it from me. I know something about it! You have no idea how much rigor and disinterest you have to have in order to seek, attack, and expose a tyrant . . . and they are among us, all the same, without knowing that we know it."

"Don Quixote?" I presume.

"Jester, if you please."

"If I were to believe that book there, folly didn't have such a bad reputation in your days."

"Don't fool yourself! On that topic, the medical discourse was as closed-minded then as it is now: strictly somatic. The doctors were already checking out the brain to find the cause. Look at Bosch's painting in the Prado, *The Cure of Folly or The Stone Operation*. You'll see a doctor, wearing a funnel like a fool's cap, attempting to extract the stone of folly from a madman's brain, just like he'd extract one from a kidney."

"I beg your pardon! You can't say we haven't made progress. Today's medicine has found the gene for psychosis in human DNA. That's Science and it's not the same."

"I don't believe you. Medieval medicine was also ahead of its time, classifying humors according to colors: yellow for frenzy, black for depression, red for mania, white for catatonia. And it had its correctors, too: a knock on the head to calm the furious, a surgical cut to air out the brain, a tickle on the feet to cheer melancholia. Stop insisting you invented the wheel. Our researchers also believed exclusively that the brain caused the problem. Similia similibus curantur—their panacea for those who'd lost their memory was, like yours, to keep them from finding it."

"You're at the right place then. Come over to the clinic this afternoon. A young doctor just back from the States is going to talk to us about universal classifications that, of course, once associated with the right drug, work miracles. Bring your friends! I insist on it. There'll be plenty to drink and eat, all paid for by magic powders."

"I don't trust American savages."

"Not to diss you or anything, but aren't you acting a little paranoid?"

"Not just a little! If novels and theatre hadn't given us a home where nobody bothers to try to treat us, you wouldn't even know we existed. We'd be like the Huron Indians who've lost everything, even their language."

"So you're a literary fool?"

"What's wrong with your generation? Do you have to label everything? Literary or not, folly is the same thing. It's always a version of one story, with a few details changed: the knight enters the forest, the space of wonder, out of space and out of time. In other words, the space of folly. Out of sight of ordinary men, he loses sense of who he is, encounters beings from another world, acquires magical powers . . ."

"You make me laugh. What kind of power lies in madness? The power of powerlessness . . ."

"Very political, all the same, as overflowing and swelling as yeast. So much so that fools' emblems include the wild man with his club, fermenting cheese, and peas that make you fart . . ."

"You're starting to get gross!"

"Just like psychoanalysis we place the seat of thought in the ass not the head. Sorry to tell you we got there first. Instead of sticking the soul in the brain, as the Academy would have it, we put it in feet, hands, stomachs, and butts. . . . Take a look at the grotesques in illuminated manuscripts or around church capitals or portals, with bottoms, tummies, and backs for heads. They relocate the psyche from its noble perch to the most unmentionable living parts. Just ask any stand-up comic, like Raymond Devos, master of quip, who makes you laugh every time he taps his ass and you tap yours. . . . Go to the Basel Carnival where wild men make the guts of their drums speak . . ."

CLERMONT COLLEGE

"Did you say 'wild men'?" Aristaeus's favorite expression made me jump. My fool was too well informed about contemporary reality to have come from the past. I wanted to get to the bottom of this farce.

"So tell me, how did you get here?"

"An odyssey, it was. When we realized streets, squares, and crossroads were not an option, we looked for the Colleges of Harcourt and Navarre. That's where mock trials first saw the light of day. But we got lost in that neighborhood you insist on calling the Latin Quarter, where there's no Latin to speak of. We finally found Clermont College and entered with alacrity, but alas, the students don't have any time to laugh there—now that it's called the Louis Le Grand High School. Apparently they work all the time in the name of Science."

"And you're against it?"

"Not in the least. But we know you can't have Science without Foolishness. Together, they've conquered the world. I'm told elsewhere there's plenty of foolishness parading around calling itself science. Once upon a time, we even created a farce about it, *The Tale of Science and Tomfoolery*. It would have made a killing today. But instead of asking us to join them, the school's crazy mothers and idiot husbands pressured the administration to throw us out. Can you believe that: us, the true natives?! They wouldn't accept a word we said, and even argued in favor of continuing to ban Carnival.

One of the counselors stood up for us by proving our tradition is alive and kicking: students still ridicule their teachers. He even praised the therapeutic worth of such mockery, because, he said: 'This year we've paid too dear a human price to the gods of Science.' But no go. It was like preaching in the desert. So they sent us on our way to your place. Sure it's a blessing. We have a lot more space in the courtyard than we need. . . . Only you can never go home again and my companions have lost interest. They're sulking and stubbornly refusing to listen to Mother Folly's rallying cry. Since she can't commence the ritual, she lies around instead of ranting and raving. Just look at her! Abandoned, her traditions forgotten, she's apt to do something awful!"

RES PUBLICA

"I take it she never expected to find herself among the mad?"

"What do you know about it? You think you're so clever. You think you know everything. Well you don't get anything at all. Those inside are the same as us. They just don't have the caps and baubles that gave us invulnerability, so they're more easily wounded than we were . . ."

"You mean you were protected from all that?"

"Yes indeed. You can't count the number of edicts and laws that forbade our feasts, our farces, our campgrounds, and our choreography—century after century. Our sketches were even censured at the Saint Germain Fair a few years before the Revolution. But folly is such that the more you chase us away, the more we come back. Those who censor us are fools who don't know it. Instead of destroying us, they guarantee a permanent renaissance.

Let me tell you a little secret (an open one, of course): those people inside are simply in disguise, protecting themselves. They look like patients, but their pitiful state is really camouflage so they can throw off social masks, poke holes in inflated egos, undercut the hyper-morality that goes unquestioned.

In their honor, we showed up to support them. Today's *zeitgeist* is strangely like our own *Insecuritas*. You remember the late Middle Ages— plague, wars of religion, Turks at Vienna's door, Inquisition? Nowadays people have their throats cut; they get tied and quartered on subways, in public places. Children are sold in plain sight."

"What are you talking about! Don't you realize we've been a Republic for the last two centuries!"

A collective laugh greeted my indignation and the assembled fools sang out in unison: "Randy reformers love to visit the door / Of res publica that ageless whore / Up and down, down and up they go / Never tiring for all is show."

"As usual you strike from the gutter. Your song is foolish."

"It's a fool's song, all right," Number One rejoined before warming up with his companions. While stretching and bending, he held forth: "So you think the tortures inflicted today in the name of freedom are more brotherly than those of the Inquisition? And you have ethnographic proof that today's rapes cause less damage than four hundred years ago? And let's not talk about the werewolves that kill children in their own homes? Who really cares about any of this if it won't get someone elected?"

"Wait just a minute. What fools are you talking about, psychopaths or innocents?"

"Is he nice? Is he nasty?" the fools chanted, hopping off the ground.

The exercises made their cheeks rosy, perked up the green and yellow of their worn-out costumes. They took their jesters' scepters out of their pockets, jingled their bells, put their fools' caps on, and cried out, while doing cartwheels, summersaults, and pirouettes: "Let's play, joke, jump, laugh, clown, and spin around."

"They're parodying a funeral," Number One told me.

That set the tone and he grabbed my book to point to *The Wake of Triboulet,* the story of the most famous of their lot, before he too, like Aristaeus, died of an overdose: *Oh he's lost and dead. Did booze turn his head*? Carried along by the melody, I too hummed as though I knew what was happening: *La donna è mobile.* "And you know that Rigoletto is really Triboulet, the king's buffoon in Hugo's play about François I."

They all started to run away, screaming like banshees. It wasn't what I'd intended. Number One was in stitches.

"You're such a blunderer!"

"What? You don't like kings? Are you revolutionaries or something?"

"We liked Charles VI, the Beloved, our mad king. He ruled for over half a century during our grandfathers' times. . . . But I'm laughing at you. You're trying so hard to be with it that you don't remember that François I, just a century after Charles, in 1516 to be precise, banned and persecuted us, and condemned us to prison."

"What did you do to him?"

"Well, we depicted his mother, Louise of Savoy, as Mother Folly, pillaging the State and governing however she pleased. You should have seen what happened when she ran things for François, who'd been captured by the Spanish. Those two didn't inherit their predecessor's sense of humor. Louis XII had learned so much from our theatre, he commissioned pro-government farces from Pierre Gringoire. In one, he had himself represented as King of Fools, and members of his Court as Lord Moon, The Abbot of the Empty Purse, The General of Child's Play. . . . Take a look!" And he signaled to one of the sauntering figures: "Over here, General, present your bauble!"

Alfred Jarry's King Ubu skipped up on his wooden horse: "Suck a muck and muck a duck," he crooned, drooling all the time. Then a group dressed in black assembled. "Into the trap," the General shouted. They sat and I noticed all had an ear missing from their fools' caps.

My neighbor prodded: "Ask them about it!"

They launched into a story about coming from Geneva and performing *The Horny Farce* in memory of their companions hanged by the Duke of Savoy: "But we've lost our taste for playing. We're waiting for Good Times to return." And the saddest said: "The one ear we have takes for bad what we've been saying for good."

"What happened to the other ear?" I asked.

Someone piped up loudly: "They lent it to the tyrant to catch his speech and now they have no speech of their own." On this day of mourning, that grumpy killjoy with his black clothes made me feel guilty for laughing at their silliness. Sadness descended as I thought about lending my own ear to the torturers who had plagued Aristaeus. Maybe I, too, had welcomed the tyrant. "Tell me," I begged them, "do you think the analyst's office might be a torture chamber? Is analysis pure torment?" Though they didn't answer, I saw myself as torturer, victim, and spectator, one role replacing the next. The man in black harangued them, rolling his "r's" the way my grandfather used to. He paid no attention to my agony, but the fools were all ears for his eloquence.

VOLUNTARY SERVITUDE

"You poor, miserable and foolish people, you nations determined to create your own misfortune and to remain blind to what does you good. You allow yourselves to be deprived of your revenues, eyes wide open: your fields are plundered, your homes robbed and stripped. Without inheritance, you live with no claim to anything. . . . And all this chaos, this misfortune, this ruin comes not from external enemies but from the enemy you empower yourselves."

Was this Antonin, whose vehemence often fueled such diatribes in the wards? Wanting to make excuses, I whispered to Number One: "That guy's a genuine madman. He always has to add his two cents."

"You're mistaken. He's one of ours. He shows off by reciting La Boétie's speech, the one he wrote when he was eighteen. You know him, right? The philosopher Montaigne's dear friend."

The man in black, ignoring us, continued his admonition: *"The one who rules you has only two eyes, two hands, and one body. Who gave him so many more eyes to spy on you, if it was not you, yourselves? Where did he get so many arms to beat you, if not from you? Did not the feet he uses to trample your towns come from you as well?"*

"And what about the ears, watch out for them!" screamed one of the fools.

At the end of my tether, I asked: "Who is he talking about?"

The man in black replied: *"A man who is a man in name only, a shrimp of a man, naked and defeated, who would be nothing without the friends who hold him up. I often pity their foolishness."*

The buffoons chorused: "You're the fool, you fool!"

But the man in black continued, unflappable: *"They serve him out of interest: as if they could acquire something, when they don't even own themselves. Nothing makes men so subject to tyranny as stealing their worth. What gives one worth is what the tyrant punishes by death."*

Startled by the expression, I bent towards Number One to tell him how Aristaeus in my dream had ordered me to retrieve his worth, a spring-fed plot that made him feel life was good—but how I had no means to do so. Our whispering continued.

Number One whispered back: "Stop that habit of acting like a slave. Act like a fool who knows, but pretends to dream."

"And then?"

Covering the ranting of the man in black, he sang in falsetto: "And then, mock the cold and don't mind the steam."

"I do know some madmen whose bare feet in winter never even suffer an icicle's splinter."

"Imagination lets us see things as they are. It frees our minds and guides our star. We speak the truth and do duty to God. The rest isn't worth a lump of sod."

A strident cry interrupted our falsetto singsong.

3

Folly's Mirror

HENCHMEN

Dressed like the Statue of Liberty, Mother Folly was proclaiming: "Where have you gone my crazy fools? Come out from wherever you are, come right here to me. What's the matter with you? Can't you hear me speak? Hurry up and fly anon."

We could hear the tinkle of a fife and the beat of a drum. A jester appeared in the foreground dragging with one hand a two-faced masked man and with the other hand an idiot wearing a mask on the back of his head, emitting incomprehensible screams. The man in black moved away to let them pass.

"We call him Each of Us," explained Number One. "He's holding double-tongued People by the hand, a subject split in two . . ."

"And the third one, with his backwards mask?"

"That's Several. He's lost face and can't speak anymore. Look closely at him, his tongue is caught in a net of three huge knots that make him dumb. One of them is called Badly Dressed, the second Lack of Funds, and the third Juvenile Anxiety. Now move on," he yelled at the figures. "And as for you, Madame the Fools' Apprentice, you'll find in our parade the land of springs for your psychoanalysis, insomuch as it's about folly's performance."

"What are you trying to say? This has nothing to do with psychoanalysis."

"I'm telling you, take some craziness in, like Mother Folly's henchmen who dance before your eyes."

"Henchmen or Hellhounds! Goodbye. I'd rather take my leave."

"*Ignorantissima! Suppositum* (*henchmen* in Latin) is the name for the subject. And we are the subjects of History, the History that doesn't get written. Subjects who get stuck, whom everybody wants to get rid of. Look, like that one . . ."

A young man, Gilles or Pierrot, was hopping from one foot to the other in front of us, his face powdered, trying to say something that wasn't coming out: "I've come to deliver a message, but I don't know what I'm supposed to say."

"What's he saying?"

"Well, nothing. The impossible . . ."

A noisy group was already starting to bump into our Pierrot who was hurrying to introduce them: "The Ripener, My Lords of Cheapskate, Yawning Wind, and Flatland, Thinking People, Seen a Lot, Suddenly Joyous, Mister from Overthere, Mister from Upabove, One and the Other who enjoy pissing together and separately, Mister Go Everywhere, Mister Don't Move." The parade group kept time in place, while Mister Moving Forward and Mister Staying in Place kept blocking the movement, pushing it left and right in order to hog the road by themselves. One of their colleagues bumped into them, adorned in a gigantic bib:

"And here's the Drooler," Pierrot started up again. "He spits out Latin more thickly than a little devil, and after him Saint Falsetto and his son Placebo, or maybe Placido. I can never remember . . ."

All robed up, the Faculty of the University had just made its solemn entrance, collectively absorbed by a question I couldn't understand.

Pierrot whispered: "They're speaking in three parts about what itches them—is it a louse or a flea? Some want to disprove, others to reprove. The truth is, everyone wants to act more the fool than the next one and scratch like fools their own itchy foolishness."

TIME FLIES

Completely illogically in terms of the reigning debate, a character strutted out in front of everyone, carrying on his back a basket full of rats. I shivered. My mentor announced:

"It's the Rat Carrier, the Tail Bearer!"

This disgusting fellow had something to add to the polyphonic Parisian Shout-Out: "I buy political dress if it's made to my liking, for you can tell a man by his clothes."

Two rowdies pushed him aside.

"Make way for Crazy Merchant and Mad Bombast," our herald cried out, feeling more and more confident in his role.

"Take this," the woman said, holding out a mallet to her companion. "Grab this club. Break the bank of All These Fools."

And from then on Everyman's Bankruptcy took over the stage. Five characters fell in a jumble: Merchandise, Trade, Little or Nothing, Time Flies, and Big Expense. Pierrot summed up succinctly the situation: "Trade and Merchandise are passing Time while complaining about Time running out. Little or Nothing encourages them to forget their miseries and eat like kings instead of spending Time. But they run after Time to beg him to stop. By dint of complaining, Trade and Merchandise attract Big Expense who raises taxes so high that in the end Merchandise ends up in the can, excuse my French, and Trade faces unemployment. Look at him take off, his bundle over his shoulder, ready to beg on the highways. What's the moral of the story? All that's left is Little or Nothing. Hey, here comes Mister Nothing, time to give in to his passion for prognostication."

And the latter cooed in his television voice: "Would you like to know how, thanks to my tremendous philosophizing, I turn the possible into the impossible? How I can make and unmake everything and turn a yes into a no? Do you know the shifty ways of transforming a city into a village? Soon the earth will hold what only the waters should: catfish and cathouses, swordfish, and pimp-pricks." Then a group of young dandies surged forth, courting our annoyance with their self-importance. Pals of Pierrot? He ran to greet them, not without telling me in a last commentary: "These are Parisians who show off with nothing to show. In Paris there are lots of benighted who sleep all day to have their nights to play."

SOCIAL PROTEST

The dandies held the stage until a small sketch by André de la Vigne was ready to go. Number One took his turn as commentator: "Remember the name, André de la Vigne from Seurre on the shores of the Saône in Burgundy—with Pierre Gringoire, one of our literary glories. And now here's the plot: overseen by the architect Abuse, some crazy masons are building a new world on a foundation stone dubbed Confusion. All of a sudden Folly arrives, furious at having been left out. Everybody flirts with her, each one trying to best the other. She proclaims she'll accord her favors to the one who sings the best ditty and jumps the highest. A battle follows, and the whole edifice tumbles to the ground. It's such a ruin that the old world returns and determines that nothing is left. So then . . ."

A fatuous fat lady cut him off and introduced herself: "I'm the Great Reformer and here are my dignitaries: Linen Closet carrying a wash bucket to launder dirty money, Chamber Pot to carry my shit, Ass Kisser to watch over when I fuck and who I fuck. In fact considering the Time, I fuck a lot."

And Time indeed ran past shouting: "I don't have time, I don't have time, I have to make war, assure big profits, sell justice, fix elections, refuse to work." Having said that, he handed out horns to everybody with the following instructions: "Spare neither your brother nor your sister, nor your father, nor your mother, from the front, from the back, stick it to everybody, and be glad of it."

A paunchy priest, horn in hand, bellowed in turn: "I'm the Abbot of Assholes. Assholes, pay your taxes. Support your Abbot and his flaming jerks or you'll be jerked yourselves! If you don't pay right now, you'll be sacrificed like a cow."

Number One applauded, saying: "Nothing will change as long as People won't change. Time is what People make of it. And Time is money. Whether in Tours, Moulins, or Paris, money makes the world go round."

HULLABALOO

Excitement was growing. One of the group came very close in order to sing a nonsense ditty at the top of his voice: "I'm dumb to speak well and deaf to hear clearly, stuck in my bed in order to walk, and dying of hunger when I'm thirsty. I'm tired from doing nothing."

As I stood there congealed like a pudding, he pointed to his fanny and erupted in more nonsense: "If the end is near when the end is here then your end is the same end as a whore's end which is as hot as your auntie's mustard sauce."

That was too much. I was overwrought by this public display of my own dead end. I screamed at him to shut up. Number One tried to bring me to my senses: "It's only the little people's small talk on the matter. They're celebrating the happiness of their own resurrection in a place that seems made for them. And celebrating with you! Look at the funny side of life, take off that funeral face."

"You're visiting at the wrong time. I don't feel like laughing today. I'd like to go away, far from here, to breathe, to change scenery, to re-center myself. Where can I go?"

"Into the woods. . . . *The laurels have been cut, here is the beauty who will go to the woods to gather them, come let us dance, see how we dance . . .*"

"So what are you waiting for? Dance!"

The order came darkly from a shadow lurking behind me. I quickly turned around. Mother Folly, implacable, was looking me over. I felt faint. Number One was singing as if nothing were wrong: ". . . And guess what is hidden in the woods—a spring where fairies live, fairies so well named from the Latin *fata*, sacred words. But watch out! Handle them with care, not just anywhere, not just anyhow."

"Or else?"

"Or else the sacred will make you silly."

The fools broke into laughter. Worried, I watched Mother Folly who found her place among them. Number One joked, quoting Rabelais: "Better to laugh out loud than to write with tears . . ." Their gesticulations were making me dizzy. I begged them to stop the hullabaloo: "You've got the wrong address. This isn't a space for riffraff. Go away, get out of here!"

They stepped back a bit. Number One frowned, disappointed: "Too bad. Last night in your dream we declared you were a real professional jokester—that is, if you'd work at it."

PSYCHOANALYSIS, THE ORAL TRADITION

So that was their verdict. Psychoanalysis could well try to disguise its origins under a ton of paper, but it couldn't deny its oral beginnings, its tradition of blunderers, madmen, jokesters, and other quacks.

"What did you say?"

"Charlatans, if you prefer."

So they did recognize that great fool Lacan as one of their own. He would have said exactly that: "Psychoanalysis should never hesitate to enter delirium."

I protested: "Where the hell did you hear that?"

Number One had heard it from the master himself. It seems Lacan even told his disciples: "If I'd been more psychotic, I would have probably been a better analyst. As for you, try to be natural instead of acting so stuffy, don't feel obliged to always brag about yourselves. You are quite justified in being buffoons. Just look at me, I'm a clown, follow my example but don't imitate me."

While I was sensitive to the master's authority, I felt it was anachronistic. I said, quite sure of myself: "It's useless to continue our conversation. If I try to talk about this someday, no historian will take me seriously. Besides, in your day, these kinds of hospitals didn't exist, a specialist told me so."

Number One sighed, seemingly worn down: "We know all that already. Foucault was also one of ours, if that's what's eating you, as well as other stars of his École Normale. Among them, that jokester philosopher. . . . Instead of wringing the neck of the system's contradictions, he found his wife's easier to squeeze. And as far as this asylum is concerned, we'll be back, don't you worry, after being charged with disorderly conduct, as they warn us in Article 122b . . ."

Mother Folly then declared we'd had enough for today.

"But can't we play one last farce for her?" pleaded Number One. "The one about 'letting sleeping dogs lie' . . ."

Smiling for the first time, Mother Folly gave the signal to leave. She halted under the arch of the gate and gave me a sidelong glance: "If you want to know why I came, look at me, I'm horned, and horning in, a horn-blower, a hard act to follow, and hard to beat. I'm arrogant, disorganized, sometimes pleasant, sometimes unpleasant, droll, malicious, scathing, stinging, the mother of discord and always full of rage, outrageous in every home, cleaning up after reason's mess, reasonable when faced with detestable facts, and detesting how things are always done . . ."

On the verge of disappearing, she thought better of it: "Rendez-vous next time right here!" She refused to tell me the exact time, counting on my sense of exactitude. And I'd better change my ways! She wouldn't stand one more minute of my being passive, seated on my bench, watching the world's folly, only good for scribbling those kinds of texts that had led to her ruin.

And with that she turned her back to me, dragging her subjects beyond the arch, where they faded away as quickly as they'd appeared. I'd had my fill of folly too. Without realizing I was already obeying her command, I got up to go to the door of the ward in order to say farewell, having decided to never enter there again.

4

The Common Ward

MELUSINE

The office was filled to bursting. In the general stupor of such an unexpected death, everyone had something to say, mostly saying that something had to be said. But what exactly could one say? A psychotherapist mentioned the recent discovery in a cellar, at last, of the body of her own analyst, who had killed himself several months before. Analyst Number One, Analyst Number Two, Analyst Number Three, like the fools in Ecclesiastes, their number is infinite.

The Head Doctor told her: "Your patient, Melusine, is being released today."

He said it to bolster her spirits. I didn't have the heart to tell him I was quitting and left without saying a word. Crossing the courtyard of the building, I ran into Melusine who was headed towards the exit. Stylish, elegant, her eyes sparkling with joy, the same eyes usually in tears since they took her children away, she told me she'd found a home, a job, and that she'd be able to take them back. I congratulated her.

"You should congratulate my therapist. Boy did I give her a hard time! So tell me, do you believe in God? You're an atheist, right?"

"Well . . . you know. . . . I mean . . ."

"It doesn't matter. What matters is not ignoring that dimension with your patients. Here, read this." And she pulled out of her handbag a sheet of paper folded in four.

"It's a poem I wrote to send to hell all those people who try to profit from everything, no matter the cost. Here's where I talk about my father, a big drunk, in front of God and everybody, and probably in Heaven now. And this is me in the third stanza getting out of Purgatory with nothing to give, except all that love I've banked for my children." She hugged me and said she hoped never to see me again and wished me lots of luck in my profession and for my children as well, if I had any. "You have to have faith," she shouted, turning to look at me, at the threshold of the courtyard.

My hand still raised in a wave goodbye, I almost decided to follow her. But I couldn't get my feet to move in her direction and instead headed towards the common ward.

PURGATORY

The common ward, the obligatory passage to get to the patients' rooms, a kind of magic circle, acts like a magnet. It attracts those who are patients and repulses the health professionals who hurry through it—going who knows where. I'm no different when it comes to hurrying. But that day I hesitated at the entrance, not knowing what to do with myself, caught up in an omnipresent feeling of futility.

What difference does it make to pry open the doors of their *great confinement*, as Foucault might say. You can say what you want, try what you want, but every attempt to mark time, to start a project, to register progress runs into the brick walls of this place's mystery, no matter how fast you go, even if you're as fast as a bat out of hell! Why? To escape from the fairy's enchantment? The one who imprisoned her lover Merlin. . . . What was her name again?

Abandon all hope, ye who enter here. That motto could have been engraved on the lintel over the entrance where I was standing. Hell or Purgatory? I chose the second. If I were to believe the book I'd been perusing that morning, the difference was substantial. An invention of the Twelfth Century, Purgatory is a timed hell. It allows you a past that skirts damnation but more importantly a future to which you can escape after purging your sins. Hadn't I been judged the night before? Declared not a great analyst but not a completely mediocre one either, what I needed was to purge my mediocrity. "To hell with this," I thought, "I'm going in."

Once inside, the mystery of the common ward seemed to be more medieval than medical. Taking advantage of the calm that resulted from my slowing down, a man seated against the wall asked me to exorcise him: "I never should have had my Opinel knife in my pocket that day, on the

Place de l'Etoile . . . an unlucky star indeed! Help me get rid of my demons. Do you know their names in Breton?"

I tried to get away. Already a woman was asking for the same thing, singing softly in a series of rhymes in *oo*. She'd come from Poitou to see a *marabout* and found herself picked up without a *sou*. I rapidly did the sums. What she was claiming as the marabout's fees were about what a session would cost with Jacques Lacan. She begged me to stop the magic that was drumming inside her head and that had made her become a streetwalker in order to expiate a crime of incest of which she could say no more. Nor did I feel competent in this case to fight against the *djinns* of her native land.

Seeing a chair propped against the wall, I sat down, as empty now as that chair had been. Was I seeing things? Wasn't that Aristaeus over there, that sloppy silhouette resembling the cartoon character Gaston Lagaffe? A shapeless sweater, a pair of wrinkled jeans, unlaced sneakers, he was moving away towards the entrance from where I'd just come. I made a move to call him and he looked back at me. He was new in the ward. Maybe he was the boxing *dervé* I'd seen just that morning at the hospital gate. Last Monday, I had crossed paths with Aristaeus at the same spot. He'd complained: "I'm fed up with that drug Tercian, it keeps me from thinking."

"Tell your doctor."

"I need to work more on French and math."

"I have a book for you, I'll bring it."

I watched him walk away. My promise was like an undelivered letter. It hadn't been able to keep him on this side of death.

Wittgenstein's words came back to me: "When the tools of names are broken, it's still possible to invent an agreed upon sign to replace the missing name. . . . As far as ethical questions are concerned, you have to take center stage and say 'I,' speak from your own depths."

But I, in my work, at that ethical moment when life slides into death, hadn't found the slightest internal sign of complicity. I wasn't even able to say "I"—and just what "I" were we talking about, for God's sake?

For fear of having spoken too loudly, I looked around. Nobody seemed to notice I was there. What's the point of swearing when the subject of the curse has volatilized? My head was as empty as a sieve. Thinking about that kitchen utensil brought me back to the farces I'd seen: Passing Time! I'd lost all sense of how to do so, as well as the hope that Good Times would return. Like the people in that ward, I didn't give a damn about the future or the past. All I could do was satisfy myself with a negative existence, with the solution of objectivation, becoming a thing. I watched how they did it.

There they were, backs to the wall, The People Who Had Lost Face. Immobile, they challenged Passing Time. Was this the *space of wonder? So much for the wondrous!* And in the meantime, little by little, like when you keep still in the forest, the space had started to come alive with a life that's invisible to the impatient and noisy walker.

VIVIANE

Viviane, a very pretty girl who'd seen her fifteenth birthday a long time ago, walked back and forth in front of me. From morning to evening, she paced the common ward, alert, looking upwards in the direction of him who might be in Heaven. She walked swiftly and swayed with infinite grace, infinite indeed as she never stopped moving. Appearing as though she were going somewhere, she never went anywhere, except back and forth like a wolf in a cage. From time to time, she let out a vigorous and resounding "quack."

That day I saw her pride take a beating and her pace slow down. She was having trouble holding her head high. Her "quacks" tumbled out as though she were imitating the siren of an emergency squad, and they ended up as tears trembling on her eyelashes as she passed nearby. I held out my arms to stop her. She confronted me directly. I told her that she didn't have to be so courageous all the time, that it's okay to cry when you hurt. She launched into a series of indignant onomatopoeia that I couldn't understand. The siren sounds increased, the tears started up again, her nose was running—snot she cleaned up with her finger and swallowed immediately while looking straight at me.

Overwhelmed by such self-sufficiency, I hesitated before looking for some Kleenex. I finally held out a tissue and she blew her nose in it, just like anybody would, and then she handed it back to me. Behind her, the *dervé* had shown up again at the entrance to the ward. Aristaeus's double, to be sure, right down to the way he looked at you without seeing.

Viviane turned her back to me in an abrupt turnabout, but didn't start her infernal pacing again. I had a thought. She'd seen something change in how I was looking, and she'd responded to my change in focus. I didn't want to put her off any longer, I had to tell her the truth.

So I said—but does she understand our language—what everybody knew but what nobody knew officially yet, that Aristaeus had died yesterday, and that I, too, would like to be able to cry. She did another about-face, looked me straight in the eyes with her blue grey ones only a few centimeters from my own, hummed a song without words, smiled, and then took off jauntily.

I tried to follow her, but no luck! It was useless to try to catch up. She acted as though I weren't there. Having arrived at the end of her race course in front of the closed ward where the grandmothers who'd lost their wits lived, she turned around and started off again at the same speed. Superior to everyone else, she floated above the common worries of simple mortals. The alleged murderer called out to her: "Go with the lady. Can't you see she's trying to help you?"

She stopped in front of him and held out her hand on which he placed an aristocratic kiss, and then she took off again.

"Fie! Enough!" as my grandmother used to say when she wanted to move on to something else. I looked one more time around the common ward.

WITTGENSTEIN

And there they were, the long-ago fools whom I had met in the honor court of the hospital. How was I supposed to distinguish the good from the evil, the rejects from the in-crowd, the dominated from the dominant? Such dichotomies didn't make sense anymore. I'd too often seen the champion of a cause become his opposite—quick collaborator in horrors he decried.

Damn! An alexandrine line! I counted the twelve syllables on my fingers. Where did this rhythm come from? From the immobile dance of these half-awake characters? Without too much effort, I could recognize Mother Folly, The Prince of Fools, Mister Nothing, The Abbot of the Empty Purse, The Abbot of Deadends, The General of Child's Play, and even Number One. Wasn't that him, over there, the quiet little man absorbed in a book? To save face, I pulled out from my bag the book meant for Aristaeus.

Stiffly and slowly, a tall young man approached me. He hadn't opened his mouth for at least twenty years, his tongue tied no doubt by Juvenile Anxiety. Every time I saw him, I thought that his pleasing face and intense blue eyes made him look like dear Wittgenstein. Sometimes he consented to shake my hand as a polite gesture of hello or goodbye. Gesturing broadly, he often flipped backwards through a magazine. Maybe he was looking for someone else who might stop while passing through. That day he was reading the newspaper *Le Monde* upside down. After making several concentric circles around me like a stalker dancing a Bûto piece, he leaned against the radiator. I felt him staring at me. What should I do? I decided to read aloud the passage I had at hand, from *The Farce of New Men*.

"In this story, World is the victim of the tyranny of reformers: First Man, Second Man, Third Man. In order to govern as they will, they obliterate the past. Here's what Third Man says: 'Who gives a shit about times past? Or about ancestors? Painters painted them, historians wrote about them. But in truth, we don't really know anything. We have another solution. We are Brave New Men.'"

My public smiled and looked away. How could I know what he was thinking? I took up the play's refrain: "Let's make birds fly without wings. Let's make lawyers give alms and refuse payment. That way we'll be New Men."

I wanted to stop at that, but blue eyes stared at me again. So I went on: "And then World, in crisis, appears. He laments: 'I'm defeated and undone. There's no longer any hope or balance. Steady and hardworking People are pillaged from all sides. Scads of crooks grab our sheep and our chickens. I fear that the envious and the incurious will devour me.'

The plot thickens at this point. New Men lead World to an inn named Bad, where World moans, 'You pillage me night and day while pretending to love me.' And after having robbed World of everything, New Men lead World to another inn named Worse. That's how World goes from Bad to Worse."

And I think about Aristaeus, whom I had led from bad to worse . . .

"Listen to World's lament. It tolls like a requiem: 'Why doesn't death come; it's approaching me from every side. I'm deprived of all comfort. I've endured multiple evils. It's too hard to bear. I wait without hope, crying bitter tears, regretting everything. Pitiful regrets, mortal tears that can't be named.'"

Can't be named!. . . . I sought the approval of those blue eyes, but nobody was there. Blue eyes had flopped down at the foot of the radiator.

THE END OF THE WORLD

Viviane arrived at that point, leading by hand yet another eternal girl, this one with huge black eyes like a doe's. Her companion was saying no, gesturing with her head and laughing and objecting with all her might. Viviane grabbed our two hands authoritatively and linked them together, then took off in her own orbit. God knows why, but the girl changed her mind and dragged me to the staircase as though I were a child. "Peepee,"

"Cookie," she kept on repeating without my being able to make out which of us was the child, which was the mother.

Behind us and following in our footsteps, Marcel brayed: "The end of the world is near. The moon and the stars have disappeared. We're about to explode. At least this morning I was able to make the sun come out."

I tried to act as if this made sense. Like a doe in the forest, the girl teased me up to the first-floor hall where Raymonde, the hairdresser, had her shop. No one was in the hall. A nurse told me that everybody was still at a meeting. Raymonde seemed to be waiting for us. Marcel sat down and the girl and I watched his metamorphosis. His hair washed and cut, his face shining, he wiped his nose with the back of his hand and made us agree that the sun was indeed where it was supposed to be.

Caressed by rays that rarely touched her in the corner where she was often parked in front of the TV, the girl lifted up her skirt and lowered her panties to offer her own sun to the day's star. Marcel threatened to slap her. She quickly pulled her panties over the furtive caress the sun had just softly given, before the apocalyptic end heralded by Marcel.

MOTHER FOLLY

I thought it was prudent to put some distance between the girl and the censor's wrath and so we were off again, me pulling, her trotting in the corridor. I was looking for my key to open the door to the landing that led to the staircase, when a woman, dressed in a black skirt and sweater stopped us: "You, there. . . . What are you up to?"

I reeled off my name and profession and asked her the same question. She had come, knife in hand, to kill everybody because there had been outrageous goings-on at her home.

What had happened? Her husband was dead, and then there was the will . . .

I put on the appropriate face for the circumstances. "Don't worry," she said, "he's well off where he is. I don't give a damn whether he's alive or dead. My daughters don't care a wit about me, do what they want without my approval, bring me twenty-year-old furniture."

"What happened twenty years ago?"

"I don't need psychotherapy."

"Has your husband been dead a long time?"

"He died a year ago. We'd been separated for twenty years. Good riddance!"

"Really?"

"He wanted to have me locked up."

Marcel had found us. The lady in black gave him a cigarette; she gave cigarettes to the two guys in slippers and pajamas from Aristaeus's gang who were not allowed to leave the floor. The girl held out her hand, even though I had never seen her smoke.

"No," snapped the lady in black. She obviously preferred boys. I thought it smart to tell her so. She agreed with a shake of her head. I took that as a sign of encouragement: "You're like a mother to them."

"Not at all. . . . Don't say such a thing."

I insisted: "Well then a grandmother?"

"I'm not old enough."

"Has time stopped then?"

"That's right, twenty years ago."

"Since you split up?"

"Twenty years ago I lost my son. From leukemia. He was sixteen years old. I know he's not dead. Good day Madame, much obliged to you."

She's not the first person I'd met at that hospital who was looking for a way to contact the other world. When a new face would come up to me in the halls, I sometimes asked: "Are you looking for someone?" How was I so sure of that? Maybe it came from the period when I thought I'd find my grandfather in that hospital in the north of France, not far from the Chemin-des-Dames, where he'd been a stretcher-bearer during World War I. He'd been assigned, like all those who were musicians, to the role of gathering up the dead and the wounded. Strange logic. . . . Or was it a way to privilege the musicians by allowing them to officiate at the doors of death?

CHANGELINGS

I didn't have a moment to think about it. The girl led me, *manu militari*, past the borders of the ward. Still trotting, she let out contented cries.

I wasn't there anymore. I was back at the age she was making me re-live, next to a cradle where a baby is crying while incessantly moving its head from side to side. He's in pain. I'm looking for my grandfather, who has disappeared from our house. I can still hear today the wheels of the little bed creaking rhythmically on the tiles. Enclosed in a hallway outside, I scribble in pencil on the door enormous figure eights, keeping time with the rhythm. Is it Möbius's strip? Lorentz's attractor? Certainly a form emerging on the threshold of catastrophe, one that worked like a magic charm, because the baby emerged intact from its crisis. As for my grandfather, that's another story.

I read in my book that in the Middle Ages, babies who cried incessantly, who were in pain, were called changelings. An old lady would help the mother pray to fairies to come take away the screaming changeling and give her back her own child. They held a ritual in the sacred woods, near the grave of a dog sanctified as Saint Greyhound, the healer of children. This allowed them to exchange the intolerable baby, given to the fauns and the fairies, for the desired child whom the local spirits of the woods vouched for. The swaddling clothes were hung on the branches of a tree. The mother placed her child between two candles, then moved far away from the sound of its cries. When she returned, the "exchanged" child was bathed in a nearby stream, a baptism that inscribed it in the mother's lineage. Was it this exchange that the lady in black hoped to realize, praying that by giving away tobacco, fauns and fairies would give her back her son? My guide wasn't interested in any of this.

There we were in the honor court. Thinking again about that woman who for twenty years had not reconciled herself to injustice, irreconcilable in any case, Mother Folly's words registered more clearly in my mind: "outrageous in every home, detesting the way things are always done."

My companion's black eyes were showing signs of fatigue. She sat down on the bench where I had sat several hours before. To make her forgive me for not having been present enough, I told her the story of the changelings, just as a historian had unearthed it from the Seventh Century on up to the 1930s, around the area of Macon, in Burgundy.

"Listen well to this story told by Jean-Claude Schmitt. He's a historian who doesn't limit himself to written sources. He went looking for those country people who knew the last little old lady to have practiced, before the war, the changeling ritual. He thus piously gave her the honors of History. He tells us that this old lady, a posthumous child born after her father's death, had also lost a child; this may be the reason why she dedicated herself to reconnecting the links between generations when giving birth makes them fragile. She herself would have disappeared in a common grave if the historian hadn't inscribed her in time, offering her a decent tomb inside the body of his book. You know what this tradition makes me think of? The moment when in analysis a subject is born into its lineage, freed of the phantoms we give back to fauns and fairies."

The girl smiled at me and took my hand to begin walking back. Clearly

I wasn't all there. I thought about Wittgenstein's advice: "Man is a ceremonial animal. Let yourself be carried by the association of practices, similar to the association of ideas in psychoanalysis."

A piercing cry brought me back to the girl: "When I think about it again, that lady in black who refused to give you a cigarette acted like the wife in *Balthus, the Lorrain*. Do you want to hear about her?"

In a hurry to go back, my companion didn't give a fig about René Bazin's novel. But, carried away, I went on anyways: "Her son was killed in World War I. Like the Crazy Mothers who circulate around la Plaza de Mayo in Buenos Aires, she combed the countryside looking for him, hanging bread from trees at crossroads, with little messages to feed him with words. She hoped the fairies and fauns would give her back her son and take on the phantoms of that unspeakable war. Nobody had had the guts to lock her up, feeling vaguely that her folly had more to do with something sacred than with a personality disorder. Her gesture was like an unrealizable sepulcher. The Balthus family was originally from Moselle, which came under Prussian control in 1870. Their son died for the King of Prussia, wearing a German uniform. Could that be the spring-fed land that Aristaeus, the Lorrainer, indicated to me in his roundabout way?

And thus we arrived at the threshold of the ward. The girl dropped my hand.

THE WATCHMAN

Exhausted by our excursion, the girl collapsed on a chair in front of the TV. I stationed myself next to her, part of the decor, quickly caught up in incomprehensible video clips. Because of them, I forgot to greet my neighbor on the other side.

With curly, flowing, shiny hair, and rouged up like a queen, she wasn't watching the screen but rather a pocket mirror in which she kept correcting her make-up. As proud as the Lady of the Unicorn, she condescended to greet me in turn with a haughty nod of the head. We'd already met in the ward where she appeared from time to time.

I felt useless between these two young women. Two interns passed: "Hi, how's it going?" Maybe they thought I was working, in the same way they thought my companions were getting better. I was the only one to realize I'd settled myself in a clandestine haven, happy to have escaped from a world of projects and progress. Of course there was the throbbing of the video performers, braying empty messages that no one could understand. Absorbing their autistic music, I jumped, dreaming of a wave theory of psychoanalysis that would abolish the corpuscles of identity we think we inhabit.

In front of me, a man was turning in circles, bent backwards, excessively taut, like a bow. With his stomach stuck out, his prominent jaw, his nose almost touching his chin, he propelled himself in a supple scansion, keeping time with the rhythm of the British drummer whose hair was frenetically shaking the screen. By contrast, his posture looked like the curve of an illuminated letter, while only his eyes were permitted to roam like radar around his body. They controlled both terrestrial and aerial space. Was he turning in rounds or making rounds? This was the first time I'd asked that question. I'd often encountered him without greeting him, imagining that his geometric abstraction sufficed to absorb him completely.

But that day I saw he was sizing me up. I was seeing a proud freedom that was telling me to go to hell. I hailed him casually when his epicycle approached me obliquely. To my surprise, he held out a hand, his arm still stuck to his body, a hand full of self-control. Then, without breaking the harmony of his movement, he directed himself, like a solitary planet, toward Wittgenstein's double, still nonchalantly posted next to the radiator. He came close enough to touch him. The latter didn't budge an inch and followed closely the trajectory that took the former to the door of the refectory where he inscribed the apogee of his curve.

During this time, Viviane didn't stop coming and going, appearing and disappearing, very busy, always looking inspired, quacking away to the rhythm of the video clips. Was she in a cage or on a tear? She came closer, rapidly looking me over, a question in her eyes. The radiance there looked like the window of a prison behind which she'd walled herself up against the champions of civilization. I tried to say something to get her to slow down. She took off quickly. Her look was that of people who can't be bought.

Little by little I saw the denizens of the common ward emerge from their camouflage gear. The odd episode in the honor court seemed near and far at the same time.

I felt good there. A small character in that huge room, who might just as well not be there. In that spectacle of vanities, my place was derisory: so little "I," so little me, even less shrink than anything else.

ENTER THE DANCE

All of a sudden I noticed a large woman over to the side, in a corner of the room, busy eating a chunk of bread with a can of pâté. She too was quick to notice I was watching her. "War is war!" she commented, while gesturing for me to come over. I headed towards her, seduced by such a hearty appetite.

"I'm too smart, that's my problem. I'm suffocating in my miserable suburb. It's just the way it is; I like to take care of people. I have something of the fortune-teller in me. I can see in your eyes that you see too. You also believe, don't you?"

"Well you might say . . ."

"That's what I thought. . . . You see," she concluded between two mouthfuls, "the problem is they think I'm a nutcase."

Marcel had planted himself in front of the television. Listening in on us in spite of the noise, he submitted that he would have liked to become a doctor or maybe even a psychiatrist. He knew Freud, Lacan, and *tutti quanti*, but given the situation, it was out of the question.

Viviane showed up again, and took the woman by the hand. "You know she likes to dance," the woman explained, putting her pâté on the floor. And they performed as a duo a couple of rock-and-roll steps.

Viviane had already abandoned her partner to come close to me in order to share her change of repertoire. "Titi tata," four new notes, had taken the place of the quacks. She was repeating them over and over, like the music of Phil Glass. The woman began to sing the Communard theme, *Le temps des cerises*, in an impressive tremolo. She couldn't remember the words. I wanted to help her, but Viviane's four notes keep resonating. Instead of remembering "Our lovelies will be mad," I heard myself singing "titi tata" as a response. What had forced me to sing her tune?

Viviane led me to the door of the courtyard. Her hand on mine, she made me open the door; she crossed over the threshold, then came back in again and waited. I sensed I'd been put in the position of the speaking partner to Harpo Marx, the mute brother of the Marx Brothers.

"So you want to go out in the courtyard?"

Once again, the enchanted alleged murderer, locked up for life, came to the rescue: "She wants to know if you're able to get her out of here."

What was wrong with me? Her problem wasn't going out into the courtyard where she was perfectly free to go. She'd shown me what it meant to leave, to get out, and had asked me a question as children do, in the affirmative. A question addressed to me who, that day, couldn't even get myself to leave. I wasn't capable of remaining a passive spectator of her deeds and movements, pronouncing from atop my high hill: "This is what that gesture means." Or rather, "This is what your gesture means to me." There was a nuance there! Her eloquent silence was addressed to me, as the alleged murderer made very clear. But again, just who was this "me" in these circumstances, "me" walking around without me, without the "qualities" to be a shrink.

Unconcerned by my internal monologue, Viviane thought of something else and brought me back to my chair. In an even more imperious act, she grabbed my hand and plunged it into the blouse of the girl with the dark eyes who chortled from the impromptu tickling. I resisted as much as I could. Viviane insisted that I feel up her breast which, like Tartuffe, "I daren't see."

Mocking me, the beauty with the mirror joked: "She thinks you're a stethoscope."

"Or my sister's hand in a soldier's pants," commented furiously a man's voice, booming from behind me.

I recognized Antonin, an ex-seminarian specializing in prophetic fury whom an inspired resident had nicknamed "Artaud." I'd confused him earlier with the man in black, the troublemaker and La Boétie groupie. This was all I needed. Here I was caught with my hand in the till, and in public.

What to do? Return to the alleged murderer's helpful method: ask myself what Viviane was trying to tell me by this gesture, a gesture seen by Antonin and her neighbor. An abusive gesture that required a response: "No I'm not a doctor, and I'm not here to play doctor either."

Viviane came close again, whispered a few words, "o, u, e," without pronouncing the consonants, words I had to reconstitute by finding the missing plosives or labials. I felt more sure of myself: "I'm trying to speak with you too."

SEMANTICS

To think that I had intended never to enter that hospital again! The beauty with the mirror began to redo yet again her face. I've forgotten her name. But Morgan, the name of the fairy, suited her perfectly. She had been roaming for a long time in her suburb, without a home, tossed back and forth by her divorced parents, like an effigy of what didn't work between them. She would arrive for short stays and would leave always in a mess and still in trouble. Like Aristaeus, she never let down her guard, never accepted even a modicum of psychiatry, even refused the role of patient. For her, the best defense was always an attack.

Neglecting for a minute her glittering eyelids, she started thinking aloud: "Speak with us, you say! Here, you're despised, you're taken for an imbecile . . ." Then, after a short silence: "I'd also like to speak about something, but psychiatry can't understand."

I was about to launch into the distinction between psychiatry and psychoanalysis when she proclaimed suddenly: "It's really a matter of semantics."

She pronounced this grand term, bejeweling herself with the studies she would have liked to have done between stays on her parents' doormats. Let's hear it for semantics! At that point, I wasn't even sure what the word meant. She explained: "It happened after a friend died. I'd gone out. All the doors opened at once and I saw it. Nobody else saw it, or maybe others saw it, but didn't dare speak. That's normal, right, don't you think so?"

"What exactly did you see?"

"Hell. It exists, all those stories about witches and devils, like in the Middle Ages. It's a matter of semantics, do you see what I mean? A figure of speech. One of them, from under my bed, wanted to make love to me through the mattress. Maybe I would have kept the baby. Why not? The other day, a guy put his hand on my thigh, a reassuring hand."

"All she needs is a man to reassure her," barked Artaud behind us.

"A man like you, Antonin, for example," she smiled charmingly. She was relaxed for a moment having been able to catch the transference ball on the rebound.

Artaud smiled back like an angel, a look I'd never seen from him before. She grew more confident: "I'd so like to take care of other people, become a psychologist. I've a gift for it."

THE CHILD WITH WHITE HAIR

Strident cries disrupted the momentary calm. A misshapen young man, who sometimes resembled a lunar Pierrot, or as he did now, a limping and drooling Quasimodo, had just thrown himself, his diapers around his ankles, on a respectable old lady. In the flash of an eye, the gyrating man intervened, slapped Quasimodo back into his pants, and began circling again.

The embarrassed old lady explained: "It's because my shop isn't open yet." Looking more closely at her, I realized she wasn't as old as all that.

Artaud got involved: "She needs fire, the fire of conception. I'll summon the Devil for her. Not the Holy Spirit, who stands for anti-conception." Like a plotter, he whispered in my ear that nothing was as good as flame to warm a woman's heart and that in that arena the Holy Spirit was useless. "I'll find what concepts I need in Pagan-Christian territory," he proclaimed, while running off to the courtyard.

The old lady came closer to me. Might I accompany her to her room? Arm in arm, I helped her climb the stairs. As she grew more confident, her tone began to change: "My word, they're all crazy in this hospital. Oh well, what can you do? That's the way it is. They told me there were psychotherapists here. I'd like to see one."

"You have one on your arm."

She looked at me suspiciously.

"Do you have an office?"

Once arrived at the entrance to the floor, I took out my open sesame key and her distrust melted away. She followed me into my office. But just as soon as I'd put the key back into my pocket, she rushed to leave. I grabbed her as best I could.

"I thought you wanted to talk to me?"

She sat down across from my chair.

"Well you see my apartment's a mess, I don't put anything away any more. I spilled water on the burners. There are flies everywhere. Is that bad?"

"Bad . . ."

I tried to call mentally on the hospital plumber to find an answer. My uptight look didn't please her. She headed towards the door imitating a steam engine: "Choo choo choo." That must have been a hit when she was a kid. I caught her and made her sit down again. A child with white hair, she laughed and recited in a high-pitched voice: "My father died when I was five. My husband, too. But he left with another woman. I've had several miscarriages. My daughter arrived very late. She took advanced degrees. I'm afraid that something will happen to her."

And then she took off again, this time around the room: "Choo choo choo." She made me laugh. I caught up with the train at the turn, just like I'd seen Buster Keaton do in *The General*.

"This is a hold-up!"

"Are you making fun of me?"

"Not at all. If *laughter is the essence of man*, why not of woman as well?"

Her face lit up and her voice grew deeper: "Rabelais? I know him, you bet! I was a schoolteacher."

"Eureka! That water on your burners, those flies, could it be the proverbial fly in the ointment?"

"I guess you could say that. Let me tell you, when I was six years old I was already too smart for my age. Don't tell anyone, but my father was never buried. Because he was an atheist, he didn't want any funeral ritual. I didn't even go."

"There must be a grave?"

"Are you kidding? In Algeria? With everything that's going on there? They want to send me to a nursing home. So I can die there, right?"

I tried to reassure her, rather than watch her substitute herself for her father—not being up to the task of making sure his soul would rest in peace. In fact, she seemed less terrified of leaving. "I'll write to you if I go and you'll answer. Promise me," she said. I promised. We left the room.

QUANTUM AFRICA

My promise had the positive effect of propelling me into the future. Had I left time behind? Looking for a marker, I decided to date this feeling from the bee's visit. Then I glanced at my watch: it would soon be noon! It was time for the meeting at the outpatient clinic, what the doctor returned from the States liked to call a "scientific" gathering. I changed my mind. I wanted to be present.

That was if Séraphine hadn't made an appointment. She had wanted to space out her sessions at the clinic. Since she'd left the ward after ten years of confinement, we'd been meeting every week. I wasn't looking forward to telling her about Aristaeus's death. He'd been like a son to that old spinster, or maybe like a tenderly loved nephew. She often asked me for news of him. Her loyalty was unquestionable. Twenty years of psychiatric care had never led her to reject the Centre National de la Recherche Scientifique, even though they'd stopped thinking about her a long time ago. How could I tell her that I'd failed to keep Aristaeus alive?

Once again, I hesitated to leave. Besides, the exit was blocked by an exhausted man, very black, wearing blue pajamas, his eyes bloodshot. He said he wanted a psychoanalyst. Madame Choo Choo pointed at me.

Jingle of keys. I opened the door for her and locked the door to the stairway. I didn't mind staying at all. Before we got to my office, the man had the time to tell me he was African, and I the time to regret not having studied ethno-psychiatry. He didn't give me time to dwell on this.

"Drugs are useless for my problem."

"Tell your doctor!" I said.

But he couldn't care less about my advice.

"And don't do the ethno-psychiatry number on me. I'd like to be Einstein or at the least Erwin Schrödinger. I'm not interested in women anymore."

"But Schrödinger was certainly interested in women." What had come over me? I was talking about the great scientist Schrödinger as though it were the latest gossip from Wittgenstein's Vienna. The African was clearly not a fan of tattling.

"I'm interested in quantum physics. My uncle the engineer told me: 'If you want to be a man, do math.' So I worked on math in my country. The first day of class, the professor warned us: 'We're doing exact science here. If anybody has any doubts, leave now.' Not very Cartesian, that guy. . . . Anyhow, I stayed."

"Don't you mean too Cartesian?"

"As far as I know, Descartes had doubts. He had his share of dreams and visions; because of them, he even cast doubt on what he'd written. *Larvatus prodeo* . . . you know the quote."

"Well . . ."

"*At the point of entering the world's stage where until then I'd been merely a spectator, I advanced masked like a specter or a ghost.* . . . Just what do you think his evil genius was? A philosophical abstraction?"

"And what brings you here?"

"Our own evil genius, the dictator of my country. I was one of the students who studied science, in other words, one of the elite. Our political movement was clandestine. But something took hold of me one day. I cracked. I wrote to that guy. Soldiers came to arrest me. They imprisoned me, *kurbashed* me."

"*Kurbashed?* . . ."

"With whips. It's lucky I'm still alive. I couldn't stop crying. Not just from pain. I cried for my people. I couldn't quit. So I left for France to continue my studies."

"At the university?"

"With not very well defined beings, a kind of army of shadows who ordered me to kill the first thing that bothered me. It's a problem. That's why I come here from time to time. You don't know me, but I know you. You used to speak with Séraphine. They told me she'd been discharged for good. We discussed physics together. She knew a ton about solid physics. Did you know she'd defended a real thesis and that the American with whom she had conversations in her head was a great specialist in her field? Poor Séraphine. She never left her 1950s lab. Impossible to get her out of there. The last time I saw her, she wanted me to explain the wave function in quantum mechanics. I remembered Schrödinger's equations for her and was pretty proud of myself.

Well now I feel better than a little while ago. I'm glad you've heard of that good old genius Erwin. You should reread Descartes. You'll see he's not all that Cartesian. He's even, if I do say so myself, a little African, capable of conceptualizing his *Discourse on Method* from working on his dreams—in addition to making a pilgrimage to Notre Dame de Lorette to disarm the ghosts, which is what I do here. So now I'll say goodbye. I'll probably be discharged by next Monday. If you see Séraphine, tell her hello from Yvain."

THE FORBIDDEN STRIP

Our conversation had cheered me up as well. I felt I could face the outside. With Séraphine I would not only be the Bad News Messenger. Yvain had just confirmed what I'd always thought; her research wasn't so delusional. Before descending, I stuck my head into the little room off the entrance to say goodbye to the lady in black. She wasn't there anymore. The young men in pajamas were sleeping in front of the floor's television which was disgorging its news to general indifference. I sat down for a minute to gather my thoughts about how to tell Séraphine.

We'd met when I'd first come to that hospital. It was the worst of circumstances. The Head Doctor, recently named director of the ward, was encountering the patients with the whole team at his side. Séraphine was presented to him as delusional, but introduced herself as a physicist who'd been forced to stop her research too soon because of insomnia. After all that time, she was still furious, despite the treatment she'd received. To say that the results of her experiments had been invented! It was the lady boss of the lab who should have been locked up! Séraphine had gotten very worked up, was still worked up, appalled.

The doctor asked her if she had proof. She couldn't defend herself. Someone had stolen her thesis, all her articles, and all the objects that were important to her. She got angrier and angrier thinking about all the things that had disappeared from her house, stolen during her long absence. She looked around for someone to support her claim, stammered the name of an American with whom she had a telepathic internet connection and went for the door, halting the introduction.

Troubled by her stifled passion for research, maybe even having seen an error in judgment, I went to find her afterwards, eager to help.

"Go fuck yourself!" was her only reaction.

A year went by. One day I heard her call me from her room, stretched out on her bed. She spent most of her time there when she wasn't seated in the common ward, unmoving, the vestal of an inextinguishable flame flickering beneath the ashes. Abruptly she asked me: "What have you studied?"

I wanted to avoid the question, but to my surprise I confessed how I'd abandoned science during my second year of math. That avowal was oddly painful after all that time. My pedigree seemed sufficiently acceptable for her to propose to teach me some physics, if I'd like. So I had my course every Monday, in the form of agreeable conversations—feeling a little guilty, as her delirium didn't bother me.

Two or three years passed like that. One fine Monday morning, she wasn't at our rendez-vous. I learned from someone else that she'd taken off to go back home, without taking the time to tell me. Her own space, up until then forbidden to her because of all those thefts—delusion or reality—no longer posed a problem for her return.

When I got that news, I thought back to our last conversation. As usual, she had spoken about diodes and about her thesis subject on "lowering the forbidden strip." A subject that had made more than one person laugh and yet, as I'd just learned from Yvain, a legitimate one. But that day she'd pushed the metaphor in another direction. She went to a strip of her native land in Alsace, periodically invaded, debased, degraded so thoroughly that her godmother, a nun, had been murdered by a French resistance group, raped and killed because of her German accent.

For fear of encountering her fury once again, I hadn't commented on this biographical detail, because we were there to do physics. But in addition to seeing how her thesis subject corresponded both to science and the history of France, I'd remembered one other detail. That day, she'd also mentioned the hospital as the only viable place to speak about the subjects dearest to her. Physics with Yvain, a young African man who sometimes dropped into the ward, Antonin for mysticism, Morgan for theatre—she had the talent, she was sure of it—Viviane, so dear, such grace that child, and finally Aristaeus, whom she surrounded with a love that only she understood, though maybe he did, too.

At the outpatient clinic where she came to see me after she'd left, she always asked for news of her dear ones. One day, without warning, she brought me a text. Some would call it her delirium. I received it as a gift.

It opened a space to give life to facts not attested to by History—as I had just begun to understand.

For the occasion, she was wearing a blouse embroidered with Vosges motifs. She hadn't been sleeping and to keep busy had written her childhood memoirs for me. Her parents weren't her parents. She had supposedly been born through *in vitro* fertilization thanks to the work of Louis Pasteur and Marie Curie. The last one was especially responsible and Séraphine remembered her native Poland well.

"Well this is really something!" I exclaimed. "I thought that your fertilization technique was a lot more recent."

She answered curtly that she'd been premature, only six months old, and that people knew things in her part of Moselle well before Paris, forgotten discoveries that her grandfather could have confirmed because he engraved tombstones. In their village on the German border, he knew a ton about the secrets that were whispered at burials. And that wasn't all. Deported to Bergen Belsen when she was six, she remembered it as if it were yesterday, as well as her escape.

I must have winced for she added: "Ask Aristaeus if you don't believe me. He too was deported to Germany. And if it wasn't him, it was his father or his grandfather, or one of his other relatives."

A tease? *Folie à deux*? At that moment, on the day of Aristaeus's death, that weeks-old declaration of deportation tolled the death knell for the civilians of Lorraine, children and grandparents included, who had perished in the camps of World War I. Was Holtzminden, the camp near Poland signaled by Aristaeus, a fiction or reality? Was this the land of the springs he'd ordered me to find?

I was pulled from my reverie in the little room off the entrance by television images of mass graves that were constantly being exhumed—all over the world.

HONOR!

I couldn't help myself from crying out: "How terrible!"

"I swear, on my honor."

A voice had just echoed mine. I recognized under the window a small character whom the shadows had hidden when I entered the room: a blonde woman, usually seated downstairs in the common ward. Her purse on her lap, she always impressed me by her aloofness and her hair—cut like Gelsomina's, the clown from Fellini's *La Strada*.

For the first time, I heard the sound of her voice. Having launched into an incomprehensible monologue, she was in competition with the TV news lady. From her flood, I could make out a few words: "Very well, yes, on my honor!" as if to place emphasis in a subliminal discourse that occasionally had sound. Then clearly: "My mother died when I was four years old."

As I asked her how, she got up to turn off the sound, despite the protests of one of the sleeping men who woke up because of the sudden silence. I pushed the button again. He told me not to bother; he didn't give a fuck about those images of the living dead. They could invade the planet; it wasn't his problem. Gelsomina closed her eyes. I went to sit next to her.

"And who raised you?"

"My godmother."

I lost the thread again. Her monologue started up once more but louder, more assertive, peremptory, and little by little I could make out several voices. Suddenly we were in a soundscape of a theatre in which she was the *tableau vivant*. A leitmotif gave her style the feel of a testimony, dictated to an impartial witness: "I swear to you, on my honor! For that, no, there was no one to answer for it. I was there at her death! With my sister, but they pulled us aside. I don't know what happened. We cried. I'm telling the truth. Just look at this!"

She looked in her bag and handed me a worn piece of rose-colored paper: it was an official certificate attesting that she was indeed the daughter of a mother, born in Amiens. The mother's name with her three Christian first names was definitely written on that paper, ready to turn into dust. It was as if she were fighting a revisionist History determined to deny the existence of her mother.

"My father was a carpenter. He married again. She was a bitch; all she did was humiliate us. Yes, but listen up! I was a good girl! I've done all kinds of work." And then she did a pantomime of how to smile if you want to be a good saleslady. She continued with a touch of a Picardy accent: she'd worked in a photo shop, sold perfume and designer shoes. "Yes Madame, in the tony neighborhoods, Saint-Placide, the Champs-Elysées—Charles Jourdan, Chanel, only quality items. I'm telling the truth. My son got married. My husband left me. I lived in a hotel. No Madame, there was not a single witness. I don't remember anymore. I was all alone, always all alone. Now I can't work anymore. I'm homeless. I'm sentenced to death."

I told her no, she insisted yes, acting like someone who really wanted to be dissuaded. Then she confided a wish: "I'd like to return to Amiens. My father is living in a house that should come to my sister and me as our inheritance. I must discuss it with the social worker. Do you know the cathedral there? Once upon a time, I did guided visits of the stalls: *'an enchanted glade, tangled, imperishable, fuller of leafage than any forest, and fuller of story than any book.'* That was John Ruskin. Perfectly, Madame, I remember as if it were yesterday. 'Ladies and gentlemen, notice the wood sculptor—the author of this marvelous piece who has represented himself on the armrest, mallet and chisel in hand. Not far from him, on the other armrest, take a look at the fool eating peas.'"

I couldn't stop myself from sharing my new knowledge with her: "Maybe that fool was part of a Société Joyeuse, the kind of fool's guild that existed in Amiens and Arras at the time these stalls were sculpted. Maybe he's the *dervé*, the fool from Adam de la Halle's *The Play of Folly and Foliage*, which was written when the Cathedral was being built. . . . I think I even met him this morning in the courtyard of the hospital."

She smiled like someone who was in the know and brought me back to reality by asking me to open the door to the stairway. She wanted to go to the refectory to eat the dinner that was about to be served.

Her hunger made me hungry too. 12:30 already! Enough folly, let's go to the outpatient clinic. The "scientific" gathering would end with a buffet graciously offered by some solicitous pharmaceutical lab. Gelsomina sped down the steps, her purse under her arm. I followed at a run. In less time than you can say boo, I arrived at the door to the ward, finally feeling like I was free from enchantment.

5

Judgment

KIDNAPPING

Firmly determined to avoid the honor court for fear of getting mixed up again in a story of fools and crazies, I surreptitiously took the back route to get back to my car. I drove past the locked wards where the author of "Head Against the Walls" had been locked up, diagnosed as a madman with literary pretentions. I remembered his name, Hervé Bazin. Could he have been a relative of René's, the author of *Balthus, the Lorrain?*

I didn't have time to dwell on these family histories. For at the very moment I crossed the back entrance, two tough guys who I first thought were nurses, stopped me. I rolled down the window and held out my hand to take the flyer surely decrying the chronic shortage of staff. What a mistake! Before I had time to blink, I was locked up in an ambulance that took off like a bat out of hell to the tune of an emergency vehicle: "You're screwed. You're screwed." I kicked myself for having tried to leave from the hospital's dead end, where no doubt unmentionable trafficking was taking place.

In the front seat, the two kidnappers were paying absolutely no attention to me and were yelling at each other in Italian. Was it the mafia? The thin one was studying a map of the suburbs and giving orders that made the other one try to turn on a dime, wheels screeching. I held on and tried but didn't succeed in deciphering their itinerary, as we crisscrossed housing projects that all looked the same.

After an eternity of this kind of gymnastics, the van stopped at the foot of a staircase. Doors slammed and the two accomplices grabbed me under the arms to lift me easily up the first steps. In a short time, my escorts ran out of steam. Getting a better glimpse of them, I saw that my musclemen guards weren't as evil as all that. They seemed more like a couple of clowns, maybe Laurel and Hardy. "Beware," I said to myself, tugged between the breathlessness of the little fat one and the athletic jogging of the big guy. They kept on encouraging each other above my head in an Italian anybody could understand: "Bastardo, coglione, cazzo, pezzo de merda, porca eva."

The staircase ended in a vast esplanade. It didn't take long to recognize the theatre of the Maison de la Culture where I'd attended that past spring a festival of Commedia del'arte starring that great actor Dario Fo. Ah hah! Weren't they the Colombaioni, Fellini's clowns? Not answering, not even a word, they headed towards the theatre. Open at that hour? That was odd! A few minutes later, I was seated next to them in the first row of a house half full.

"What's playing?"

The answer sounded like a guillotine.

"Your trial."

So I'd had a premonition! In a lightning flash I saw again the dream of Aristaeus arriving in my office with his escort of fools to warn me I'd been judged. By the kind of temporal juggling in which folly is so expert, the judgment had only now become imminent. But I was better prepared.

I quickly saw that Mother Folly had her place on stage as the chief interrogator. From a distance she looked a lot like Sissi, my old patient. Wittgenstein, haughty, the Prince of Fools, exactly like the silent man in the ward, was at her right. Antonin, more ferocious than ever, was at her left. Each one had an acolyte, a *therapon*, a ritual double, no doubt.

Neither one of them bore any family resemblance. Neither the calm man in wire glasses smoking his pipe sitting to the left of Artaud, nor the man to the right of Wittgenstein, as peaceful as the other double but much more colorful. His mauve tweed suit stood out from the neutral colors of the other three.

Mother Folly's scream made me jump again. Her henchmen answered her call, joked, did clown tricks—a sense of déjà vu. In fact, I hardly paid · any attention I was so worried by what they might want from me. Number One was leading the charge, as was fitting, but this time instead of sitting next to me, the traitor pointed an accusing finger.

"Charlatan," they yelled out in chorus.

It was time to judge psychoanalysis. I protested that I was not psychoanalysis. I'd never taken myself for psychoanalysis. To which they responded that if they were the crazies, then I had to be the psychoanalyst, whose head was as hollow as the cage Magritte depicted in his painting *The Therapist*.

GESTUS: FORBIDDEN GESTURES, FORBIDDEN JESTS

"First offense," announced Number One. "You condemn our acting out and you keep us from doing our work as fools, jugglers, and *histrions*. You're collaborating with the accusations the Church levied against our jests and our gesticulations, accusing us of diabolical paganism."

My eyes opened wide, never expecting to hear such a complaint: "You're very much mistaken. Psychoanalysis is not a Church, maybe a bunch of Chapels, but . . ." I asked permission to give my rebuttal a little later.

"Permission denied," Mother Folly proclaimed. "We want to hear right now what you have to say about this."

"Well you might say that gestures are forbidden in order to give free rein to speech. On the other hand, gestures really aren't forbidden. . . . This is a groundless trial. If you want to wipe out psychoanalysis, you should say so right away. I think I'm the subject of a witch hunt."

A reproachful reaction drowned out my words.

"Shut up!" yelled Number One to the audience. He shot an angry look at me: "Don't speak of something you don't know anything about. I'm talking about gestures that are certainly not vulgar groping, but rather gestures that are permissible, that are considered socially acceptable. And you condemn that kind of gesturing as acting out."

I bowed my head, thinking that they were accusing me of not having seen the empty cage that Aristaeus had shown me, when we were no longer able to speak to each other. Even worse, I'd neglected the gesture of giving him that book that spoke of the time when men were never left alone, but always connected by language games in a community of jest and gesturing.

"And you don't know anymore, either, what lofty dreams are," an odd type in the courtroom with a cat in his arms shouted at me. "You're only capable of low dreams. You're afraid of the visionary practices of allegory that Old Europe knew how to cultivate. In Dante's time, it was a lot more coherent. Despite the filth and the fights, despite the different languages, we all saw with the same eyes."

"Shut up, Eliot," the man in mauve tweed cried out from the stage. "Mind your own cat!"

The man laughed and sat down with his cat. "What does this have to do with our subject," I asked my neighbor, who was astonished that I didn't recognize the author of the poem "Cats"—T. S. Eliot.

"You mean the musical comedy?"

I didn't hear his answer. I was under fire again.

VULTUS: THE FACE AND THE LOOK

"You psychoanalysts don't look at your patients enough. Isn't that right, Drury?" Wittgenstein spoke, tossing the ball back to the man in tweed. The latter continued in a French-English creole.

"*Bon*, it all depends. When a patient is studied in hospital, everybody looks at him, even the psychoanalysts. I used to do it myself in my own ward, when I worked at Saint Patrick's Hospital in Dublin. I even tried all kinds of weird experiments with my patients. Really *étrange* and *inquiétant* it was, too! Just uncanny! Nevertheless, my mentor Ludwig, and I salute his presence, warned me against such aberrations. For my graduation, he sent me *en cadeau* the *Traumdeutung* and recommended that I take time to do face-to-faces with my patients. He's the one who convinced me at Cambridge to quit philosophy for *la psychiatrie*, so that I wouldn't give up thinking. When he came to visit me in Ireland, he insisted on seeing with me patients who had been institutionalized *depuis longtemps*. And he had long and frequent conversations with them. Some of them were *beaucoup mieux*, really much better because of it. That was in 1938, the year of the Anschluss. In Dublin I actually saw him read a newspaper for the first time. He found the mad a lot cleverer than their doctors."

Wittgenstein smiled slightly. So the man in tweed was Maurice Drury, one of Wittgenstein's favorite disciples. For the first time that day, I breathed a sigh of relief. My adventure was taking a turn for the better: I felt my courage come back. Escaping was a matter of now or never. But my two guardian angels forced me to sit back down. Mother Folly called Fool Number Two to the bench.

PHALLUS

Chewing on a cigar, wearing a bow tie, the latter came forward sighing heavily, affecting an imitation of Jacques Lacan: "I'm a couturier of words. . . . I can do everything, there's nothing I can't do, cure girls who are too frigid and those who are hot-to-trot. I am amazed at my own great mind, my great understanding, at my great knowledge, at the imagination and the memory that are mine."

Excited by that pantomime whose gestures were anything but enigmatic, another fool jumped on stage: "Get out of my way, let me get to it." It was Fool Number Three. He proclaimed that all those "rhymesters" of *fabliaux* had invented psychoanalysis. Freud had plagiarized their dream theory. They weren't angry with Freud, though, because in their day plagiarism wasn't a crime. And he gave two *exempla* as proof: two examples of wish fulfillment, low dreams at that, and he hoped Eliot would forgive him but they were as Freudian as one could get.

I was on the edge of my seat, delighted with this development. Number Three announced: "The Monk's Dream," an adventure that had been told to him personally. All the fools grew quiet, as though at a meeting of psychoanalysts. Half speaking, half miming, Number Three began: "A monk rode a palfrey in the streets of Nesles, disturbing everyone. He spied many pretty girls all around. So much so that his manhood grew so taut it almost jumped off his body. Arriving at the inn, he stretched out in his white sheets that smelled so sweetly of a fresh cleaning he began to dream. He was at a fair where the stalls only sold punctured cunts. After a very long discussion, because the merchant was trying to fob off a worn-out one on him, he managed to choose a young English girl's. He even managed to haggle him down 100 *sous* (and a few prayers) because after the Hundred Years' War, the English weren't worth very much. Just as the deal was about to be sealed, he hit his hand on the thorny log between his bed and the fireplace and was awoken by a terrible pain."

"Analyze that one!" Mother Folly ordered me.

I argued knowledgeably that it wasn't anything to get your knickers in a twist about or even to move the Acheron, as Freud would have said. And besides, there was no theory in that story. Number Three should have spoken about repression.

Number Three interrupted: "Listen now to 'The Repressed Wish,' which is the pendant to 'The Monk's Dream,' because in these cases everything proceeds in twos. Due to confidentiality, I will not divulge the name of the Douai couple. But the man, in business, came home from a long trip. The woman, who wanted to celebrate his homecoming, prepared a gourmet meal of meat and fish, with wine from Auxerre and Soissons. Unfortunately for the woman, their celebration ended pretty quickly because the wine got the best of her husband. Not wanting to be seen as piggish, she didn't dare wake him or fondle him in bed. And so she fell asleep from boredom and disappointment. In her sleep, and I'm telling the Gospel truth here, the woman dreamed a dream. She was at the annual market fair. Imagine what they were selling! She saw one so big that even if someone had thrown a cherry in its eye, the cherry wouldn't have stopped its flight before descending into the balls. No one had ever seen anything like that before. Less tight than the monk, she didn't haggle. And in any case, the object was neither worn-out nor ragged, and certainly not English. In fact, said the merchant, it was the best that Lorraine could offer, and Lorraine's balls that year were having a bullish market. Just at the point of sealing the deal, the woman's hand fell on her husband and gave him such a blow that her five fingermarks stayed imprinted on his cheek. He woke with a start and awakened his wife who would have slept if she could have for her joy had turned sour. Waking up this way wrecked her desire which had been wondrous in her dream. The husband asked her to tell him her dream. She made up her mind to do so—either by force or willingly. I don't know which. Completely awake, he suggested they exchange her dream for reality. And that night, it seems, they had a very good time together. It was so good the man bragged about it to Jean Bodel, the Arras poet and rival of Adam de la Halle, and Bodel told it to my ancestor."

As I was distracted, thinking about that fair, Number Three lectured me with other fragments of analytical theory he thought I should know:

"Do you want to hear one on castration? On that delicate subject, we have 'The Unballed Lady' and 'Béranger of the Long Ass.'" He winked knowingly at the audience. I wanted to trip him up.

"What do you have on the foreclosure of The Name of the Father?"

"'Jennin, Son of Nothing!' A simpleton asked his mother, 'Tell me how I'm supposed to believe that you made me all by yourself?' For the foolish mother never stopped denying that he was the priest's son—something the boy knew only too well. Just as Erasmus was the son of a priest, he too was a henchman of Mother Folly."

Mother Folly cut us off: "That's enough. If she doesn't know anything, let her go look for the answers."

SIMPLE MEDICINE

She called to the bench Fool Number Four. Without a modicum of introduction, he announced "The Tale of the Herbarium," a parody of Rutebeuf's tale about medicinal herbs. He was going to make fun of my love of traveling; my heart fell to my stomach under his direct attack.

"I'm a medicine man and I've traveled from here to Japan. I have herbs that pick up pricks and herbs that cool down cunts. My supplier is Lady Trot Good-to-Go from that Italian town known as Salerno."

I was laughing with everybody else, watching him mime his mule, trotting and moving its long ears, when two wild women burst out of the audience, one young and one old. They leapt onto him and threw him off the stage. Taking me to task, they sneered I was a traitor to listen so approvingly to this phallocratic ditty. Had I forgotten the stakes on which they'd been tortured repeatedly for close to three centuries?

I had to admit, shamefacedly, that I'd enjoyed the bawdy tales, forgetting for the moment Big History.

We'll forgive you this time, the young one conceded. But at least know whom that jackass is making fun of: Lady Trotula de Roggeri, the most famous matron of the University of Salerno, where women were great intellectuals during the Twelfth Century. *Mulier Sapientissima*, her knowledge was as great as her husband's, Johannes Platearius, one of those rare men, *viri rarissimi*, who aren't afraid their wives will overshadow them.

I objected: "Not as rare as all that. A lot of analysts have a female responder—Lady Dolto for Lacan, Frieda Fromm-Reichmann for Sullivan, Anna for Sigmund . . ."

The young one cut me off: "Don't change the subject. We're targeting you. Our women doctors knew how to protect their patients from the omnipotence of apothecaries. You push them into submission."

I protested violently: "I've never prescribed drugs."

"Of course you haven't, you had no power to. Don't be hypocritical; you close your eyes to whatever your colleagues are prescribing. Don't you see the apothecaries have sworn to do you in? They will stop at nothing to conquer the market of human souls, and they'll end up making your folk remedies illegal."

"Folk remedies? I don't believe in that garbage."

"How can you say such a thing? So you don't know that the expression 'folk remedy,' in French *remèdes de bonnes femmes* comes from the Latin, 'bona fama,' meaning 'good reputation.' And your reputation, whose strength comes from words, indeed from giving one's word, has been prostituted. It's happened by accepting unacceptable methods: an abuse of drugs, electroshock treatments, sterilization of the mentally ill." In my heart of hearts, something told me she was right. Hadn't Sissi paid the price of eugenics? Yet I cried out: "But I don't have anything to do with that!"

"Tsk, tsk, tsk, tsk."

They left the stage to take the place of the hoodlums sitting next to me, both of whom had gone out for a smoke. Then they opened up before me a magnificent book, illustrated with several color plates. *The Great Herbarium of Salerno*, now in my hands, offered people who couldn't pay for complicated drugs a "simple" medicine—so-called simple because the herbs were not combined with expensive spices. I had no difficulty recognizing common flowers from the woods, the prairies, the hedges, and the byways, with their winged guests: butterflies, dragonflies, beetles, and ladybugs that the young woman pointed out to me.

"Spend some time reading the texts that go with the drawings. You'll verify that Trotula didn't only look at the biological virtues of the plants. She tested empirically how effective they were, and what precisely linked the flower to the organs needing treatment. That was their signature. And she counsels that one must speak to the patient as well as to the plant. Don't be so arrogant! She understood transference as well as you do."

I smiled at that kind of naivety, assured of my superiority over such superstitious beliefs. But I consented to read the text that the old one was indicating so as not to hurt their feelings: "So that gathering herbs will not be reduced to a predatory act, you must ask permission of the plants, 'for man is in some ways brother to the plant.'"

"And woman is their sister," added the young one.

I wanted to please them but also to test them: "Do you have something for anguish?"

The old woman replied without hesitating: "We have valerian, cat nip. It makes cats drunk, you can test it. Gather it in the springtime. Then there is betony, which you can find all summer. When you cut it, you must say, '*Betony, lady of all the herbs, whom Aesculapius first discovered, I beg you through this prayer to help me in all the ways I desire.*'"

The young woman didn't want to be left out and proposed sagebrush, or artemisia, for nerves. "It was named for the goddess Artemis who found three types. One of them, called tansy, makes children happy and beautiful when you burn it under their beds while reciting their names."

"Your recipe seems a little dangerous to me."

"Think again. The time spent looking for sagebrush in the countryside and burning such a lovely-smelling flower under the beds of children while reciting their names calms a mother's nerves. Children aren't happy when their mothers are on edge."

Where had I seen such mischievousness before? I couldn't remember. "And what's Aesculapius doing in all this?"

"We're calling on Hippocrates' accounts as we can't name our own ancestral medicines, the knowledge of which has been wiped out over time."

"Like the medicine of American Indians, forbidden in the United States until the 1960s."

THE POTTER WHO WAS NOT JEALOUS

Mother Folly leapt up, enraged by that harmless remark: "You really are like the charlatan who travels the world over. You want to impress us by singing the praise of the Red Skins, but you only have scorn for the natives of our own plains."

I felt the sting of their accusations. The old woman especially never stopped staring at me and I saw in her eyes a familiar light. Indeed, in spite of everything I felt myself take off for Canada—too bad for Mother Folly—where I saw a similar light ten years ago.

It belonged to a woman whom I had thought quite odd. She had first approached me with a commonsense idea: "If you've come from far away to learn about our medicine, it's because in your country there is something similar. . . . Besides, your coming was announced by a prophecy."

That word "prophecy" put me on alert. That encounter had taken place on the Island of Manitoulin, on the banks of Lake Huron. I was participating in a colloquium organized by the Cultural Foundation of the Wikemikong Indian Reservation and by the Niobrara Institute. It had been an idea of Jerry Mohatt, a cowboy-shrink. He had invited some analysts to share their experiences with medicine men from the Sioux, Ojibwe, and Athapascan nations.

Terrified about being the first one to speak, I finished my oral account at last, evoking as a kind of conclusion the pansies that a young woman, judged to be delirious, had planted around her mother's tombstone to calm her ghost with sweet thoughts (*pensées*, of course, in French). The mother had died without warning. After waiting a moment, I gave myself permission to explain to the assembly the importance of the signifier in Lacanian theory. The long silence that followed my explanation made me take stock of how poorly I'd judged the situation.

During the break, some nearby Toronto ethnologists confirmed my impression by accusing me of laying waste to their academic field. Some American and Mexican analysts made me take tests on Lacanian theory that I probably failed; I was so preoccupied by the Indians' silence. The latter, still keeping their mouths shut, sipped their coffee and ate their fried bread while I stood there, lonely, in the midst of all those people. Then the woman began to speak to me with her visionary words.

That was just my luck, I thought, while, without a second thought, she talked to me about a tree under which war weapons had been buried. It had an eagle on its top. Its roots extended to the four corners of the horizon. Strangers were supposed to come, as I had from the Orient, looking for the source of their medicine. Disoriented by having been taken for an Oriental, I wanted to take my leave and so I asked her her name before saying good-bye.

"Sara Smith."

A man came over to offer us some warm doughnuts. I recognized Art Blue, an Athapascan Indian, a former fighter pilot, and now a psychologist in Manitoba. "You can't tell by her name that she's a famous Iroquois potter."

My appetite came back in a flash and I swallowed two doughnuts, one right after the other.

"And a grandmother for a few weeks now," the potter added. "I've come from the nearby Six Nations Reservation of Ontario. Now that I have the right to stand and speak, I'm not going to deprive myself of it. What I liked the most in your story were the flower-thoughts. Their double meaning is proof that spirits speak through you. What is the name of that medicine man you call your mentor? Jack . . ."

"Lacan?"

"His wordplay fits perfectly into our traditions. Our medicine men have always interpreted dreams and visions that way. We call them 'false faces.' Unfortunately, the masks we employed for these rituals were stolen in order to psychoanalyze museums."

I'd found my equilibrium again.

"And what about that tree with its immense roots?"

"It's the tree of the Iroquois Confederation. One of the oldest confederations in the world. It symbolizes the ties between nations that decided a long time ago not to fight each other anymore. The Federation of the United States copied us. And after that, our tree was transplanted to your country during the French Revolution to be the roots of all Liberty Trees."

Since we were telling secrets, I confessed I'd been very afraid to speak.

"Wait until you're a grandmother. You'll speak the way I do, all over the place. At my age, we Iroquois women have a lot of power. We're the ones

Swanson Branch

Tue Aug 19 2014 05:24PM

33149044582761

GUTE

ELI

Hold Expires: Thu Aug 28 2014

who choose the chiefs who stand in elections. Nobody knows better than we do what they're worth, because we made them. Come with me, I want to give you something."

In her first-floor room, she showed me a little vase made of red earth on which the famous tree, the eagle, the roots, and the arms had been etched with her signature in the shape of a turtle.

"I'm a Mohawk. This is the mark of my clan. Remember us in your country," she said, giving the vase to me. "By following the roots of that tree, you'll find the source of your medicine. It isn't so very different from our own."

"So there's a potter without jealousy!" the young wild woman gloated. "She completely contradicts Lévi-Strauss's 'Jealous Potter.' Too bad for the specialists who love to stoke our rivalries. She knows that both of us are experts in dreams and visions!"

"This is a happy coincidence! Since minds can meet across different cultures, could you interpret a dream I had in France, when I got back from that conference? In a spring-fed pond, in the woods, I saw a white mask settled on the stones at the bottom of the pond. Water came out of its mouth in bubbles. They were words that wanted to speak to me. Since you speak to plants, can you tell me what that water was saying?"

I had asked the old woman, feeling she'd know more than the young one. She answered right away: "What does it make you think about?"

"Maybe Aristaeus's spring-fed plot. . . . And what do you think?"

"Those bubbles are telling a secret you've come here to confess."

"Oh no, you're not going to join in too. . . . Wait a minute. Are you the sorceress who takes care of changelings?"

She only smiled, pulling more confession out of me.

CONFESSION

"You mean it was a death mask, foretelling Aristaeus's death? What do you want me to confess? I don't believe in premonitions."

As she kept on smiling, I went into free association: "A confession. . . . In the 1930s, Henry Stack Sullivan modeled himself on the Plains Indians to inspire the caregivers in his ward—where he welcomed young schizophrenics—not to be afraid of speaking about themselves to their patients. The idea came to him during a discussion with his friend, the anthropologist Edward Sapir. Sullivan had queried Sapir about the odd tie that links the youth of a secret society of warriors, the Crazy Dog Society. When, in small groups, these young men went on the warpath to court danger, they swore that all of them would be ready to die if one of them were killed.

Sullivan wanted to know about this type of transference, of a tie so strong in life you could choose to fight to the bitter end. Sapir answered, 'Among themselves, before leaving, they confessed the times when they had broken their word, especially concerning sexual behavior.'

'Just like in my ward,' Sullivan exclaimed. Pressed to explain what he meant, Sullivan compared the young warriors to his young patients, also caught up in courting danger at the limits of language and of survival itself. Sullivan explained that on that path, he or other staff members were sometimes led to tell something of their own stories. But he never said any more about it, leaving us wanting more information."

I waited for the old wild woman or the young one to make a few comments. They said nothing. What an idiot to have launched into telling them my dream, as if they were analysts!

After a long moment, Wittgenstein stood up and began to speak. He too had had a decisive moment when he was courting danger, in which he felt the need to confess. He remembered the year well. It was 1937. Austria was on the point of being led by a bunch of gangsters. At his hasty return from Russia, where he'd had the bad idea of emigrating, he couldn't stop confessing to a small group of friends that he was Jewish, as well as telling them about certain sexual and other transgressions that weren't worth spending much time on. Drury could be his witness. The latter acquiesced without saying a word. Wittgenstein asked in a rush: "Does anyone have anything to add about those associations of practices, those links, I've been talking about?"

TELLING SECRETS

I continued my story: "In Manitoulin, the Indian anthropologist who spoke after me gave an oral account called 'telling secrets.' He was originally from British Columbia—also an Athapascan—from the same linguistic family in the north of America as the Tarahumara Indians of Mexico."

I'd added that note while glancing in Artaud's direction, because in the 1930s he'd gone to visit them. His seat was empty. Where had he gone?

"So then?" croaked Mother Folly.

"So those Indians think that a person's life is like a pathway for telling secrets. In that way, the most extraordinary childhood experiences are known little by little, like a public good shared by the community. The social link is articulated around all these secrets and is as solid as the structures of kinship theorized by Lévi-Strauss."

"Tell your story first," the old wild woman broke in. "We'll take care of the interpretation later."

"Telling stories is precisely a crucial art of observation and theorization, in which individual experiences accrue the status of collective knowledge. So the speaker recounted the story of critical moments where, traditionally, children left home in search of a vision. Entering into the bush, the wild space of hunting and the wondrous in order to encounter spirits, children came back without knowing how to talk about what had happened to them. During that time, an Elder might dream about the child going through a trial. Thus the Other's dream connected the unspeakable experience to the words of the tribe, by passing through the filter of the unconscious. Far from any manipulation of the child, the Elder would share the dream he had had about him, without interpreting it. The child had to find the interpretation by himself. But the fact of expressing that such a dream really happened was already the proof that the unspeakable is a part of a language game. *Little by little such stories take on reality in the theatre of storytelling,*

This is literally what the Elder said. I find that sentence to be wonderfully true, without really understanding what it means. Can you interpret it?"

The old one avoided my question: "Go to Basel during Carnival," she suggested, "and tell that story to old Benedetti. You'll see how it will become real in the theatre of his storytelling."

"I intend to do so. I already said so to a bee," I answered brusquely, fed up by her not telling me more—by her Indian silence.

"We know, don't lose the thread," she added.

How did she know about that? From the apiary of the Luxembourg Garden where she hid behind the beekeeper's veiled face mask?

"The thread of the story links childhood trauma to unknown knowledge that takes an entire life to be transmitted publicly to a larger and larger circle of people. Far from exhibiting their errors on television as youthful mistakes that seek absolution, those people work through their secrets in the rigorous field of transference and the unconscious. They call themselves *Dene*: 'the People.'

They pay special attention to adolescent dreams that witness a return of childhood visions. And, also, to moments of physical or psychical survival, in war or during hunting when dreams and secrets will first be received within the framework of the Other's speech, which the Elders put into circulation."

The old one said: "Spare us your subliminal allusions to Lacanian myth. We all know he plagiarized the Indians."

"I thought you didn't care about plagiarism! Still, that's how myths are made; it's therapy for social ties at the points where they have been broken, where the painful secrets of childhood are registered."

"Nonsense!" vociferated Mother Folly. "If you want myth, I'll give you myth! Come along quickly my fools, my henchmen, come quickly; make that scatterbrain shut up and let's put an end to this judgment. Help! Herla! Harlequin!"

6

The Theatre of Cruelty

"What did she say?" I asked my "colleagues."

"She called on the King of the Dead, Herlequin."

"Again? I've had enough of this!" I leapt towards the exit before they had time to think about holding me back. A man just entering, his face hidden by a huge monk's cape, blocked my way: "Do you think this hood suits me?"

Forgetting that morning's lesson, I shoved him away with no thought of being polite. In *The Play of Folly and Foliage*, that phrase announces a spirit's arrival from the nether world.

"To hell with your coquettishness, let me through!"

"I've come to hear your confession . . ."

I wasn't going to let myself be cowed by that voice from beyond the grave and wanted to move away from him. He grabbed my arm to draw me back. The Inquisition? My blood froze: "Stop it! Are you crazy?!"

The troll-like specter wouldn't listen to me and kept insisting that I take my place on stage. Facing Mother Folly and her imperturbable court, I was begging for some kind of sympathetic glance. Wittgenstein and Drury stared at a spot over my head. To the left of Mother Folly, the person who'd said nothing until then smiled a little, crinkling his eyelids behind his tortoise-shell glasses. I felt a jolt of kindness. But then, I said to myself, Artaud was still missing.

"Enough laughing!" ordered the evil thing behind me. "Can't you hear the moans of the specters from my wild hunt? Make way for the Knight of Black Metal."

"The what?" I stepped back instinctively, ready to flee into the wings of the theatre. But the other caught me, and shoving his diabolical monk's cape off his face, Artaud appeared, laughing hilariously: "Now I've really got you! I've enlisted you for my Theatre of Cruelty."

Seized by a sudden nervous urge to cry, I must have looked a sight. On the contrary, absorbed in his work, Artaud started to tell me what to do: "Don't move. You're great like that, playing the part of the frightened double, passing through enchantments you don't understand."

"But I don't want . . ."

His look stunned me, and Mother Folly completed the thought: "Do what you're told; we're not asking your opinion."

I had the impression of embarking on a script whose text I'd never seen but that I knew perfectly, something my patients often talked about. What could this be? I asked this question silently of the man with the glasses. Placid, still appearing benevolent, he kept on smoking his pipe; and its tangy smell had the virtue of calming me down. Consequently I was able to understand better what Artaud was trying to do. To illustrate what he meant by the Theatre of Cruelty, he had in the past used the example of Balinese theatre. Now, he wanted to demonstrate that his theatre wasn't exotic at all and that a French farce in the shape of a trial could serve his design just as well, and be understood by anybody. I started to understand in a confused kind of way that I could, in fact, be that anybody. What did he want from me? Luckily he'd launched into a monologue that kept me from having to do anything while he was still speaking:

"Confusion is a sign of the times. Now I see at the bottom of that confusion a rupture between things and words, ideas, and signs that represent them. We can't even keep track of the systems of thought and ideologies that empty us of our vital energy. So much so that we've never spoken as much of civilization and culture as we do now, when life itself is fading away."

People were nodding their heads, encouraging him to continue: "In this context of general breakdown and of culture with no depth, wherever we turn, where our mind only encounters emptiness, I'm proposing a theatre that uses living instruments and continues to disrupt the shadows that have never stopped shaking up life."

Was he using me as a living instrument? I suddenly felt awkward—like a wooden puppet incapable of moving. He didn't notice and started pacing up and down the stage. In their seats the spectators, including Fools Number One, Two, Three, and Four, and the others, were delighted by this new farce. On the stage, there was only Artaud, the jury, and me.

HUBRIS

The man in the tortoise-shell glasses gestured with his pipe that he had something he wanted to say. He spoke slowly, in a German accent: "In this context of general breakdown, are you referring to ideologies born from the principle of objectivity? In the sciences of the psyche, for example, we might say that the rupture between neurons and words contributes to the undoing of subjectivity. If I'm understanding you correctly, your theatre brings back as a shadow the ghost of the subject that science has banished, and the subject demands to know why it has been rejected."

The house was whispering: "Who is he, just who is he?"

A medicine man, I guessed. . . . Impossible! In less than a second, I was again carried to Manitoulin where Joe Eagle Elk, a Sioux medicine man, had asked the same question: "What do we do about Western medicine's unpaid debt to its accumulated knowledge?" For the hubris of Western science seemed to dispense it from offerings of tobacco, even of the minimum necessary to appease Wakan Tanka, the Great Spirit, the Great Manitou, the Great Mystery or the Great Other . . . or whatever name we want to give him. Eagle Elk wanted us to know that we were irresponsible and that the analysts present at the conference had better answer for their recklessness.

Unaware of his relationship to Lévi-Strauss's "savage mind," the mysterious character in the glasses with the pipe gave a backhand answer to a question nobody had yet asked: "Don't make me say what I didn't say. I'm not suggesting we start science all over again. The world can't be a play performed for empty seats, existing for no one in particular . . ."

"And just who is the particular person who is supposed to sit down on empty seats," I asked, the words rushing out of my mouth.

"Why not you? You had hardly sat down on your seat to watch the world's folly when you were thrown on stage and ordered to perform. I'm curious to see how you'll make out. I called on psychotherapists and psychoanalysts myself, once upon a time, to do something."

I couldn't hear the rest of his words. His face disappeared suddenly from view, as he bent over to pet Eliot's cat who had shown up on stage and was dancing around his legs. I thought I heard him speak over the purring of "Vedas," those five-thousand-year old poems. . . . Words about the power of words. . . . To put time back into motion . . . when the moment is so chaotic. . . . Having put the cat on his lap, he sat back up: "It would do you good to have a transfusion of Oriental thought, a homeopathic dose, of course, to avoid thrombosis . . ."

He laughed all by himself over his own cleverness and the cat accompanied him with a meow. It occurred to me that he might be a Sanskrit scholar. I was about to ask him when that chatty Artaud made me swallow my question.

"I had that transfusion a long time ago. My theatre indeed takes its inspiration from Oriental theatre, with its ferocious warriors in states of trance and perpetual battle. . . . For, as I'm sure you agree, the return of the subject can only be ghostly, like the spectrum of light you talk about that is both a wave and a corpuscle at the same time."

Could he possibly be a physicist? Artaud commanded his attention again: "We must create a space where poetry and science can identify with one another. Start from the necessity of the word rather than words that already have shape. Make gestures speak, give back to language its ancient symbolic function . . ." Artaud was growing frantic. I saw that nobody would be able to stop him from now on: "My theatre starts there where the impossible begins. It gives shape to all the great social catastrophes, to conflicts between peoples, to forces of nature, to what chance brings us, to fatality's attraction."

Mother Folly cut short his enthusiasm: "Your theory's a little abstract. Let's have action."

Artaud looked undone: "That demands preparation. . . . I need new scientific means. . . . Besides, the only ones who understand me are the ones who understand what language is . . ."

"You're just paranoid!" A woman's voice had erupted from the house. The young wild woman was on edge.

Artaud paled. Was he going to stop and do the mad number he'd done when lecturing at the Vieux Colombier?

REVERSIBILITY

Wittgenstein came to his rescue: "Be quiet, all of you! I've said it too, the only one who can understand is the one who knows what language games are; only their precise use gives meaning to them."

"Just what use are you talking about?" shouted the young wild woman aggressively. "That's all we're asking you."

"About showing what can't be said," Wittgenstein yelled back, fueled by the same impulse.

The man with the pipe lowered the temperature by speaking to him in their mother tongue: "'*Wovon man nicht sprechen kann, darüber muss man schweigen.*' Didn't you yourself write that what one can't say should be kept silent?"

"Since you and I left Vienna, I've changed my mind. That's all."

I suddenly worried that the most sympathetic among these men was one of those logicians, a member of the Viennese Circle, whose work I couldn't grasp.

"Neurotics!" The young wild woman called on the assembly to bear witness. But Artaud had recovered: "It's not a question of knowing whether we'll be able to make love well, whether we'll go to war, or if we'll be so cowardly we'll make peace, of how we make do with our petty moral anxieties, of if we're aware of our complexes, or if our complexes are smothering us. . . . Nothing to do with social or political theatre that changes as epochs change. I don't want to solve societal or psychological problems. I want to create a space of danger, even if conventional, and make felt through living gestures the truth hidden under forms when they encounter their own becoming."

In a flash, I thought I'd understood what he was saying: "A different royal road to the unconscious than dreams?"

"And modern psychoanalysis would do well to take some interest in it," he added fiercely.

"I was wondering if your theatre could provide access to excised truths, as the Freudian dream does for repressed desires?"

Only the man with the pipe seemed interested in this: "So you are theorizing two forms of the unconscious."

His sentence was lost in the riotous behavior of the house. The public was hysterical, stomping its feel, clapping its hands, demanding at the top of its lungs the theatre that had been promised, no longer staying in place, grotesquely miming the academic debate it had been witnessing. That's when Mother Folly, followed by her court, decided to descend into the house where Carnival had reclaimed its rights. Artaud was in Heaven. Eyes closed, he rocked himself with rhythmic phrases that I alone could hear on stage, standing next to him.

He chanted: "Just as it's not impossible that the pent-up despair and the cries of a madman in an asylum be the cause of the plague, by a kind of reversibility of feelings and images, we can also see that exterior events, political conflicts and natural catastrophes, revolutionary order and the disorder of war, once released in theatre can contaminate the sensibility of the spectators with all the strength of an epidemic."

THE CARRION MAN

"Amen," I agreed promptly in the general chaos, trying also to get off the stage. Shrill cries stopped me in my tracks: "Shit on you Davoine. You're crazy, a simpleton. A nurse! A nurse! May Day!"

That was Sissi's voice! How did she know I was there? The more I looked at the public, the more the house took the shape of a mirage. Twenty years already! Well before Aristaeus, I'd failed her too. . . . Why try to keep it secret? "I have something to tell you . . ." I yelled.

"Silence everyone," Mother Folly screeched, "let her make her confession or we'll never finish this farce."

Before me I felt an opaque wall of silence from which I could hear the strange sound of my own voice. I pulled back: "But I don't know how!"

Artaud tried to be conciliatory: "Don't do psychology, look directly at the unconscious."

"I don't know anymore, nothing's coming to me."

"That's not important. Every real and profound feeling elicits the idea of emptiness in us. Don't try to speak clearly, speak a physical language, mix the abstract with the concrete, let yourself speak in mystical incantations."

There he was in his own agenda again. I was blocked: "Find somebody else who can hallucinate. I don't have the powers of Tarahumara Indians."

"That's not a problem, help yourself to the nightmares of the Flemish Renaissance, let yourself be inspired by the monsters of which I myself never dared dream, how about Bosch and his *Temptation of Saint Anthony* or Breughel's *Mad Meg*?

"So you know her too?" That wasn't such a bad idea. What if I recounted my arrival in the hospital in the north of France, a neighboring country to Brueghel and Bosch? I tried to draw the attention of the man with the pipe. He was looking elsewhere, in Artaud's direction, who continued to work me into a tizzy: "A complete depersonalization! That's what you're feeling. Don't worry about it, as a marionette you'll be all the more able to stage inhuman reality and make room for socially hostile acts."

Instead of helping me, his comments paralyzed me from head to foot. He took advantage of my state to go way beyond the permissible: "Don't make a single move. You're in an ideal catatonic posture to express hallucination and fear."

I was under the baton of a madhouse ringmaster, staging the presentation of a mental case. Artaud was using me: "Let me insist on the spectacular aspect of staged conflicts that never represent men but rather events.

The person you see in front of you is the result of a historic occurrence in which she played her role . . ." What kind of fatal historical epic could that be! I started to get really mad. Against all odds, the public was drinking in his words. They had what they wanted. I was making a spectacle of myself: "That's enough of this game! Aristaeus did not die because of me . . ." It was getting hard to breathe. I was on the brink of a meltdown.

Artaud took on the stance of a carnival barker: "Look at her! The theatre she's performing is analogous to madness, a theatrical crisis that will resolve itself by death or by cure. It's a theatre that tears off masks, invites the mind into delirium, exalts our energies, reveals to communities their dark power, their hidden force . . . for our societies are drifting away and committing suicide without even realizing it."

There's no chance he'll kill himself without our realizing it, I thought meanly to myself.

As if he could read my thoughts, he turned towards me: "Didn't you ever ask yourself if our social and moral systems weren't iniquitous? All your psychological preoccupations stink of what you call man. A provisional and material man, a carrion man! Everything that made life livable has disappeared. We're all crazy now, desperate and sick. I'm inviting us to react to that."

EQUATIONS

You bet I would have liked to react to him, except I actually agreed with what he was saying. Of course an analysis of folly shattered not only psychology but also the limits of psychoanalysis. Of course in addition to the Oedipus complex, it revealed the hidden force of society. To think that analysts believed they were safe in the shadow of that desperate and sick Oedipus, in his tragedies where madness appeared in every page! And here I was, ending up the guinea pig in the Theatre of Cruelty—a strange fate!

Artaud didn't care a wit about my mental torture and harangued the house as if he were trying to work them up into a mass protest: "I say we're not free and that the sky could still fall on our heads! We must find the centuries-old traditions and the extraordinary intellectual level of those peoples who understood civic festivals as a battle of souls with ghosts from the beyond. We must refuse the dictatorship of the writer!"

This dictate struck me in the gut, as I'd always dreamed of writing. No longer able to contain myself, I exploded: "Shut up! Everybody knows you're mad. You're sick. You won't succeed in terrorizing me!"

PROPHETIC FURY

I was so outraged that, trembling, I took refuge in silence.

"Perfect," said Artaud, without concession. "You're coming around to my Theatre of Cruelty. I've never denied it was therapy for the psyche, and you, yourself, are starting to use it for you own good."

"Keep your sadomasochistic scenarios to yourself!"

Suddenly changing his violent tone, he put on an angelic smile to explain: "You're misjudging what I'm trying to do. It's not a matter of vices or perversions but, on the contrary, of a detached and even pure feeling, of a real movement of the mind, rigorous as well as spiritual. I want to unhitch expression from how psychology pounds and molds it and create a passionate equation between man, nature, objects, and society."

"An equation, that's my expertise!" piped up the man with the pipe. "Can I see it? Do you have a blackboard?"

Fearing that this circus was going to degenerate into a mad game of mathematics, I tried to stop it: "No way! You won't get to me with your purity and your detachment! Mark my words. I'll never offer you the ghosts of my own story, even if they start to equate themselves with my patients' unknown."

"All the same, this concerns scientific rigor," the man with the pipe observed.

I felt I had to confide in him: "Don't put salt in the wound. I abandoned the scientific field years ago and I'm not about to return to it now."

Who knows why, but my bluntness provoked one last crisis of prophetic fury: "We must know if here in Paris, before the catastrophes hit, you will pull together what's necessary to make this theatre live or whether we need some real blood right now to demonstrate cruelty."

Artaud was shrieking. He bumped into Mother Folly who was trying to stop him: "Let me pass, I'm returning to have myself locked up again." The door slammed shut behind him. A livid Mother Folly snapped at me: "See how much progress you've made. He already lashed out like this in 1933 before he returned to the asylum in Rodez for institutionalization. Six years later his prophesy came to pass. Real blood ran everywhere."

7

The Esplanade

REMORSE

Horrified at the idea of contributing, even in my small way, to the beginning of the next World War, I went running to try and stop him. Having crossed the anti-panic bar of the theatre, I found myself on the esplanade. Its concrete was even more opaque than when I'd first arrived. In front of me was a wall covered in graffiti, resembling a cabalistic rainbow of signs. I thought I should turn back but the door had closed behind me; my way out was cut off.

Remorse overcame me. It was my fault the play had stopped. I should have given myself over to the role of madness's double, something I had so often performed before. Why did I pretend to know nothing about this familiar mayhem, especially when psychoanalysis is at its wit's end?

When nothing works anymore; when the analysis can't go forward but can't back up into a healthy anamnesis, the void takes over, the slow slog of a suspended present, the prelude to the entrance of a faceless character who reactivates unsuspected mental cracks and fissures. I'd been dishonest with Artaud, refusing to recognize his theatrical crisis as a familiar moment, a therapy for the soul . . .

On the grey esplanade, I expected to see the ghosts of the sleeping suburb disembark. I queried nervously the windows of the projects that looked at me with empty eyes. Were they heavy with coming events? Was there apt to be blood again in Paris's streets? Had Artaud foreseen some germinating *Führer*, waking up in us the sleeping, snorting pig?

SCIENCE HAS LOST ITS MIND

"What do you have against pigs? When compared to us, they smell good."

I pricked up my ears in alarm. Nobody. Then I heard voices: I was in trouble! And yet I felt someone's presence. . . . Behind me, the man with the pipe, his legs crossed, was leaning against the frame of the opened door. He gestured with his thumb that I should re-enter. "Don't look so gloomy. Your judgment is almost over. . . . You're wrong to want to run away. This trial is about the subjects of folly, a cause that's very important to me."

"Because you are also a militant for the Cause?"

"You are correct, a *cause grasse*, as they say in French, the medieval name for parodies of trials, like the one you were subjected to. They just explained all of it to me."

"What are you doing here? You don't seem to belong to their company?"

"My wife Anny pushed me to be part of the jury. She'd been the patient of the Irish psychiatrist Maurice O'Connor Drury, who's also officiating today. Between her and him there's transference, you know, so I wanted to make her happy."

"And you are?"

"A physicist and a poet, in any order you like. Allow me not to reveal exactly who I am. I'm here incognito. If somebody were to find out that I frequented this lot, who knows what would happen. . . . I don't want trouble. We've been political refugees for a very long time on Irish soil . . ."

"Is that how you met Wittgenstein, through Drury?"

"Not at all. Our paths must have first crossed in Vienna, when we were young. Maybe it was 1906 in that genius Boltzmann's course, the year he killed himself because the scientific community wouldn't take him seriously. What folly! It nearly did me in."

"Ah! I would have thought that you and Wittgenstein . . ."

After thinking for a few seconds, he started up again: "He's really changed. A little while ago, in the midst of all those fools, I wasn't very comfortable. Wittgenstein told me not to be afraid of folly, to let it come to you like a friend. That's easy enough to say. Especially when you've, like me, been married to Folly. . . . But I have to admit that the hullabaloo made me look at my wife with different eyes. I would never have believed madness to be so close to today's scientific research. Shall I explain that to you?"

"Not right now. . . . I have to go to my clinic for a scientific lecture."

I looked at my watch. 12:30. That's exactly when I'd left the ward. A little lost, I queried him silently. He told me mockingly what he thought: "As long as it's not your watch hands moving backwards. . . . You do know that thanks to Boltzmann it's possible to think about the inversion of the arrow of time?"

"Seriously, you mean you know something about that?"

"A little. The other reason I'm here is because there's a wind of craziness knocking over all the old paradigms. Think about it! There's no more boundary between the stage and the house from which the researcher observes. So what's happening to objectivity! Even the identity of particles is no longer obvious. We're seeing the propagation of a field or a wave that gives form to space/time itself. Are you following me?"

"Not in the least, but what I do get is that since this morning a series of catastrophes has been set in motion, like a tidal wave, and the result is I'm living in a different space/time. Even my own identity isn't obvious anymore. If it were, what would we be doing here on this esplanade, when, in normal times, we would never have met each other at all? To tell you the truth, I don't find the identity confusion you're worried about all that shocking. We analysts know that the unconscious subject of desire always appears in the gap of the ego's illusions."

"In my own humble way, I'm also interested in the return of the subject in the sciences, especially since the tiny particles in the physics I study appear and disappear like your egos."

"You can tell me about it another time. I'd rather that you help me find the staircase I came up on."

"Not before we clear up an urgent question, the real reason why I'm here. I insist upon it. Artaud predicted blood in the streets of Paris; a deadly gas has been released in the Tokyo subway; psychologists and doctors work on behalf of torturers; genocides are perpetrated under our eyes, even as we speak. Science has lost its mind. . . . Now that we're alone, will you please tell me what you think about electroshocks? I accepted such treatment for my wife for a very long time and I'm not proud of myself for having done so."

THE GREAT MAN'S CRAZY WIFE

"Oh it's very fashionable these days. Psychiatry is into retro," I answered, laughing at my own joke.

He was not amused.

"All the same those 'retro-objectives' enlisted my wife as the object of experiments."

"And with what kind of results?"

"Variable. At the end of a seism, she was sometimes smiling, sometimes exhausted. Incapable of remembering what had happened to her. She asked stupid questions, for example, about what we were doing in Ireland. She'd forgotten how we'd managed to escape, the fight I had in front of a Jewish shop in Berlin. What was its name? Wertheim's, I think. I can still see the sidewalk and the hate in the eyes of those boys from the Hitler youth group . . .

Sorry. Where was I?. . . . A few days after a series of seismotherapies, Anny would come back to herself. Then she'd start to drive Drury and me crazy again. He tried a whole lot of drugs on her, but after that nothing worked. Dear Anny! She got into the habit of driving herself to his unit. Her comings and goings resulted in one positive thing, curing her psychiatrist of psychiatry. So she left him. Mission accomplished. She went on to get her treatment, like Artaud, in another hospital and to use her talents on the next doctor.

It's amazing the kind of progress Drury was able to make—between Wittgenstein for the theory and Anny for the practice. As for myself, every time I had problems, I experienced my wife's gifts for psychotherapy. And God knows there were plenty of those! I had a scrape with an attempt at suicide in 1956, just before my famous Tarner lectures at Cambridge. Have you read them? I would have thought so! I don't mean to brag, but you should take a look. I speak in them about scientists' anguish. Anny was magnificent!

When I wasn't doing so well, her so-called depression disappeared as if by magic. You might say that her melancholia was like an antenna that captured the warnings of a malaise or a misfortune to come. She stopped being depressed as soon as that unknown thing showed up on the horizon and she was able to take care of it without hindrance.

Dear Anny! How much fun she must have had playing the go-between. A real Mata Hari! Determined to foment a psychiatric revolution in the name of the new paradigm we call quantum physics. I began to suspect this when I heard fragments of my own theory come out of Drury's mouth. Not satisfied by citing his master Wittgenstein, he took hold of my ideas to apply them to his field, without asking me what I thought about it."

"I know who you are! I bet you're Heisenberg."

"You lose—and I'm insulted. He and I never stopped squabbling with each other. He stayed in Berlin under Hitler, and justified his choice copiously in his autobiography. I took off. . . . But let's talk about you. I have to tell you that on stage you really seemed troubled. I even asked Drury how we should label your case."

"I saw you were talking to him under your breath."

"Just think about how far we've come since his electroshock period in the fifties. He explained to me that psychiatric categorizations were more a symbol of our ignorance than of our understanding. And he summarized psychiatry's attitude in all this using Voltaire's witticism: *That animal is very dangerous; when you attack it, it defends itself.* While we were waiting for Artaud to finish his performance, we did some more chatting.

He confirmed that in time, under the influence of his patients and especially my wife, with whom he had many long discussions, he had become—yes, even him—very suspicious of shocks and tranquillizers. In fact, he had renounced statistical typology to trust only what he had witnessed in his personal encounters with his patients' madness. I wanted him to tell me more about Anny. But that's where he played an Irish joke on me. He told me his religion wouldn't let him talk about his cases without having allowed them to age at least a dozen years, like Irish whiskey.

I asked him, since we were on it, what his favorite brand was. And we ended up agreeing that shrinks could not possibly, without tasting of folly themselves, recognize the land, the year, the cask, and the number of years it had been fermenting.

I felt very close to his way of thinking. So much so that I couldn't really detect whether his ideas were coming from me via my wife or if, instead, he'd invented everything himself. He made me laugh when he recounted a session of experimental psychotherapy to which he'd been invited. He sat behind a two-way mirror with a supervisor connected by a headset to a student therapist talking to a patient who was pretty far gone. The patient's delusions seemed to signal the presence of some kind of spying operation: each time the young doctor made a mistake in interpreting the patient's symptoms, his supervisor let loose with a beep in his ear. Drury made me see that at another time the same patient would have been famous for his prophetic visions.

Now if you'll allow me to sound a little delusional, I've become more and more convinced that my wife had him read my lectures about the return of the subject in scientific studies."

"Why didn't you ask him?"

"I didn't want to get in the way of their relationship, or introduce a topic when I had understood from what Anny had said that I wouldn't really agree with him. As a good Irish Catholic, he thought it was impossible to bring the subject back into the question of the natural sciences without invoking the supernatural."

"And you?"

"I'm a poet. I told you. I imagine the subject in science like a small character. . . . How can I make you see this? Have you seen the painting *The Adoration of the Trinity* by Dürer in the Kunst Historical Museum in Vienna? It represents a celestial vision, but the artist has painted himself as a humble side figure that might as well be missing. Unnecessary to the scene, he could just as well not have been there, can you see? Nevertheless, without him, the painting would never have existed. To me this is the best comparison with the bewildering double role of the mind."

"The tiny analyst in the corner of a painting of madness, that figure was the double Artaud had wanted me to play. I should have at least tried . . . a character without standing, without stature . . ."

". . . Insignificant, but without whom the picture of science would never exist."

"Are you suggesting that the subject of science and the subject of folly are related?"

"I don't know, but I have to admit that I'd thought I'd gone crazy the day I discovered. . . . Well we were skiing in Arosa. My equations came to me as though out of time, like a present a fairy was offering me. And I'm not the only one. Heisenberg also told me he was in a pretty odd state when he discovered the principle of uncertainty on the Island of Heligoland—where he'd gone to cure his allergy. Do you think that science and madness come together in their attempt to create a formula for the impossible?"

"You go too fast. Could you repeat that formula? You aren't listening to me."

MAD MEG

The door to the theatre had just opened wide, as if thrown by a violent wind. Caught in a trap, I looked all around me. Where was that damned staircase that got me up here? In backing up, I ran into someone passing by, a huge silhouette, surely Mother Folly, who was swearing under her breath about pedants and their books. I ran after her. But she'd disappeared into the rainbow of mysterious inscriptions, and I was stuck in front of the wall, in front of that obscure writing, unable to jump and unable to read, as knocked out as if I'd run into it. I had to fight my inclination to stretch out and sleep, to dream maybe of Oz and over the rainbow.

Enough of this joking! Since this morning my experience had taught me well that The Garden of Earthly Delights could at any time turn into the Garden of Torments. And indeed an optical illusion had just changed the colored tags in front of me into handwritten letters formed from florescent tormented bodies and sardonic death heads.

In the foreground, I thought I recognized Erasmus's skull, laughing up-roariously at all my misadventures. There were all of his teeth! He'd kept them intact until his death at the age of sixty-six. I'd been able to ascertain this a year ago while visiting his house in Anderlecht, near Brussels, where a plaster cast of his skull held the place of honor. It was he—and I was now certain—disguised as Fool Number One, who'd seduced me earlier with his praise of folly.

How could I escape from this satanic jumble? With no clues to help me descend the staircase, I dreamed of rappelling down and sat with my back to the wall to think about it. Goddamn that textbook! I should have crossed the honor court in a flash, not paused in the common ward, never tried to exit from the rear of the hospital, and gone like a good girl to the clinic. What was I doing hanging out with mad delinquents?

For a moment, I could imagine the Father of Humanism as a tough guy from a Renaissance suburb, street-smart and capable of making his way in the margins. Erasmus, the son of a priest, had lost both his parents, dead of plague when he was a teenager. Placed with his brother, Pierre, in a monastery, he took off the first chance he had. And from then on there were a series of moves to escape from the men sent to find him by the convent, from various centers of contagion, and especially from the Inquisition's pyre, where Berquin, the French translator of his *Praise of Folly*, had nonetheless been immolated.

When he was fifty years old, a Papal bull had finally purified the "incest" responsible for his birth. And to think that I, at the same age, was petri-fied by a wall of graffiti—when no one had yet declared a witch hunt for analysts. . . . Although in such a period of fundamentalist thought, some-times the analyst's couch had begun to smell of smoke and brimstone. That threat completely disoriented me. Where was I? I had to find a way to calm down! So I tried to remember the survival techniques that Eras-mus had mastered.

First, don't listen to Artaud, and get the hell out of there. Flee the plague as if your life depended on it! Seduce an editor: Erasmus had simply installed himself with his publishers, whose names I recited as though a ballad of bygone times: Aldus Manutius in Venice, Froben of Basel, and in Louvain, Thierry Martens. Profit from the situation by telling the truth, just as he did. One of his techniques was to publish large excerpts of his correspondence, flattering the big wheels of his world and compromising them in public. The problem was I didn't know many people and even fewer big wheels of this world or any world.

I felt discouraged again. Maybe Erasmus was the folly in his praise, as Flaubert was the Emma in his Bovary, but I was just the clown in the farce. What had I done to end up there? I started to feel the pull of Aristaeus's death again, followed by the visit of the messenger bee and then the arrival of the fools in the honor court.

Thinking about Erasmus's Flanders brought me back to Mother Folly: gangling, disheveled, she was just like Brueghel's *Mad Meg*, a painting I'd wanted to see a year ago. I'd found her, still in place, in the Mayer van den Bergh Museum of Antwerp. She was pacing a burnished red landscape devastated by war and by plague.

As she was not a woman to be pinned down, she'd obviously left the frame to teach me a lesson. I tried to make sense of it. Looking at it from the right angle, *Mad Meg* was only a war-like image of the end of time, returned to claim her place at the turn of the Twenty-First Century. I suddenly realized I was speaking to the wall behind me, as though it were a seated analyst in the place of Meg who had disappeared from the same spot.

Fuck You! Fuck You!

The meaning of the rainbow tag became clear to me all at once. In a minute I was back on my feet and looking at the letters to verify the inscription. The taunt started coming at me in stereo from the theatre's doors from which the troupe of fools were tumbling into the esplanade right in front of me.

The third déjà vu of the day! Just as he had under the arch of the honor court, and on the stage, Fool Number One came towards me, a mirror image of Erasmus only more severe. He asked me brutally: "Where has Mother Folly gone? It's your fault we're orphans."

I indicated the inscription behind my back: "She left that way, but I had nothing to do with it. She was mad long before she met me."

"It's useless to try to flee the blame. In farces, as in tragedies, the fault is collective and today it looks like the carrier of the fault, for us, is you."

"Oh my!"

Some jokesters armed with mirrors and bellows teased me from behind, while Number One continued his lecture as though everything were normal.

STRIPTEASE

"No one responded to Mother Folly's cry in the honor court this morning. The moment to do so is now or never. Normally with farces we hand over to the public the mirrors you see here, magic mirrors to reflect back indirectly what can't be seen otherwise. Then we drag onto the stage the most important political person present who pretends he's not crazy. Today, you're it. Of course the fellow loses steam, like this bellows right here, *follis* in Latin, is losing wind! We're all the same faced with nothingness—just as you are now, like a crazy blade of oats that sways back and forth in the slightest breeze."

"*Let him who has nothing stop worrying, if you have nothing, you lose nothing,*" the chorus of fools chanted. I sighed with relief: "So the farce is over?"

"All that's left is the striptease."

"Oh no, not that!"

"Too late!"

They rushed towards me. Terrified, I'd forgotten we were in the theatre and that this kind of farce always ends with the disrobing of the accused in order to expose the fool's clothes underneath—well-hidden under official garb. They all seemed to be trying crazily to pull on my sleeves. I had to take off my coat, and under it I was wearing a green sweater and yellow skirt, the very colors of folly.

Who would have believed that for that mad day I'd dress in their uniform purely by chance? Crying out joyously, they let go of me to skip around the esplanade. That was when I finally realized that by playing at being an analyst, I really was part of their collective body.

Number One couldn't keep himself from pronouncing an epilogue: "Neither bad, nor good, you're just another fool."

And after happily kicking up their heels in all directions, the fools sang a ditty: "All men are fools / And he who can't see clearer / Should stay on his stool / And break all his mirrors." And then they obeyed a signal only they could decipher and disappeared down the staircase.

During that whole time the man with the pipe remained at a distance, not coming to my aid, amused. He called to Eliot's cat who was funambulating above the fateful "Fuck You." I was mad at him for not lifting a finger.

"You might have done something . . ."

I tried to keep him from leaving, anxious not to be left alone, stripped of all my theoretical and practical bits and pieces: "You know . . . one day I'll have to write about what happened."

He removed the pipe from his mouth: "Your patient is dead and all you can think about is your own immortality?"

"Do you think Aristaeus was hiding among all of those people? They're demons, aren't they?"

"If you like, in a manner of speaking."

"What did they want me to confess? I don't get it. . . . What do you think? There must be some sort of confession ritual. Joe Eagle Elk always began his ceremonies with the story of his inaugural vision, the one that inspired him to become a medicine man. Should I confess how I became an analyst? It's true that patients always ask you: 'What are you doing here?' 'What do you want from me?' 'Why did you pick this job?'

If that's what they want to know, everything started in a hospital in the north of France. . . . Maybe that really is the confession they seek from me. I didn't dare open myself in front of all those people, so they sent me to hell. Read those two words, right under the cat's paws. A little rough, don't you think?"

The cat jumped between us. Falling on its feet, he stretched in all directions, then dutifully began to wash himself. It looked like he'd be licking for at least a quarter of an hour. Lost in thought, the man with the pipe waited for him to finish.

I tried everything to keep him from leaving: "And what if the spring I'm looking for were History? Not the one that gets written but *the one that hides behind the two-way mirror of our silences, on the very place of our betrayals?*"

"Charmingly expressed!"

"It comes from Jacques Le Goff, a renowned historian cited in a book I was reading this morning. . . . If I were to take my own advice, I'd tell you now how I became an analyst."

MAD AS A HATTER

"If you think it would help . . ." The man with the pipe walked toward the staircase, sat down on the first step, packed his pipe carefully with tobacco, then raised his head, surrounded by the smoke from his first puff: "I'm listening."

"To begin with, I should tell you about my arrival. Every psychiatric hospital has its doorman. One of the 'long-time inmates,' as they called them back then, opened the door to the ward, made as if to take off his hat, and begged: 'I work from my hat, could you give my noggin a vacation?'

Troubled by the absent hat, I must have felt in a confused kind of way that one day I'd be the mad hatter. So I crossed the threshold without looking at him, acting as though the man, not to mention his hat, had never existed. I'm only just realizing now that my behavior didn't guarantee any peace for my own noggin."

"I know what you mean. It's not easy to enter a psychiatric hospital the first time."

"The most disturbing element is the physical language that requires you to be 'an athlete of the emotions,' as Artaud once put it. . . . And yet I had learned to look: 'Watch me, you're not doing it right; you've started from the wrong end. Go on; don't stop now. Take your time; you have all the time in the world. Damn! You're clumsy! It's by doing that we learn how. Come on, get with it; take your hands out of your pockets. Don't be afraid to bend. Easy, this time you've got it. Not like that; you're not watching what you're doing. My God, what a knuckle-head! Just do it. Don't stand there like a statue. How can you know if you don't try? Good Lord, she's still reading!'"

"Who's speaking?"

"Voices from my past. I thought I'd find one of them in the hospital. Now you know everything."

"Your story is not clear. Can I go now?"

"Wait!"

"Then get on with it!"

THE SOCIOLOGIST

"I'll begin at the beginning. Imagine the courtyard of a palatial abbey, founded in the Twelfth Century, restored in the Eighteenth. Nestled in a forest. During the Nineteenth Century, that abbey becomes a mental asylum. Imagine again that after having crossed the only street in the village, lined by low houses having sheltered several family dynasties of nurses, a car stops in front of the gateway to the honor court. The cast-iron gates forged in the Century of Reason are open on each side. At the steering wheel the head doctor says to me: 'This is it.' I understand that I'm supposed to get out; and I open the door smack into a sign clearly indicating 'Dead End.' My boss points out the path to a building situated on the right: 'That's my ward, we'll rendez-vous back here at 2:00 P.M.' I look at my watch. It is 8:00 A.M."

"Were you there as a psychologist or as a doctor?" my confessor asked.

"Neither one nor the other. It was a kind of obsession and an inexplicable impulse, helped by a bit of luck. I'd heard my new boss at a conference defend the idea that analysts should learn their trade in an asylum. When he left the podium, I introduced myself as a sociologist researching 'Madness and the Social Link.' I remember I'd added that being a simple observer was unthinkable . . ."

"That's also what I believe."

"Especially when confronting madness. I also confided in him my hope to become an analyst in a psychiatric hospital. My obvious lack of experience didn't seem to put him off. He accepted: 'Come to my place next Monday a 6:00 A.M.' I quickly jotted down his address at the other end of Paris and took the first metro on Monday—never losing track, given the look of my taciturn, bearded captain, of the fact that if I were late, the ship would leave without me.

'Are you the sociologist?' Those were the head nurse's welcoming words to the ward, when I finally dared ring the bell to the entrance of the building— and when I pretended not to see the invisible hat of the man at the door.

In the halls, I kept encountering figures dressed in faded grey, blue, and green uniforms, who either stared at me or looked without seeing. A very heavy young woman, quite pretty, gave me a look to kill. The head nurse explained she was nearly fifty years old. The daughter of a regional grandee, she had been stuck living here after having been sent with busloads of others, at the age of eighteen, to Saint Anne's in Paris where she was lobotomized. Another woman, very tall, dismissed me with an unmoving stare: 'That's Elisabeth, nicknamed Sissi, the Empress of the Austro-Hungarian Empire,' whispered the head nurse.

I can't be an analyst here, I thought to myself. What the hell am I doing? I want to leave. The warm voice of the head nurse pulled me away from those thoughts: 'Come over here, let me introduce you to the nurses.'

We entered a small room where a dozen white blouses were drinking coffee. I shook hands with everybody: 'Hello'. . . . 'Hello'. . . . 'Hello'. . . . 'Hello'. . . . 'Bonjour' one of them insisted while I turned red.

'My name really is Bonjour; I'm from the Jura Mountains; don't pay any mind to that bunch. In this region, they're all idiots.'

The head nurse announced: 'She's a sociologist.'

'Good for her,' said someone else, a little heavier and older. 'We haven't had many sociologists lately. The last one ran away with his tail between his legs.'

Everybody talked at once to give his or her version of what had happened. I think I understood that the nosy interviewer in question had become a little too interested in the local black market for wine.

'You might as well take on the Cosa Nostra,' laughed Bonjour, holding out a cup of coffee to me. 'And just what are you studying here?'

I explained I was an apprentice analyst and interested in madness.

'So you've come to give us a few lessons? We already have one Lacanian who comes once a month to speak to us about the object small a. Do you know that essay?'

I tried to laugh and spilled my coffee. Bonjour got up and came back with a rag at the end of a broom, like a flag lowered at half-mast: 'Just a swipe with the *wassingue,* as they say in Picard, something to clean up your act, the primordial therapeutic tool.' Break was over. He suggested: 'You should go up to Building Five and visit the locked ward.'

'On the top of the hill,' added the head nurse, clearly relieved to get me out of her hair: 'The last one on the left. Leave by the door at the end of the hall.'"

WRITE!

"Finally some fresh air! The hospital's atmosphere didn't quite smell like antiseptic but rather like something musty and indefinable, a new smell to me. I tried in vain to identify it. On the way to No. 5, I ran into men in faded uniforms pushing carts full of laundry or food, accompanied by white blouses. They all said hello to me. I was grateful for their civility. It had become so rare in Paris.

My nose detected something. No question, piss and shit had added themselves to the odors that assailed me five minutes later when I opened the door to the old building where I had just rung the bell. I put on a pleasant face, shook hands with all the people hovering around a white blouse, who was ostentatiously carrying an enormous key ring. I stopped for a minute, alert, because of the noise of the lock being turned behind me. No insane wild person jumped on me—so far so good. It felt as though they'd been waiting. I had to admit my reputation had preceded me.

A loud voice behind me shouted: 'Write! Write! We're all writers.'

I turned around. The man who was speaking was leaning against the wall next to the door. He wouldn't take his eyes off me. The nurse put the keys in his pocket and introduced him: 'George.' We all shook hands. 'I'm a lifer,' he explained, 'because of a crime I didn't commit, that is, not really. So you're a sociologist. How'd you like to have me in your institute? My dream is to be a guinea pig. I gave permission once for a trial drug. Rats, white rats, do you know something about them? How can I help you? I'm giving my body and soul to science. You can do anything you'd like with me.'

'Come this way,' the nurse urged to help me out. Then lowering his voice, 'Prison psychosis, do you want to see his file?'

Overwhelmed by too many impressions, I answered no. We ran into a man smoking a pipe in the middle of the hall. He also stared intently at me. Who did he make me think of? He didn't resemble you: he had brown hair and black eyes. We crossed a room my guide called 'the Quad,' as though he were showing me a historical monument. In fact, as you will see, the place was like a sinkhole that swallows time and history, a quadrangle harboring on its entire perimeter unmoving silhouettes slightly quivering. From one foot to the other? I couldn't really see any movement at all. In the center was a young man in a dirty white hospital gown coming apart in the back. Stretched out on the ground, his ass was in the air.

'What's going on?' I asked the nurse.

'Haven't you ever seen a chronic case?'

The place didn't lend itself to pretense: 'No.'

'We're all chronic cases here. My mother and my grandmother were nurses.'

We passed a group of little old ladies, very well behaved. A clean white sheet attached them by the waist to their rattan chairs. Somebody called to the nurse from the hall: 'Take a look at this. I can't get a needle in. Her veins are collapsing.'

We entered a room where, on a white bed surrounded by bars holding back what didn't amount to much, a very skinny body was protesting: 'You're hurting me. What did I do to make God abandon me here?'

It was more than I could take. I took refuge with the grandmothers, introducing myself by way of starting a conversation with the one who was closest, at the end of the row. She pronounced her words as though she'd been trained at the Comédie Française: 'My father was a tailor. We had two homes. Please give us something to do.'

Looking for something to say, I asked her the name of her neighbor who wouldn't stop chewing her gums. 'I don't know the lady. No one has introduced us,' the seamstress answered coyly.

Then a little man in a grey gown, face glowing, emerged from the group. Like quicksilver and without reservation he introduced himself: 'Undertaker and proud of it too.' He liked it when people died, it meant work: 'I can feel death coming; it's for tonight, she'll have a big dough tomb.'

'Dough from the region?' He must have taken me for an idiot.

'I mean she'll have enough money to buy a beautiful tombstone; she deserves it, given how long she's been here, not spending anything. Her children never came to see her, so nobody's come to steal her savings. This is all well and good, we talk and talk. But I have things to do in the ward next door. A guy swallowed his watch last night. So long.'

He moved away, youthful in spite of his age. All of a sudden I felt the weight of static time threatening to swallow me up. Without waiting any longer for my guide, I tried to find the exit, crossed the Quad, ran into George near the door who was handing the half-naked young man a pair of pants and a loose cloth belt: 'There are ladies here. Get dressed!'

The fellow refused energetically, got up and grabbed the cloth belt that he waved in every direction. George commented: 'He likes belts.'

Raising his whip like a coachman to give the signal to depart, bare ass started to trot softly and grabbed my hand as he passed to bring me along.

Where were we going?

George said: 'Don't be afraid,' while following close behind. 'A schizophrenic smells things that other people don't smell: feet, paint, hair. And what he can't smell or stand he'll hit in the face, and the other person will never see it coming. They smell, they sniff until they get to the origin and then they chase the odor down.'

Were we already talking about a land of springs?

My new guide picked up the pace. I wondered if he could smell me or not, but instead of feeling afraid, as you might expect, I felt certain that, led by that firm hand, I would come back to work here; this was my rendez-vous. But with what?

I'll never know where we were headed. Having arrived at the end of the courtyard, where the showers were located, all of them grimy and moldy ('My kingdom,' George exclaimed, responsible for their upkeep; 'Just see how impeccable they are!'), we were stopped by the supervisor of the ward who introduced himself and asked me what I was doing there. I knew by then I wanted to stay in No. 5. He advised me to ask the doctor to bring me here early in the morning and accompanied me to the door, jingling his keys behind me.

Waiting for the afternoon to arrive, I strolled around the hospital property like a tourist, until two o'clock sharp and my arrival at the 'Dead End' sign.

'So?' asked the doctor.

'So I'm coming back tomorrow.'"

REVENANT

"Every morning at 6:00 I met the doctor at his car in order to pick up psychiatry on the way to the hospital as best as I could, learning from being tested by concrete reality. On the second day on the job, I was told to go to the laundry to choose a white blouse, for which the supervisor of No. 5 had given me a ticket.

'Are you a new nurse? An intern?'

'No, a sociologist.'

'Just what is that?'

I tried to make sense one last time of what I did for the laundry workers, while they marked my name in blue ink on the collar of my uniform. Then I returned to No. 5. Little by little I got into the habit of washing the grandmothers, of wiping up messes (a little *wassingue* here and there), and of drinking a cup of coffee in between. I learned how to shave men in the shared sinks, where I laughed with the nurses who were able to laugh at the general madness—to which the chorus of inmates responded in stereo.

Day after day, like an onion losing layers of skin, I shed my attributes. I was less and less an analyst. Was I a sociologist? The name stuck, like an empty shell. Myself—who was that? A name on the inside of a blouse that had hardly any importance at all. What was important was to laugh with that one or the other one, to make fun of the situation and especially of oneself. In the evening, I returned to Paris totally exhausted. People said to me, 'What's wrong with you?' Nothing. Nothing was more tiring than that nothing. As soon as I got near my school, La Maison des Sciences de l'Homme, I had to drown that nothing in hot chocolate, incredibly thick and made like they used to, in the nearby Café de Flore, famous for it.

'What's the name of that place where you work in Paris?' The man with the pipe, the one you don't resemble, asked me one day, out of the blue—leaving his silence behind for a moment.

I answered: 'Le Centre d'Etudes des Mouvements Sociaux.'

'Ah,' he said, 'you're single!'

The man in the tortoise-shell glasses smiled at the allusion, emptied out the bowl of his pipe by tapping it against his heel, and echoed the question: 'I was going to ask you that myself . . .'

I had noticed, indeed, that I was the only one working for these social movements. I alone wanted the walls to crumble, the doors to open, the chemical controls to stop. In sum, I was 'antipsychiatral.' It was really true that the walls in question, a thesis subject for a Foucaldian student, oozed the *great confinement*. As in the story of Bluebeard, there was a large forbidden room 'up there,' and I wanted to get in.

'At your own risk,' I was warned. 'We've leveled and realigned the floor but the floorboards are still rotten because of the soiled straw from the patients' bedding. They were moved out not all that long ago.'

Once, at lunch, I expressed my concerns out loud at the table, while serving myself a piece of badger meat that some nurse had illegally poached. It tasted all the better for being a forbidden food, marinated and simmered.

Shortly after that, nobody was surprised by what the man with the pipe, your homonym, did. He made an appointment with the intern on his forty-sixth birthday. Contrary to his usual behavior, he actually went to the appointment, but he demanded nothing less that the termination of his treatment, a treatment that hadn't been changed for years. The intern accepted. The hero of the day took me aside in the corridor: 'I stopped the medications to see if there'd be any change,' he said.

'And what happened?'

'There wasn't any.'

That man, with his intense eyes, had some influence on the others. What he had done provoked a copy-cat flurry. We called a meeting.

'In any case, most of them don't even take them,' argued the nurses, philosophically, having found the colored pills that came out of the little boxes with the patients' names on them in sinks, bras, toilets, and gutters. The cats had their pick of drugs. In the past, the boar that fed on slops at the neighboring farm had become completely impotent because of them.

'Just like the male pig from the Ville-Evrard psychiatric hospital,' somebody, whose great aunt had worked there long ago, commented.

To foment our revolution, it was decided that the distribution of medications would rely on demand. A 'meeting of the patients' ratified the decision. As their names were called out, the question was asked: 'What about you, do you want them or not?'

Most of the patients took them only to throw them out afterwards, as usual. The man with the pipe refused and paced back and forth in the Quad, puffing away. Seeing me arrive, he noted, 'I could stop if I wanted to.'

'Why don't you try to get out?'

'What's the point?'

Everything was back to normal in two weeks. It would take more than that to stop the silencing machine from functioning."

INSIDE OUTSIDE

"Sometimes my heart wasn't in it. I remember one of those grey winter mornings, lost in an enveloping fog, where neither my ears nor my words were able to grasp anything. I was seated in No. 5's kitchen. A nurse was ironing, another one read the obituaries in the local paper. She saw the name of a childhood friend, went on to talk about the death of her husband four years before. A third one came in, pregnant, wearing a black vest. She recounted the accidental death of her eldest son on one of the iron spikes surrounding her house, which prompted another nurse to fret about his wife's depressing heart condition.

Sometimes the social worker would take me with her on visits to the countryside around the asylum. She knew thoroughly the geography of the region's madness, spanning several generations. One day we went to see people who had been farmers. After three devastating wars, those fertile plains had seen any number of small farms go under, to be replaced by agribusinesses specializing in sugar beets and potatoes.

It was the usual story. The grandparents had had a small farm. The parents had to stop working their own land and take work as day laborers or farm hands for others. Some had tried to turn themselves into factory workers. They became city workers without any urban culture, and ended by filling up detox wards. When their social survival became impossible, whether because of accumulated debt or because all the old people who'd served to connect them to their traditions had died, their small farms became hovels, like the one we parked in front of that day. In the courtyard, next to a rusted tractor on which a few hens were roosting, an abandoned motor scooter seemed to be waiting for someone.

'It's been in that place for twenty years,' the spinster social worker commented. 'It's the only sign of the person in the asylum.'

His craziness claimed him when he saw the horses he was responsible for start to disappear from the farm where he'd been working since he was fifteen years old. His boss had tried to help him learn the new system, but he got stranger and stranger. And then one night, he stunned the boss by making the tractor do circles and backfire in the farm's courtyard, as he had always done when the horses were having trouble with gas. He was diagnosed as psychotic, went into the asylum, and all the responsibility for his family fell on his wife. She survived with their children, like a bohemian, thanks to what her traditional gypsy family had taught her to do.

She invited us to have a coffee in the shambles of her house where we talked about the 'absent one.' She didn't bring him home anymore as he'd gotten violent. In leaving, I thought about what the patient had said to me when I'd announced I was going to visit: 'What's the use?'"

PSYCHOANALYST?

"More and more often, I hung out in the Quad, leaning against the wall, not doing much, just passing time. I found it restful.

I could finally recognize all of the permanent denizens. From time to time, one of them did pirouettes in the middle of the room. Two old fellows, always the same, argued ceaselessly over incidents that happened when they were still in their right minds. Others smoked and offered me unfiltered Gauloise that I accepted with pleasure. Others stayed silent, rocking constantly and softly humming. Bits of popular songs began, then faded out like will-o-the wisps. A fat man was sleeping, stretched out on the ground, his powerful snoring providing rhythm for the 350-pound body that acted like a resonating chamber. Sometimes the Prince of Monaco, crowned by a fur bonnet decorated with a Communist star, came to sit in the middle. That was when he wasn't busy sending his interminable and unreadable coded letters to the Principality.

One day—who knows why that day—I realized that the rocking, humming rhythms and songs that seemed to be addressed to nobody were, in fact, addressed to me: 'It's really *concerning*, as the Swiss would say. . . . Of course that's French, no it's not a made-up word.' Bonjour attested to that linguistic innovation from a cousin on the other side of the Jura Mountains. He was our guest that day from the other ward, where I hadn't made an appearance since I'd first arrived, except for required staff meetings.

Helped by some wine from Arbois, I recounted at lunch what I'd been able to make out of those words thrown out in a circle like waves, without anyone looking at anyone else. They finally made sense to me: 'Sociologist . . . ' 'What's that?' 'It means you're not married.' 'She comes by car from

Paris . . . ' 'It takes a lot of gas . . . ' 'It costs a lot . . . ' 'What's a sociologist?' And someone had suggested the answer: 'It's like a nurse, only free.'"

THE MAN WITH THE PIPE

"No one wanted to believe me, but we toasted to my visions anyway.
From that day on, nothing was like it had been. Even though nothing had
changed in appearance, I started to act differently. I started looking for
what was meant for me in this mountain of nothingness. And all of a sudden, the man with the pipe wanted to talk. We sat down together in No. 5's
big common room. It was empty. Everybody else preferred the Quad, a
veritable monad, eight square yards without windows or doors. (The door
had been kicked in and never replaced.)

Facing him, in that vast deserted common space, I could clearly see the
place's faults. The Quad was a geometric space that provided a locus for
all conveniences. Ideally located between the dormitory and the refectory,
not very far from the toilets, at the foot of a staircase that led up to another dormitory and the infirmary, it was less a crossroads than an obligatory crossing. From there, you could enjoy, without even seeming to, the
spectacle of busy white blouses, elegant residents rotating through twice
a week, and especially, the highlight of the day, the daily visit of the head
doctor, followed by the head head nurse, and all their 'court.'

The man with the pipe said, 'You shouldn't try to understand. Well, you
should try to understand. Do you think it's worth it? In Paris, there's Saint
Anne's psychiatric hospital, right?'

'Yes.'

'But others, Charenton and Maison-Blanche. Places like that should
be destroyed.'

'And everyone who's in those places . . . how will they live?'

'Outside, like everybody else.'

'What about Biba and his belt?'

'Oh he understands what's going on. Do you know Maison-Blanche?
That's where I went the first time.'

'Why?'

'I don't remember; I wasn't doing well. I'd wanted to get married when
I was twenty-four.'

'And so?'

'It wasn't easy.'

'But I bet you were good-looking.'

'That's not it. Even ugly people get married.'

'So what was it?'

'Money. I worked the land for my parents. I went to Maison-Blanche, only for fifteen days. They gave me electroshock. It helped me. The second one made me worse, then I left and things weren't good until I turned thirty. After that, I came here. You think it helps to tell you all this?'

'Yes, I do.'

'I'm pretty old now. Before I lived in a fog. Now, since I've been here, I've understood some truths I thought were lies. Don't you think they lead us up the garden path? Other people like to earn money. They're happy, I guess. You're looking for truth in books. You'll write a book.'

'I don't think so.'

'Books are the devil. Nothing wanted to stay in my head in school.'

'You didn't like to learn?'

'I was always the first, but for me I was the last. I thought the others were acting like jerks on purpose, so they wouldn't do well. They all understood better than I did, even if I acted like I knew more than they.'"

MY ANCESTORS!

"That night, I remember it well, I dreamed about a man behind bars and I woke up with a start. Was it grandfather? That was too easy. Impossible, I repressed the thought. My grandfather had disappeared before I could imagine what had happened to him. I used to see him in dreams, stuck behind a gate, same intense and serious look, same gesture of packing his pipe, reluctant to speak.

Stuck in fact in a hospital far away because of hardening of the arteries. . . . Do you think they were afraid he was losing his mind? I see you don't want to answer me. His presence was eclipsed, his gestures rubbed out, his look erased—truths became lies, it was all about the garden path, and my 'absent one' was covered over by meaninglessness.

When he came home for the last time, I saw him in his pajamas in the kitchen. He was asking for the trumpet he'd brought back from World War I, so he could play me a tune. No one answered him. I could tell by how they were all looking at each other that the adults thought he was lost for good. So he started to whistle like men did before gramophones were invented. They led him back to his room. A week later, he was dead before I could see him again, writhing in circles on mattresses covering the floor.

That day, I went all by myself for a walk in the countryside. 'Do you think I went to that mental hospital looking for the absent one I had hoped to find in the countryside when I was eight? Or, rather, looking for a vision . . . going on a vision quest, like the Indians of the Far West? . . .'"

"Who knows," said the man with the tortoise-shell glasses and the pipe, quite unmoved. "But now, you'll have to excuse me, I have an appointment at a school. They're going to be speaking about the French translation of my Tarner lectures. The book has just come out, *Mind and Matter.* You should read it. Goodbye."

"I doubt if we'll see each other again. . . . Could you tell me your name?"

He was already out of sight. To think I'd told my life story to a stranger whose name I didn't even know. Oh well.

I had to pick up my car from the hospital. Just about to descend from the esplanade, I thought I heard someone yell behind me: "Fuck you! Shit on you Davoine! You're an idiot. You're crazy! Get the hell out of here."

This time I stayed cool: the Empress's voice was simply my imagination. Sissi had been trying since that morning to make herself present to me. But to protect my ego, I'd carefully avoided recounting my spectacular failure with her to the stranger with the glasses. I was sure she was cursing me, just as Mother Folly, whom she resembled by her gait and brutality, would also have done.

To put an end to my escapade, I quickly ran down the stairs. I spied a bus station. It was already 1:30 P.M.! I was famished. Rocked by the ride on the bumpy streets, I dreamed of the buffet that the apothecaries were going to offer me.

8

The Clinic

"Holy Smoke," I said to myself arriving late, "he hasn't finished yet."

Accusing looks accompanied me to the chair from which I listened to the expert, a former doctor in our hospital, just returned from the States. Driven by a mission to convert all of us, he laid out his conclusion. Thanks to the overhead projector he was using, we could even visualize it. I focused on the screen, as if I weren't smart enough to grasp without this apparatus the hyper-simple ideas he was slowly and pompously illustrating. All his science was in his tone and transparencies. From which we could conclude that:

1. Our psychotherapy methods were incapable of producing any statistics, thus any evidence-based data. They were poorly served by our verbal hype. ("Excuse the expression," he added.)

2. They didn't cure very many people according to the assessments effectuated in the United States (which my lateness had prevented me from having to follow on his colored charts).

I'd had a taste of all of this from an earlier return from the U.S. of a specialist in follow-up studies. Very sure of himself, even though he'd hardly encountered a patient, he opined about mental health according to norms that were as exciting as the number of times one goes to the movies, or the frequency of phone calls one makes, and the variety of TV programs one watches. You didn't have to be a genius to see in all of this the shipwreck of fifty years of illuminating discoveries in the Anglo-American arena of psychodynamic psychotherapy of psychosis. The official discourse of the *Diagnostic and Statistical Manual of Mental Disorders* had adjusted the language of U.S. analysts to reflect the American way of life. While I was remembering this, the lecturer continued enumerating his conclusions, adding:

3. If we French really want to be scientific, we must give up our obsession with clinical histories, indeed our obsession with History itself, with its terrible confusion of details that are unverifiable by a computer. Such a waste of time compared to short-term therapies, the "rich and quick" ones, as they say over there, and the only ones efficient enough to avoid the variable of time.

(Thus from Nevada to Mongolia, *l'homo* of the *DSM* would be *psychiatricus* or would not be—just like dinosaurs are thought to be, with the exception of a few details, exactly the same monsters from the steppes of Asia to the American plains.)

4. Consequently, we must get rid of our bad language habits, use a psycho-correct vocabulary, purchase the American classification system (that he could indeed sell to us in its brand-new bright green edition).

He picked one up, and to prove to us that his bible had thought of everything, read a vague sentence out of the introduction about the importance of clinical experience. No one understood it. Then he gave us marching orders: all the old nomenclature had to be dropped; it didn't scare anybody; it had no impact anymore, given that anyone could, without a second thought, call his neighbor manic, a melancholic, a schizophrenic, or paranoid. However, notions such as "dysthymic disorders," "bipolar illness," especially if combined with the label "genetic," which could be proven although it never was, now had the same force and efficacy that magic concepts, such as fatality and destiny, used to.

5. Finally, at last mastering their own subjectivity (as well as the universe, quoting Corneille), new-style researchers would be able to observe a patient's symptoms much more objectively—now that they no longer had the kind of troubling relationship with suffering subjects that psychiatrists such as Bleuler and Clérambault couldn't avoid.

6. To sum up, he preached austerity, reminding us of how terribly expensive health care had become (without a word about the huge

amount of money wasted on inept assessment experiments). The moment was dire. The economy was in major trouble, and folly a true illness that should be treated quickly, with molecules adapted to each computerized symptom—or even better, with electric shocks capable of shortening stays in hospitals and of calming a population already pretty far out there (thanks to diverse drugs that would soon be distributed like tap water). Today, de-institutionalization obviously meant saving money. And furthermore, an armada of U.S.–trained lawyers was preparing their D-Day to launch the malpractice market in France, a pretty profitable one.

Then his threats became patronizing. Our guru was ready to talk with anybody, especially to hear what worries the psychoanalysts had about all of this, given that he, himself, was one of their lot. (And just what wasn't he?) He'd even had, God knows why, some encouraging results.

The greatness of his soul, his humanity touched me to the bottom of my being. I hadn't expected such compassion, and the drop of psychoanalysis he allowed us in his implacable rigor was like a balm, an unhoped-for elixir, especially in light of what I'd been through that morning. I could finally relax. Aristaeus's death was forgotten, my morning phantasmagoria nonsensical, the man with the pipe and the tortoise-shell glasses repressed. This psychiatrist knew where he was going. He was the man for me. Smiling, well-dressed, warm, athletic, not bad at all, my God, what more did I need to feel better.

I almost applauded, I so much hoped to join an unquestioning cohort of bigots devoted to a cause. Humanity, for example, which he couldn't stop talking about. What a man! Indeed! I had to control myself, seeing that everybody else was looking at their laps, except for the head doctor whose beard seemed to be looking out the window.

DISCUSSION

"A patient from our ward died yesterday morning. How will your statistics help us face our immeasurable mourning? I imagine you'll say we diagnosed him improperly." A young resident had just gotten to his feet.

The expert took on the role of the sincerely moved: "I don't deny the human dimension, but when it comes to assessment, we owe it to ourselves to be Cartesian."

"You are no doubt alluding to visions that came to Descartes that fa-

mous night of November 10, 1619, during a nightmare, s<
ago—since you like numbers. According to Descartes, *the*
admirable science—which you seem to be caricaturizing h
fertile results of this visionary episode. God's spirit visited D<
his reason, for he was being tortured by ghosts and terroi
all around his bedroom. 'What path should I follow in lifε
dream, just as we do today.

And do you know what a guardian angel recommendε
poem by Ausonius, entitled 'The Yes and No of Pythagoras'
poetry and science. That's what founds his *Discourse on Me.*
he wrote eighteen years later in French, instead of Latin, in o
by 'women who are the health of the world.' In that case, pc
you put it, helped inspire scientific findings. How do you think your *DSM*
would classify his experience today?"

The head doctor seconded his resident by displaying a book meant as an
antidote to the *DSM*: "In fact, delirium isn't so bad. It's not I who says that,
but Erwin Schrödinger, the inventor of the equations in quantum mechanics. It's all here in his *Mind and Matter*, which just came out in French."

So put that in your pipe and smoke it, I thought, jumping up at once.
I grabbed the book and shoved it in my bag as witness to the morning's
encounter.

Not seeing the state I was in, the head doctor continued: "Schrödinger
affirms that the maddest theories have led to the best results. First, because
it's better to have the wrong theory than to have no theory at all. Second,
because the more a hypothesis is arbitrary and unfounded, the less it risks
being responsible for future intellectual debacles, because experience will
eliminate it much more quickly—while your science, cut off from experience, thinks it can reinvent everything, starting by 'new' classifications that
come from the last century.

You should take your inspiration from Pythagoreans. Their faith, even
more mystical than yours in terms of numbers, prompted pretty delusional theories that led to the belief that the Earth spun around a central
fire. That lasted until the great Hipparchus, President of the University of
Alexandria, disproved their system in the name of reason."

"Don't think I don't know the writings of Pythagoras and his belief in
the transmigration of souls," the Cartesian Dr. I-Think-Therefore-I-Am,
riposted with a knowing air.

The normally taciturn head doctor couldn't seem to keep quiet: "As for metempsychosis, Schrödinger counsels us to hear in it modern resonances. He recalls what Pythagoras said watching a dog being beaten: 'Stop, for I hear the voice of a tortured friend who's calling for help.' Schrödinger wants us to acknowledge that their joys and sorrows are closer to our own than we suspect. So those three-thousand-year-old cries sound to him like the echo of voices being tortured across space and centuries, right up to our times."

An Argentinian analyst supported this idea: "Like the voices of the *desaparecidos*, carried by the Crazy Mothers and Grandmothers who circled around La Plaza de Mayo in Buenos Aires with the portraits of their disappeared children, whom they asked to have brought back alive—because no one would confess to having made them disappear. I work with autistic children. The analyst Frances Tustin speaks about predation, or a brutal survival of the fittest, as a way of describing the world where these young patients live. At the same time, she believes they are rationalists, not so far from having a scientific outlook, provided that their therapists have enough intuition to share their inquiries. Maybe they're specialists in the field of catastrophe?"

This was a prompt to the young resident who recently had been swearing by catastrophe theory. For a moment I pictured Viviane's moves when she turned her back on me as Aristaeus's death crossed my mind. The resident took the bait.

"Why not? Autistic children are sensitive to the least little change, to even a suspicion of differential. They thus invent forms in order to communicate. According to what René Thom says in *Morphogenesis and Catastrophe,* catastrophes generate forms. We shouldn't think of 'catastrophe' in its negative sense: any discontinuity on a continuous background is a catastrophe. The edge of that table, for instance, is a catastrophe. It holds within, one might say, the memory of the saw that cut it. Along those lines, René Thom evokes manic-depressive psychosis."

"The analogy with brutal breaks and the beginning of folly is of course tempting," answered the head doctor. "Without quite going there, I might add that sudden breakdowns after a big success are also frequent. I heard that your mathematician Thom had the courage to recognize he was really in trouble after having received the Fields Medal—the very year that John Nash, another beautiful mind, lost the competition and his mind as well."

The fan of quantitative methods tried to find his footing in this discussion: "That was a long time ago. You can object as you want to experimentation. . . . But today positron cameras can analyze objectively our mental images. Pretty soon our unconscious won't need a couch."

"Can your camera take a picture of the edge of a word that's never been uttered?" I asked timidly. I was hoping that this James Bond cognitive type would help me resolve the enigma of Holtzminden. The resident went on, heatedly: "For Thom, folly is prey that takes itself for predator. What do you think of that definition?"

"But what's the relationship between math and hunting?" I asked.

Scandalized, he looked disappointedly at me. How could I not know more than that? I tried to justify myself: "It's just that in the hospital you often feel not at all like a hunter but really like prey. . . . At least I do."

I didn't dare mention my morning's adventures, the vague sense I had of being relentlessly tracked, of having constantly eluded my pursuers. What a damned comparison! All of a sudden I could imagine Aristaeus like the mythic Black Hunter, Herla, the King of the Dead, leading the wild hunt or Mesnie Hellequin, with his Valkyrie companion who resembled Sissi, the Austro-Hungarian Empress.

The head doctor stood up.

"Let's have a drink to clear our heads of this wild hunting."

Everybody happily joined him.

CHEESE

Raising his glass, the head doctor wished us a good Samhain, the Celtic feast—according to the calendar of his Breton ancestors—that prefigured All Saints' Day. Paying no attention to the solemnity of the moment, the resident and the returnee continued their argument.

"It's easier to start with the continuous and move on to the discontinuous than the opposite. Try, for example, to make Gruyère cheese by making the cheese stick to the holes. René Thom couldn't do it, and he's even from the region of Franche Comté where Comté, a kind of Swiss cheese, is made."

I added what I'd learned that morning: "In the Middle Ages, cheese in French (*fromage*) was called *formage* because of the form of the wooden mold."

The all-knowing resident had already learned that: "They thought cheese was a symbol of spiritual gestation, as we see in a vision of Saint Hildegarde from the Twelfth Century. Several kinds of cheese appeared to her, held in vessels by the world's inhabitants, separated according to taste, from strong to sour to mild, according to the degree of ripening and in keeping with the diversity of the world's people. And that's not all: because of that kind of mystical belief in cheese, a miller from Frioul, Italy, was burned four centuries later by the Inquisition. So cheese was also a symbol of folly, along with the club of the wild man. Quite a subject for catastrophe theory, don't you think? Blows from the club to quell anxiety and yeast to make transference rise."

Then the "scientist" attacked the "Thomist": "But if your brain is destroyed, you won't be able to think anymore."

"Here you come with your knock-out argument. Obviously if you come after me with a cudgel and squash my head, I won't be able to think anymore. But if your club stops me from thinking, it's because it destroys the forms that are ideas and the words that express them—as well as the neurons. Instead of reeling off your classifications, you'd be better off reading Plato's *Phedra*. It deals with folly and the forms, that is the ideas, perceived on the brink of the fall of the psyche."

Encouraged by the champagne, I tried something else: "Talking about hunting and clubs. . . . A long-term patient once told me that schizophrenics can trace odor to its origins."

SHE'S OUT!

"It was George who used to say that."

Surprised, I turned to the unknown voice behind me.

"Have I aged that much? Don't you recognize me?" And then I realized it was the head nurse who had originally welcomed me to my first hospital and my very first ward.

"What happened to Sissi, The Empress, I mean Elisabeth," I blurted out forgetting all about being polite.

"She's out! She's living outside. She has her own place now."

"Really?"

"After you moved, we picked up where you left off. One step at a time. She recently was able to leave the hospital for a half-way house. I've left too; I retired. Your head doctor invited me as a guest today. I'm often at my daughter's who lives pretty close by."

After a few moments of celebrating our reunion, I left the clinic, lighter than I'd almost ever been in that place. I urgently wanted to read the notes I'd taken under Elisabeth's command. She had ordered me, as George had, to write. Scribbled under her dictation, my papers had been sleeping since then in a folder. Euphoric, I decided to go home and look at them.

PART II

THE RETURN OF THE SUBJECT

An investigation is possible in connection with mathematics which is entirely analogous to our investigation of psychology. It is just as little a mathematical investigation as the other is a psychological one. It will contain no calculations, so it is not, for example, logistic. It might deserve the name of an investigation of the 'foundations of mathematics.'

Wittgenstein, *Philosophical Investigations* (II, 14)

1

Asphalt

UNPACKING

In a hurry to pick up my mail, I parked my car in the bus lane in front of my place, needing just the time to enter my building and leave again. Among the many envelopes, I finally found the only real letter destined for me.

Dear Madame Davoine,

Thank you for participating in our collective volume on de-institutionalization. After having read your text, however, the editorial committee has several suggestions to make: As far as the title (*Madness and the Social Link*) and inter-titles are concerned, they are far too ambiguous and will not guide the reader sufficiently. Your style is far too literary, even subjective, and differs in its general tone from the other contributions. It disrupts the hoped-for harmony of the volume. Unfortunately, and despite my enthusiasm for your original proposal, your text cannot be published as is. Would you please adapt the style as suggested; the content remaining nonetheless more than adequate. To that end, I'm sending you a sample outline and guidelines to help you in revisiting your work. Hoping that you'll be able to make the necessary adjustments so that we can publish your piece, I send you my very best.

A second sheet provided the guidelines and model:

Chapter I: Propagation of Fiber Optics

All that electricity and I didn't even feel a spark. I'd completely forgotten about the article the editor had solicited and even accepted "enthusiastically" the year before. A promise isn't always a promise! Anyway, who cares? Stuffing my mail in my bag, I crossed the sidewalk to my badly parked car.

It was almost dark and very damp and cold. The sidewalk was slippery. My bag simply refused to give me back my car keys and vomited its whole contents onto the sidewalk.

"So you're unpacking? You're emptying out?" A young man was on his haunches next to me. Despite the shadows of the end of October, I could see his worn clothes, his fatigue. Some tinkling coins were rolling about in the gutter and he picked them up, collecting at the same time letters and envelopes, various ID papers, and scribbled notes. I had tried to catch *Mind and Matter* as it flew out of my bag, but the head doctor's book ended up torn and in the gutter. Wiping it off with the back of his hand, the young man took a look at it. The torn book seemed naked to me without its cover. I confided my bad luck to him. He didn't seem that surprised.

"This isn't such a strange occurrence for Samhain Night."

As he was getting up, I wanted to offer him some money. He wouldn't take it and started to leave. Had I hurt his feelings? Was he in a hurry? I suddenly remembered the head doctor's toast: "Samhain, you mean All Saints' Day, don't you?"

"It's the night when the passage between the living and the dead opens up."

Thinking about it made me sad. Aristaeus had waited for this opening to leave. . . . And what if he took advantage of it to come back?

The man frowned: "Is something wrong?"

"Well I don't believe in ghosts. . . . But I guess you never know. . . . Where do you think this passage is? In psych wards? At the openings of metro stations?"

"Where do you get such crazy ideas?"

"From the hospital where I work. So much happened this morning, kidnappings, disappearances . . ."

"You have too much imagination. The only name that is somewhat historically verifiable is Avalon."

"You mean the exit after Vézelay on the Highway to the South?"

"Of course not. Avalon is a lost island governed, they say, by nine women. The fairy Morgan is their leader. The only possibility of finding one's way there is not to look for it and encounter it by accident."

"I know. In the hospital where I work, there's a room like that. I found it this morning by pure chance. But tell me, since you know so much, would you be able to help me find a land of springs?"

"I'd like to find it myself. I'm very sorry; I can't help you. So long then! Maybe we'll see each other again."

I wish I had learned his name. Maybe he caught mine from my papers. Eyes glued to his silhouette disappearing in the shadows, I stayed planted in the middle of the sidewalk. And I was invaded by the feeling of déjà vu. And yet he looked nothing like Aristaeus. Nothing at all.

THE JUGGLER

Maybe he was like that mournful and weary man I'd met the summer before in a parking lot in Germany . . .

Crossing the country during vacation, I'd seen Holtzminden on a map. The guidebook praised it as a tourist spot, citing "its greenery, its climate"—without saying a word about a World War I concentration camp. Aristaeus must have made that up. In my revisionist history of his story, fate also had a hand: it must have been written that I was never to see that enchanted site. A wrong turn at the interchange had sent me to the East, to the former border between the two Germanys. I got off the highway at Eisenbach, known for "Bach's childhood home," and "its famous Wartburg Castle, the site of poetry contests of the Minndesängers, including the famous Tannhaüser."

In the parking lot, I waited for the bus that my guidebook told me to take to the castle. The bus wasn't coming. Nobody was around, except for an unknown man sitting on a bench watching me out of the corner of his eye, while appearing to be absorbed in his newspaper. Was it a Stasi agent? I was being delusional; those days were over. But I no longer knew what I was doing on that cracked asphalt in the middle of nowhere. The parking lot and Wartburg Castle were as unreal to me at that point as the pavement and my badly parked car when I dropped my bag. No bus, no *Burg* in sight—and added to all this, to put the cherry on my bad-luck cake, that Looney tunes man standing in for Tannhaüser.

It seemed he was making magical signs, because at the point I'd lost hope, the bus arrived, an old, bumpy jalopy out of which an Old Regime driver unfolded himself. He tapped his watch to signal that we had to wait the scheduled time before he would take off again.

During the whole wait, the bus remained hopelessly empty. Nevertheless, the unknown man couldn't find a better place to sit than on the seat facing me. I tried to behave like a tourist, and as we bumped along going higher and higher I watched from the window the construction sites that were wrecking the roads.

In an English that he didn't speak any better that I spoke German, the man asked me if I were American. I think my being French disappointed him. Then he took a piece of cloth out of his bag and put it on his head. It didn't have any more color than his clothing. "Musik, Musik," he laughed like a simpleton. Crowned by this ridiculous hat, he made a series of grotesque gestures that I couldn't understand and didn't want to understand. So what if he were crazy? I was on vacation. No transference that day!

After several twists and turns, the bus stopped in another parking lot, this one with a brand-new blacktop, and filled with Mercedes that had been able to climb up there—how on earth? I understood that my guidebook from East Germany dated from another age, a time before untamed individualism. It was the moment to dump my companion. But he gestured again for me to follow him through the woods. Completely illogically, I obeyed him despite my reticence, prompted by an enchantment that felt more like disenchantment.

The path wound up the steep hill to open up onto Wartburg Castle, as medieval as one could hope for, indeed as it truly was. No longer paying any attention to me, the man put his excuse for a hat back on, which, in this context looked more like a fool's cap, took a recorder out of his pocket and started playing a few notes. It didn't take much for him to become a jester. I took this opportunity to slip away beyond the draw bridge and join a tour—of which I couldn't understand a word except for a few names: Elizabeth of Hungary, Luther, Wagner, Tannhaüser, Minnesänger. All good company! But not for long. The neo-Gothic frescos of troubadour life in the great hall ruined my pleasure. I crossed it at a run, pushed forward by groups of adolescents plugged into their Walkmen and tearing through the suggested itinerary. One last wave of people swept me to the exit.

The man was still there. He had crossed over the portcullis and was holding forth in the first courtyard, coiffed by his ridiculous fool's cap, juggling three balls. I watched him for a long time, throwing, catching, running after his balls, starting over again; then I approached to give him some money as other people had done. He signaled no with a shake of his head.

Still the only passenger on the bus that brought me back to the parking lot, I could see better how the city was making itself up in Western colors. The brightly repainted walls contrasted with the dull colors of the inhabitants' clothes. And they seemed overwhelmed by the devils invading their city. The driver indicated that, despite the rules, he'd take me for a little visit. Once passed Bach's childhood home with its splendid golden walls, I suddenly had the vision of my comrade left up on the hill. A Renaissance juggler, tired from having slept for such a long time, emerging from a barely erased border, he'd begun juggling again like the real ravished fool he was, trying out gestures that had grown stiff from several centuries of sleep.

I could see myself descending from the bus to the parking lot—finally reassured by the man from long ago whom I thought I'd been able to glimpse under the features of the unknown man who'd helped me collect my papers in Paris.

THE CAT!

The noise in the street had stopped. A light caught my attention and I turned my head in the direction of the building I'd just left. With its windows all lit up, my building looked like a Halloween jack-o'-lantern, laughing with all its might at my misadventures. What was that orange death's head doing there? I thought it had immigrated for good to the United States after World War II and after being judged undesirable in Paris—while it still appeared to our forefathers in Savoie and Britanny, at crossroads on the eve of All Saints' Day. The one I was looking at seemed particularly cynical and worrisome. Through its bright openings, many animated shadows were wandering.

A passerby taking giant strides was coming towards me. I looked at him without seeing. Like lightning, a yellow streak cut him off and disappeared in the shadows. Probably a cat. Arriving to where I stood, he stopped.

Hearing his voice, I knew right away that he was the man with the pipe and the tortoise-shell glasses, but without the pipe this time. I felt at home! He made the first move: "We've already met under other circumstances. I can finally tell you who I am." Bowing as they do in Germany, he introduced himself: "Erwin Schrödinger, one of the founding fathers of quantum physics."

His title left me cold. I'd always known what he'd done since my time hanging out with science students at l'École Normale Supérieure. Sometimes I even took a tunnel under Erasmus Street that led to the labs where they were conducting experiments in wave mechanics. He was the one who could have written that article on waves and light particles. . . . The sample outline and guidelines I'd just looked at came back to hit me in the gut. His powers of observation didn't miss the fact that I'd changed color: "Don't make yourself sick because your ego's taken a beating, especially when we're in the midst of a crisis, close to a breakdown. I want you to hurry up and revisit the initial gambit."

Impressed by the imperious tone of that great scientist, I didn't even try to understand what he meant by "gambit." But I suddenly suspected something: "Tell me, is it because of you and how you play with the dimension of time that I found myself frolicking among the fools?"

He shrugged his shoulders and gave me a modest look: "Well it wasn't really so very difficult. . . . If you'd like I could, for example, summon the RSI from Vedic India."

"You mean Lacan's patented RSI, the acronyms for Real, Symbolic, and Imaginary?"

"What are you talking about?" I mean the Rishi, those inspired poets who authored the *Vedas*. I already suggested you read their *Treatises on Sacrifice*. You'll find in them the way to put speech and time back in motion; they're especially useful in the midst of the periodic apocalypses that hyper-nationalist times specialize in. Allow me to repeat myself, if we don't revisit the initial gambit, we're lost and done for."

"But just what is this gambit?"

"A bold stroke that gave birth to science twenty-five centuries ago by evacuating the subject and his passions. I'm just coming from a debate about this in a school not far from here."

I wasn't listening to him anymore. The keys to my car miraculously reappeared in my pocket, and I had to hurry to move the car out of the way of the bus, which was arriving like a comet. He must have been at the famous Collège de France to present his book, I guessed jealously, while I headed for my garage . . .

2

School

In an instant, I was home. The telephone rang in the entrance. What catastrophe was next?

My "hello" was far from warm, but neither was the man's voice at the other end of the line who introduced himself as the friend of one of my colleagues, the resident in the clinic. He apologized for calling so late. Could I see him right away? It was now or never. He only needed one session; he hated things that dragged on.

For a second, I thought it might be the unknown man from the sidewalk, as if in the mess of my papers he'd had the time to note down my name, my telephone number, and my profession. The uneasy feeling of leaving myself open to just anyone made me give the anonymous voice a hasty rendez-vous for the day after All Saints' Day. Then, remembering I was on vacation, I tried to change it. He'd already hung up without leaving me his phone number.

What was I thinking of? I tried to make sense of this. It was all normal, a patient is just a patient, just like an editorial committee is just an editorial committee. There's nothing to make a scene about. But that absence of drama, about which one should not fret, still kept me from falling asleep.

As a sleeping aid, I opened the book I'd lifted from the head doctor. I checked the subtitle: it was indeed the Tarner Lectures, delivered in 1956 by Erwin Schrödinger. The man with the pipe hadn't lied to me.

Comfortably tucked in bed, I hoped to finish my rough day by communing with the book and surrounding myself in sweet illusions. Who knows, I thought, the master of equations might even help me understand my disarray.

And then something came over me and a dialogue started up—which I'm about to recount—realizing that Descartes himself ceded to the temptation, he too privileging this moment between sleeping and waking for his investigations. At least, as Yvain the African physicist had told me, he'd taken care to disguise his writings and not to reveal the names of the ghosts who'd communicated that "admirable" science on November 10, 1619, the eve of Saint Martin's Day.

CARTESIAN DREAMS

It was practically the anniversary of that date! Jumping from one thing to another as the fools had taught me, I got up to verify whether, in the editions of his works I owned, Descartes's nightmares were cited. In fact, the biographical note reported that he wasn't sure whether he was dreaming or having visions, but that the dreamer "decided it was dreams, and interpreted them while sleeping, before he could fully wake up." After two nightmares in which ghosts and great winds from the beyond chased him down, a huge commotion filled him with panic—and he saw sparks everywhere in his bedroom. A third dream dragged him out of his frightened state. In it a huge quantity of books appeared and disappeared, including a *Dictionary of All Knowledge* and a *Corpus poetarum* or *Poets' Book*, of which he was able to read the first sentence: "Quod vitae sectabor iter" (What path shall I follow in life?).

Little by little his deathly fear diminished. The note told me that among the ghosts, his mother perhaps appeared. She had died when he was only a year old, after having giving birth to a stillborn baby boy of whom no one ever spoke. But Descartes had always believed he'd killed his mother through his own birth. The *Poets' Book* especially delighted him. As Lacan would say, it was the "Discourse of the Other," and gave him a treasure of signifiers after a horrific nameless dread. He found within the interpretation of his own wish and the path to follow in life: *for he didn't believe that one should be astonished to see that poets, even those who were just fooling around, produced many thoughts more serious, more sensible, and better expressed than philosophers. He attributed that wonder to divine enthusiasm and imaginative force, both capable of producing the seeds of wisdom more easily and more brilliantly than even philosophical reasoning.*

So Descartes was advising me to fool around, according to my dialogical inclination. After the rejection of my anti-scientific foolishness, I was in need of this Authority. Who knows if his "evil genius" wasn't related to that sardonic pumpkin who'd wounded me by making both my article and identity papers disappear. And I would have let them go if the helpful unknown man hadn't picked them up for me from the pavement.

I stopped myself from going farther down this manic path, tormented once again by the morning's trial, worthy of the . . .

"Inquisition! Just admit it, but don't get too carried away, and remember it's the Inquisition seen through the Enlightenment and pretty watered down."

"I wish I believed that . . ."

And we were off again! I was talking back to Schrödinger who, smoking his pipe, had made himself at home in the armchair facing me. He explained he'd just come back not from the Collège de France (where had I got that idea?) but from a high school in the neighborhood, where his book had been presented alongside another one, by a biologist, to young students supposedly passionate about science. No, it wasn't Clermont College, but a different one, even older, whose name he couldn't remember.

PSYCHO-SCIENCE

He was all excited. The presentation and the young crowd reminded him of his own youth in Vienna, and the time he spent in discussions with his father, who was much more passionate about biology than about the oilcloth business he'd inherited. Indeed, after World War I, both his father and the business had disappeared, leaving his mother in financial trouble. As a young researcher, he'd been too broke to help her. In those days, research hardly put any bread on the table. So all his life, he'd been anxious about not having enough, but for the moment, he was in a great mood: "I have to congratulate that colleague. He did a good job. Believe me, it wasn't easy. I've been there. I always thought it my duty to tell the public when we were triggering a scientific revolution. And in that regard, the eminent colleague seemed to be a little behind. I can't judge his experiments, but I think his idea of science relies too much on a stimulus and response kind of conceptualization. Whatever the case, the 'Tout Paris' seems only to have eyes for neurons and neuronal man. You missed a chance to learn something."

He reacted joyously to my alarm.

"Is your brain functioning on the low setting? The most farcical moments happened during the discussion. There were even some shrinks present who challenged the role of the encephalon. A mathematician squashed them by speaking about the chaos equation that regulates neurons. No one understood whether he was speaking literally or figuratively. I was pretty baffled myself. And the biologist got up on his high horse. With brio, and I do mean brio, he commented on our splendid cerebral connections and disconnections. He almost persuaded us he could locate our psyche inside our skulls. We were under his spell. . . . The god Mars had spurred him on to make war with your profession."

"Well he's probably already encountered some pretty dogged soldier shrinks who love sparring with him. Freud was always spying on the territory of neighboring biologists without realizing how he was provoking them. And it's an unequal fight, in any case because, despite its attempt at jargon, psychoanalysis can't help expressing itself in everyday language, whereas nobody understands the biologists' formulas."

"Indeed! But you should have seen the psycho-mathematical monsters your colleagues produced. In any event, the neuro-scientific hubris knew no bounds. You would have thought that Rabelais's Picrochole was attacking all the knowledge in the world. Moving effortlessly from neurotransmitters to psychology, then to mental disorders, through a succession of unpredictable macroscopic quantum leaps in his model of cognitive psyche, our famous biologist gradually left physiology to enter the fields of psychology and linguistics—deploring that biological data was sorely lacking in these domains. Nevertheless, he had 'courageously' formulated a few hypotheses and was hopeful that sooner or later someone would realize how important it was to test them."

THE MISSING LINK

"What is it you find so shocking? Do you refuse him visiting rights in neighboring disciplines?"

"Quite the contrary. I'm very much for it."

"Then what are you complaining about? Through psychological or linguistic experimentation, he must be planning to find a way to speak to the subjects of his experiments."

"You're speaking for yourself, now. He could never think like that. The subject doesn't interest him. Whatever—he really did have a lot of courage, for he set about, unabashed, producing the missing link between the basic synapse and the thinking mind. He audaciously took on microscopic organisms such as aplysia or daphnia, those tiny charming crustaceans you feed to your goldfish, without ever realizing they are closely related to us. You should have seen with what skill he peeled, bit by bit, synapse by synapse, psychic disorders from the cranium, just like you and I shell a crayfish. The most reassuring aspect of all of this was that he claimed that's how it is and no other way.

With absolute certainty, he sees our soul in our head as a little housewife tirelessly doing housework for our neurons. When you're about to cry, she quickly sweeps the path of the lachrymal glands up to the source of secretion, thereby clouding over your poor sad globes. Everything happens through chemical exchanges and other as yet unknown reactions from the central organ, animated by an endless hammering of regular electrochemical pulses, conducted from nerve cell to nerve cell, through tens of thousands of contacts opened and blocked every split second. . . . And all of that to make you feel bad inside, in your private sphere, supposedly unreachable by others . . ."

"It sounds like he took as literal truth Freud's *Project for a Scientific Psychology* and made it fit the inside of the brain. Freud describes the psychic system in rough sketches representing neurons, dendrites and synapses thought to filter the monstrous energy coming from the real through a series of sifters designated by Greek letters. Your biologist has mixed up words with things and the Freudian grid of the functions of Psi, Phi, and Omega with the imagery of a scanner. He had no clue that Freud used neuronal images to speak about the psyche and its speaking ability that is, according to Freud, located not only in the brain but also between people engaged in speech and language games. You should have told him to read Wittgenstein."

"Oh he made Wittgenstein serve his own purposes."

"Everybody has his pets and makes others' theories and passions fit like a fool's cap! At the time Freud wrote his *Project*, he was enthralled by Wilhelm Fliess, who thought he could calculate the date of our death and so on from our biorhythms."

"My pet passion is to be a poet. My equations wouldn't have seen the light of day without that hobby. As Baudelaire says, 'Nature is a temple.' I can't quite remember the rest . . . 'a forest of symbols . . . of confused words . . . ' Wait, the last verse is coming back: 'to unite the transports of the spirit and the senses.' That's what matters to me. I've written a few poems on the subject and I think they're pretty good. I don't know if they were passed down to posterity."

I didn't dare tell him the truth. Posterity, represented by Stephan Zweig, judged them good for the toilet, just like Alceste when he evaluated Oronte's verses in Molière's *Misanthrope*. Luckily we weren't communicating telepathically, so he could continue as if I hadn't had such thoughts.

"That biologist is so little concerned with uniting 'the mind and the senses' that the grey matter he's examining under his scalpel can no longer emit any confused words at all. I assure you, the forest of symbols has been cut down. He swears only by the neuron. He's fixated on it, like Molière's medical idiot, Dr. Diafoirus, was fixated on the lung."

MISLEADING COMPARISON

"Aren't you being a little harsh? You said they were only hypotheses . . ."

"A purely precautionary rhetorical trick. . . . Through his eloquent loggorhea, his position of authority seduced the audience. Don't forget we were in Sorbonne territory, in a school founded by Robert de Sorbon in the Twelfth Century. I saw the date engraved in the pediment."

"You can criticize him all you like, I find your guy visionary! He's part of an avant-garde that already revolutionized the Middle Ages. I learned this first hand this morning in the honor court. Psychiatry at that time wasn't so magical after all, but quite rational, and even then fascinated by the brain. Today, Hippocrates would have to accept seeing his sacred illness fall from on high."

"You aren't telling me anything I don't know. I already told you, my wife Anny suffered the most insane treatments. It seems that folly was a family trait."

"I see you've become a geneticist to save your own skin. I don't mean to push you, but they say she suffered from your infidelities."

"Are you lowering yourself to gossip? I'm disappointed in you. She introduced me to her friends and nearly forced me to give private lessons to two truly ravishing twin girls. I went out of my mind, and when I say 'mind'. . . . Poor Anny! But she had her Prince Charmings as well. What she must have told Drury! You know, he had a book project he wanted to call *The Danger of Words*."

He published it.

"Strange times! When Wittgenstein went, like me, into exile in Ireland, he was just as depressed as I was. The Nazification of Austria drove us crazy, so much so that the least little skirt caught my imagination. He went wild about your profession. . . . Psychoanalysis for the mad, what an idea!"

I frowned: "Let's drop the subject."

"Stop sulking. If you're going to pout, I'm leaving. Drury told me that his great man Wittgenstein agreed with me: there will never be an accurate enough knowledge of the nervous system that will enable us to see clearly into the mind. My friend Scott Sherrington, who received the Nobel Prize in 1932 for his work on the reflex arc and neurons, also proclaimed to anyone who would listen that physiology didn't lead to the mind but to the brain, which is like a telephone switchboard. There are wires but no messages. Of course today the telephone is out of date. The brain has become a computer; and any of the kids at the school I was just at could show me up on it. The latest gadget of our internal life is that camera the biologist mentioned that registers our thoughts before we even articulate them. Soon you'll see the mind feel, think, maybe dream, as projections on a screen. Still, whose mind are we talking about? The scientist's—who's looking at someone else's synapses? He'd do better to follow the motto 'Know thyself' spoken by the god of Delphi. This makes me think about this morning when Wittgenstein cited a rather comical paragraph where he compared psychology to physics. Do you think you can locate it?"

I got up reluctantly to look through the *Investigations*. I quickly found the paragraph he was looking for:

Misleading parallel: psychology treats of processes in the psychic sphere as physics does in the physical sphere. Seeing, hearing, thinking, feeling, willing, are not the subject of psychology in the same sense as that in which the movements of bodies, the phenomena of electricity, etc., are the subject of physics. You can see this by the fact that the physicist sees, hears, thinks about and informs us of these phenomena and the psychologist observes the external reactions, the behavior of the subject.

"He accused psychology of being more royalist than physics, the queen of science."

"Not the queen, much more humble than that. We physicists have always known we were dependent on our senses, even when relayed by the most sophisticated devices. Whereas the human sciences act as if nothing of human matter ever touches them. They believe they are imitating us by justifying what they do as objective, supposedly as in physics. When in fact they miss the subject of their subject."

3

Schrödinger's Call

He got up to pace the room, stopping every once in a while to think out loud: "Of course a rationalist could be tempted to deal quickly with that question, as in the discussion at school this afternoon, through the analysis of nervous functions going back to the beginnings of organisms. . . . But all that is pure fantasy, as irrefutable as it is improbable, and without any use for the advancement of knowledge."

I thought I'd hurt his feelings without realizing it: "Let it go. Shall we talk about something else?"

His agitated state was making me dizzy. I warned him if he didn't stop, I would turn off the lights. Wasted effort! Even in the dark, he kept on pacing. I could catch on the fly bits of things he'd already said on the esplanade. He was talking about shadow performance, of the uncanny gap that might not have happened, of the price to pay, of wandering, and again of a strange reality. He finally stopped and in a loud voice called me to witness: "Do you see it? Do you feel it? Do you hear this world that science renders colorless, cold and mute, so horribly objective as to leave no room for the mind and for its immediate sensations?"

I couldn't take it anymore and I turned the lights back on: "That's just how the world is, scientifically speaking, isn't it?"

He responded, sarcastically: "So are you saying that you believe the world exists objectively?"

"Don't you?"

"And if no one looks at this world, does it still exist? Isn't it like a play before empty seats? Can we even call 'world' a world that no one contemplates? Did it ever exist?"

"Please calm down! It seems that all I've been experiencing since this morning are worlds that no one contemplates. Have you already forgotten my confession? In the Quad or the common ward of the hospital, I tried to sit on those empty seats you're talking about. Because nothing was happening, I was tempted to leave. Too late! I finally understood why no one wanted to sit in that empty seat. In the time it takes to stand up, the battle has already begun with the shadows you mentioned. Even if you try to make yourself very very small on your seat, huddled in your neutrality . . ."

"There's no more boundary between the stage and the house, or even between the actor and the stage. Is that right?" he asked more softly.

"Don't you think this is dangerous?"

Schrödinger stared at me: "I know the risks of this kind of exploration. Understand what I'm worried about. I wonder if our science has become a Minotaur asking for its share of human sacrifice. I've seen this monstrousness develop for a long time. As far as brain science will progress, we will never encounter the personality, the dire pain, the bewildering anguish I've felt myself."

"Yourself?"

SCIENTIFIC NEMESIS

He looked me right in the eyes, strangely calm now: "The men and women for whom this world is lit by an unusually bright light have been more torn up than others by the pangs of inner discord. . . . And yet, without this conflict, nothing lasting would have come about. I'm arriving at the essential: if I'm here this evening, where I thought I'd only make an appearance, it's to launch an appeal to psychoanalysts asking them to lead us out of this impasse where we find ourselves."

"This is unexpected coming from the hard sciences."

"The ignorance and scorn shown towards your discipline does not come from people who know too much about it, but from those who overestimate their own knowledge. In my days, we hardly dared admit curiosity for psychoanalysis. It would have been an outrage, a crime of lèse-science. My compatriot Kurt Gödel, as you know, paid the price. He starved to death in 1978 in a hospital in Princeton, persuaded that his doctors wanted to poison him. And he wasn't the only one to have suffered from such a mental state—supremely qualified as a scientist but unskilled for living life."

"Rumor has it that he was interested in ghosts and in extra-terrestrials, that he wrote philosophy in secret."

"That's exactly right. His only confidant at Princeton was Albert Einstein, with whom he liked to go for walks. After Einstein died, Gödel was left to himself and, if I understand correctly the rumors from the scientific community, started to grow delusional. In Democritus's time, it would have been different. Imagine that Gödel had visited him in Abdera. I'm sure that in addition to questions about atoms and the infinity of the universe, Democritus wouldn't have hesitated to ask him about the simulacra that were bothering him. Unless Gödel himself would have confided his anguish after the success of his theory, or even asked Democritus what path he should follow in life. Could one possibly imagine such a conversation today, as varied and as rich, between, for example, a science geek from the school where I just spoke and his professor?"

"It would be an exception."

"For my part, I've always hated the way Westerners proceed through polarizing opposites. I prefer, as happens in the East, to look for an underlying commonality among different doctrines. That resonance is even more urgent now that our epoch is going through an excessively critical phase concerning basic science and the emotional life of humanity. Entire populations are deprived of ordinary comfort and security by massacres, genocides, overwhelming stress, destroyed hopes, fear of an imminent catastrophe, and especially by lack of confidence in the thoughtfulness and honesty of our leaders."

"But what can we do? It is what it is. Demagogy is now thought of as a media science, supported by statistics and surveys. We only have to be flattered to believe anything they want to tell us."

"It's partly our fault, mine and my colleagues from the Copenhagen School. Because of what we did, science isn't what it used to be."

"Don't you think you're giving a little too much importance to that revolution you like to brag about?"

"So you think you have something to say?"

He was intimidating me again. I thought I'd better prepare a retreat: "You started to talk to me about this on the esplanade. I've forgotten some of what you said, I have to admit."

REVERSIBILITY OF THE ARROW OF TIME

"The first thing I told you was that in the world of particles, space and time have lost their status as frames of reference. They're no longer the stage on which we represent what we think of as their mutual movement and inter-action. The distinction between actor and stage is no longer relevant. For, and I'm repeating myself, it's the propagation of something in the form of a field or a wave that becomes the form of space/time itself. Time is no longer an inflexible Chronos, and we can even imagine reversing its arrow. It means the dethronement of the rigid tyrant imposed on us by outside, a liberation from the unbreachable realm of before and after, of causality itself."

"I know. I learned that at my own expense during catastrophic mo-ments in the course of an analysis. That was when the distinction between past and future, inside and the outside, here and there lost all their sense, and the territory defined by the session became the only frame of refer-ence, the unique form of space/time. Do you see what I mean?"

"Not really. Can you give me an example?"

"I first experienced this a long time ago with a patient who'd been hos-pitalized in the first hospital I told you about. She wouldn't stop shaking up the boundaries between us and turning time upside down, even going so far as messing up how she used different verb tenses. It was impossible to find any signposts. Sometimes she made herself younger. Sometimes she was older than the earth itself. She would say, I remember: 'We're going to talk about nomadic time, about fluid time, it's time that floats within us.' We called her Sissi."

"The Empress of Austria? I would have remembered that name."

"I was careful not to mention her on the esplanade. I was too ashamed of how she'd dismissed me. She was as furious as Mother Folly. But when I listen to you, your new paradigm would seem to suit her. . . . I know I shouldn't be jumping over the boundaries of our disciplines . . ."

"Feel free to steal from our orchard. I've always thought the geography of separate regions deplorable, each one functioning like the other's hell. The wall that separates our branch of science from other ways of knowing is a dead end. I used to say to my students, between the wars, that they mustn't lose sight of the role their research plays in the tragi-comedy of human life. Don't lose touch with life, and make sure life stays in touch with you. If you aren't able throughout the years to explain to just about anybody what you've done, then your activity will have been useless. We're living a strange moment. As the Oxford Hellenist Dodds pointed out to me, the rise of rationalism and scientific progress has always been accompanied by a parallel rise in the brutality of fundamentalisms. So much so that we've never tossed as many babies out with so little bathwater than in the periods we like to call enlightened. That's where the danger is—when an incoherent conglomerate that calls itself a culture is about to collapse. He also pointed out that tormentors across the globe don't have our scruples. They're happy to poach in all disciplines in order to be able to debrain as many people as possible."

LOSS OF IDENTITY

"This brings me logically to my second point, which relates to the loss of identity. Let's go back to where we started when we were talking about infinitely small particles. Up until today, the fact that they constitute identifiable individuals was considered to be a fundamental property of matter. It wasn't even mentioned as it was considered so obvious. But now we have to renounce this idea of their individuality. Now matter has ceased to be something simple, palpable, that moves in space and whose trajectory everyone can follow while stating the precise laws that regulate movement. We now find this property limited: when a corpuscle moves at sufficient speed in an area where the same kind of corpuscles are in motion, the property of individual identity is fairly unambiguous. But in most other cases, the notion of identity is indeed confused."

"Sissi tried to warn me about it: 'Working like this, you're going to wear yourself out, your skin will disappear, your mouth is already disappearing.' And she added, 'How do we move from one instant to another?'"

"In effect, if you observe a particle, then a similar particle very shortly after that, and in very close proximity, with many reasons to suppose a causal connection between the first and second observations, you will still not be able to affirm that it's the same particle. Of course you have to deal with a slew of intermediate cases, but at the level of elementary particles, the notion of individuality really has no meaning. At that level, materialism, which relies on the belief not only that matter really exists but that it has always existed and is indestructible and can be counted on, is completely metaphysical. Habits of daily language lead us to say otherwise, but matter in that case escapes from the hands that attempt to manipulate it. It doesn't obey the rigidity of our laws. It's impossible to predict its evolution."

"If objects are composed of non-individual elements, how can we even conceive of the notion of individual?"

"It relies on the form: individual identity only plays a subordinate role. And that form is not the form of something. . . . The truth is we only recognize specters, spectrum rays, and not the atom's structure. We can only seize interactions. It's the interaction that takes the form of small particles, quite identifiable as long as that interaction is perceived as a small wavelength of weak intensity. Are you following me?"

"Sort of. If I take Sissi as an example, she had turned this vision of forms into a real method. She would say: 'Putting yourself into a vision to know means putting yourself into a strictly official position.' I thought she was talking about her hallucinations and I felt left out of that world. You're making me understand. Maybe her visions seized the specters of interaction between her and me, as the only permanent thing in a world without apparent logic."

SUBVERSION OF THE PRINCIPLE OF OBJECTIVATION

"The boundary between the actor and the stage isn't the only one to collapse. It's the same for the space that separates the spectator from the performance. The observer, in other words, is inseparable from what she observes. So you see the problem! The foundations laid long ago by Galileo, Huygens, and Newton don't hold anymore and we're all confused, as if science had lost its way after many years of the same mental habits.

This, then, leads me to my third point that attacks the tyranny of the principle of objectivation. Observation leaves a stain on the object observed. It perturbs it, making it impossible to know precisely the elements affected by the observation. The access to certain characteristics is forever blocked and they'll consequently remain forever unknown."

"That touches on something very sensitive. Some patients, not satisfied with imposing on me another conception of space and time, become champions of reification, of 'thingism.' I've never gotten used to the moment when they threaten to throw their corpses at us, as if they had become a thing. Think about George saying: 'I'm your guinea pig; my case should interest you.'"

"That's exactly it. We researchers had to exclude ourselves as subjects from the field we were trying to understand. We can only step back into the role of non-concerned observer. But this principle of exclusion reduces the world of science to a shadow theatre, where, as a result of sacrificing our senses to our equations, we finish by becoming shadows ourselves in a life once familiar to us. Believe me, the various totalitarianisms we've known would never have been so seductive if people hadn't started accepting the credo of reification. That's why I'm appealing to psychoanalysis. Is it a good idea? I'm not sure. Nevertheless, if psychoanalysis wants to make a place for itself in this world, it must accept examining again the initial gambit that brought science into being two thousand years ago, rather than submitting to pseudo-theoretical dictates."

"Who told you about this? The cat I saw on the boulevard when you arrived?"

SCHRÖDINGER'S CAT

"To just what are you alluding? Eliot's cat left when he did. I don't see. . . . Well, I did invent the story of a cat some time ago . . ."

"Now we're getting there."

". . . To illustrate the Psi function of my equations."

"A cat who's been following you for a long time?"

"No, a purely imaginary cat, closed up in a box, without the possibility of contact, with a kind of hellish set up. A Geiger counter is placed near a sample of radioactive substance, so small it's possible that only one of its atoms will disintegrate in an hour. But it is also possible, and with equal probability, that it won't. In the event of disintegration, the counter crackles, and through a relay activates a hammer that shatters a flask of poison. But let's let this device work by itself for that hour. Then one can predict that the cat remains alive, provided, of course, that no disintegration has occurred during that time."

"Otherwise it's been poisoned?"

"Exactly."

"And so what is the Psi function that poisons cats in your imagination?"

"In the Psi function, the living cat and the dead cat are, if I dare say so, blended together in equal proportions. The dictatorship of measurement no longer pertains. Up until now, it was enough to play with an apparatus displaying a counter near almost anything for a sufficient number of times to appear to be scientific. But the Psi function makes repeatability unpredictable. Between the form in which one knows something and the form in which it springs back up again, there is a gap."

"I know I'm obsessed with analogies, but here's another one. In an analysis of folly, that gap has to happen. At every session we have to start from zero again. But I'm getting off the subject. . . . Your Psi function lets you off too easily. To think you accused that poor biologist a few minutes ago of horrendous crimes. . . . How could you imagine such torture for a cat? I'd like to see you locked up in that box with a Geiger counter. And first off, what has to happen to find yourself face to face with a single atom?"

"OK, I plead guilty. We hard sciences have a knack for torturing the real with our words without feeling the least little scruple. Like that scientist who imagined being able to predict voluntary actions. He fancied obtaining in the near future the configuration and the speed of every elementary particle of the human body and especially of the brain. My friend Niels Bohr, one of the nicest men I've ever known, anticipated the apocalyptic outcome of the process, for such an observation would imply such a strong interference with the object that it would ultimately break it apart into elementary particles. The interference would kill so efficiently, there wouldn't even be a corpse left for a funeral.

So that's how we scientists martyr the world: I target a cat with my atom and someone else targets an aplysia's synapse. It doesn't bother us. And really if I seemed to go overboard tonight, it's because I've been thinking about the price that science has to pay for its lack of scruple."

"You're championing austerity now?"

"Not in terms of research monies! I'm talking about how many lives it costs. Boltzmann argued that if the universe is sufficiently vast and lasts long enough, time could very well flow in the reverse direction in the universe's farthest parts. He paid with his life for this blasphemy about the reversibility of time. You don't get away with attacking old Chronos who, of course, eats his children . . ."

"Tell me more about the influence the observant subject has over the observed object. This is really fascinating."

LADIES AT COCKTAIL PARTIES

"Be careful! You're starting to sound like a society lady at a cocktail party! Well, I'm going to disappoint you. That influence isn't what you think it is. Just follow me now: I wonder if we are using the right language when we call a system interacting physically with another a subject? You should understand this. The mind that observes is not a physical system. It can't then really be placed in interaction with a physical system. That's why I don't like to call that physical interference the influence of the subject on the object."

"But I thought you were worried about the fate of the subject mistreated by science . . ."

"We must envisage other perspectives on the subject that take into account our own mind. Because if the subject is something, it's the thing that feels and thinks. It doesn't then belong to the world of energy whose structure is granular."

"Then what do you call the 'subject'?"

"The thing that made the students' eyes sparkle at our discussion this afternoon, when after the lectures the specialists were tearing each other apart. What would you say about a physicist who'd argue that in fact nothing in reality makes those eyes shine? That in reality the ocular function is only that of being continually struck by light quanta? That's what reality is. Some strange reality, don't you think so? Something seems to be missing . . ."

"Indeed. . . . Your theory has done the trick. My eyes are closing. I think I'm going to fall asleep . . ."

"Me, too," yawned Schrödinger.

4

The Transference Box

DULLE GRIET

I must have dozed off for a second. Somebody rustling papers woke me up with a start.

"Are you snooping through my things?"

Schrödinger had picked up the reproduction of *Mad Meg* from my bookcase. "Where have I seen this painting? In Vienna? This woman is the spitting imagine of . . ."

"Mother Folly, I know. Her Flemish name is *Dulle Griet*. She hangs in a museum in Antwerp. I've known her since I was thirteen. She was reproduced in black and white in my history book with the museum's name written in small caps under her image. When I saw her in color, as big as life, gangling, with her red nose, in iron-toed boots, helmeted, and armed with her sword and a basket with all the tools of her wild music, I realized she was capable of jumping out of the frame and going into action. She's thinking about an attack, wouldn't you say?"

"What are you looking for in this painting? The little person who should be there without being there?"

I examined it very carefully. *Mad Meg*, through folly, was reflecting the shadows of a world no one contemplates. Behind the giant Meg, women were fighting with monsters assailing their city. "Ouch!" I yelled suddenly, feeling a sharp pain. Outside of the frame, one of those women had just struck me. I could identity Sissi, without hesitating, under that bite of remorsefulness. She had attacked me for abandoning her to her Gehenna, after I'd dangled in front of her eyes an escape from her asylum fortress.

I knew she'd gotten out a short time ago, but I couldn't shake the feeling of having betrayed her, while she fought with her monsters, including the "chopping block," as her roommate liked to say.

A voice hurtling through the air made me jump: "Fuck off, Davoine. Shit on you. You're stupid. You're an idiot. You're torturing me! Help! Enough! That's enough!"

THE PRINCESS

Not again! Turning towards *Dulle Griet*, I was determined this time to fight back. But she was as quiet as a lamb. Before I could explode, Schrödinger said: "You'd do better to take a look in that transference box on the last shelf of your bookcase. Something's screaming from inside there." Red, green, and beige file boxes, in which I'd collected different administrative papers, seminar lectures, notes, and abandoned drafts, were lined up neatly on the shelf. Rummaging in the box Schrödinger indicated, I pulled out a bunch of notes dictated by Elisabeth-Sissi—the notes I'd told myself I'd look at as soon as I got home from the clinic. I waved them in the air with a flourish, as proud as an archeologist finding inscriptions that had been saved from an earthquake: "Here's something to spark your interest! There are traces here of a subject petrified by a cataclysmic event. You're going to help me decipher them."

The notes ended with the deluge of swearing that chased me out of the first hospital I'd worked in at the moment I was deserting Sissi. Unable to look at them until now, I saw that these paper odds and ends stuffed in haste in a folder and held together with an elastic band were insisting I break the seal of silence.

FORMS OF LIFE

On the top right corner of the first sheet, I'd written: "November 15th, Elisabeth, 30, in hospital since she was 17." I started deciphering aloud what had already been the beginning of our conversation: "Why don't you make any effort to leave this place? Why do you always come back after you've gone to visit your family?"

"That was the head doctor questioning her, the one I told you about on the esplanade. We were in the first ward where the head nurse had welcomed me when I'd arrived. I can see it all clearly: we all hurried into a small office. The team had thrown up its hands and asked the head doctor to see the patient who'd already worn out at least a half dozen other head doctors. A nurse opened the door of the arena, and Sissi made a stunning entrance.

'I want to get well,' she said right away, 'but there are conditions. Getting well means choosing the life I want to have. The life of an artist, not everyday life. The life of great queens, the life of Archdukes, the life of all forms of life.'

Changing your form of life is a matter of changing your language game, Wittgenstein might have answered. I remember well the silence after that declaration. Everybody knew that when the ruler of the Austro-Hungarian Empire consented to speak, there would be no room for anyone else's comment. Sissi had the same character as Erasmus's Folly; she struck everyone dumb with her almighty knowledge. Submissive to her power, the assembled group was waiting for the end of her tirade, when the head doctor tried something: 'Tell us a little about life in your family, when you were a child.'

She turned the situation around: 'Actually, I've been wondering, ever since I was a child, what kind of lives you all have. I bet the grandmothers know, as we can hear them crying. I can't live like a dog and a person. I'm the only one who reacts. I'm my own family.'

And with that, imperiously, she left the room.

I don't remember what we said about this, but I remember very well approaching her a little shyly after that encounter. She anticipated my questions: 'You're a great queen as well. There are a lot of great queens. You must be one of them.'

'What makes you say that?'

'We can dream!' Then she turned on her heels.

The next week she accosted me in the corridor and suggested: 'If you were to bring a pen and some ink, we would write out our pride. We'll note every day the sense of a being who could become normal and supple.' Without hesitating, I took out of my bag a ballpoint pen and the notebook I always have on me. I remember transcribing in it week after week—without ever having the impression of understanding—what I'm going to read to you now. Then we'll see what we'll see."

EUGENICS

"'I'm wounded in my stomach. I don't have a stylish head. Mademoiselle Sissi has ears that itch her. There's another Elisabeth in another skin, the one who's stupid and fights against me. My intelligence eats up my head. My intelligence will kill me. My life wants to be independent and not live with me. Something makes me unhappy, it's my giving birth.'

I get it, I thought, full of the advice of the manuals I assumed I had to know by heart; this looks like dissociation and delusion . . .

'Take a look at her file,' a nurse to whom I'd confessed my rudimentary psychiatric findings said hauntingly to me. In her file—I can still see it—written in capital letters: 'THERAPEUTIC ABORTION + tubal ligation of a 27-year old *primigravida primipara* at 3 ? months pregnant, due to incurable schizophrenia, institutionalized for 10 years at this point.'"

"So what's so wrong with that?" exclaimed Schrödinger, a little too eagerly, thereby exposing his discomfort.

"Eugenics doesn't bother you?"

"You're on your high horse again. I've already said it: you're as much a prude as the society ladies in Vienna. How do you know she didn't decide for herself? And what shocks you about this, given the situation?"

"My clear sense that she wasn't given a choice nor did she even know what was happening. Later on her mother confirmed it. Neither she nor her daughter was told anything about this. And what's more, by one of those frequent coincidences that happens within the interactions of psychotic transference, I'd just given birth myself, in the same unit in the same hospital, six months before I met her.

I remember as if it were yesterday how floored I was seeing this piece of paper, administratively exemplary, announcing the sterilization of a mentally ill person without her consent. . . . My recent maternal happiness left me open-mouthed in front of a document that stared back at me like the dead eyes of a hooked fish. I'd started to come to grips with serial lobotomies because, you see, they were a thing of the past. But sterilization, try to understand. . . . I was new in the ward. . . . Is something wrong, Monsieur Schrödinger?"

"I want to tell you about the dream I had. It included some strangely similar circumstances."

"Later, not now . . ."

"When I arrived the following Monday, without even asking a question, Sissi gave me the answer. She came to meet me, and before I could open my mouth to say I'd looked at her file, she made me take notes: 'One day, I went to Paris. I had an abortion. They told me I was pregnant. They didn't tell me I was expecting a baby. Whose baby? The President of the Republic's? It was taken out of my body. I wonder what happened between my son and me. Who wanted to take him away? Who had the right to say they had to take him away? I guess it was a frame of mind. Maybe he was worth something?'"

WAR

"The following week, I noted down for the first time my own impressions. I got to the hospital completely exhausted and depressed; the morning light was too strong; familiar objects were of no interest. I dropped things. I wrote: 'Uncanny feeling. I'm a thing. Everything has changed but nothing has changed.' Sissi was waiting for me on the steps of the ward, and said to me as soon as she saw me, as if she were speaking in my place: 'I'm exhausted. I can't take it anymore. I didn't make my bed this morning.'

I answered her mechanically, 'You will, when it'll be your own.'

I noted then that she began to scrutinize me, as you are doing right now. And then, out of the blue, 'What have you been through to understand me so well? In the street the sun's light doesn't penetrate me. Should I admit how well we get along?'

I answered evasively, 'Why don't you admit it?'

She insisted, 'Try to understand what I'm saying. I want to know if you had a lot of trouble getting yourself back together again.'

I tried another feint, something more universal: 'Who'd ever say the contrary? Who'd ever say that one day or the other he didn't find himself in trouble?'

She was holding on like a pit bull: 'If you want to understand me, understand me. I'm going to confide in you. When I was five, I didn't want to be like everybody else. And if you would adopt me for eight days, you'd see I wouldn't be like everybody. And you wouldn't be like my mother, crying all the time. She debased herself in front of less than a banana peel, even the cat's food. It was too heavy. Was she an imbecile or not? I don't accept war. But it wasn't me who started it. She's the one. That's the reason I'm sick. If I'd dared kill all of them, maybe I wouldn't be here now.'

Her war was all merely a metaphor to me; and I de-realized what she was saying in order to protect myself from her harshness. Today I would ask about the war; I would try to follow her advice, try to examine rigorously what I'd been through to have arrived at that exhausted state. Reading my notes again, I now have a couple of ideas. Maybe we can talk about it. At that time, I would've been frightened to find so many bridges between her madness and my private life."

"You're starting to see what I mean by the limits of the initial gambit," Schrödinger murmured. "It protects research against subjectivity."

"I see the moves I must have had to make to stay neutral and consequently to understand nothing. These notes concerned me too; but I only see that in rereading them. Positioned as her secretary—I remember this well—I felt I was invaded by a fog. No doubt it was the smoke screen necessary to censure the messages targeting my intimacy. I felt such a terrible discomfort with how these words were stirring me up, that little by little I built a wall to keep me safe. Lacan said it and he was right, resistance comes from the analyst."

FLUID

"The following Monday, she came back from a weekend leave: 'Life will always be the *meanie*. I won't go home again for millions of centuries. Who could expect me to marry my mother! For good reason. She debased herself in front of men to see herself as a man. How complicated life is! My head is heavy. I don't know how many kilos it weighs. They complained to me and I can't stand it. At home, there are only imitations of a mother and brother.'

Then vehemently, 'They don't pay you enough for the work you do. You're going to wear yourself out. Even babies do too much for their age. I have to tell you, your skin is going to disappear. I'm afraid of losing you. Your mouth is already disappearing.'

Nearly struck dumb, I must have stammered, 'Who have you lost?' She answered, or rather answered tangentially, which turned out to be right on target (as you'll see later): 'I'm afraid of tuberculosis. I have too much pain. I'm invaded by a paper illness. It's always been like that. You aren't just anybody.'

'And neither are you,' I replied politely.

'Everybody has their thing. My thing is to cure myself of death.'

I stared at her, but she wasn't seeing me: 'They let a human being suffer as though she weren't going to die. She's born for that. I'll tuck her back in. She asks me to die in peace. I have to tell her that. The nurses change my mind. I have to tell her to act her age, to die in peace. I need to tuck her in. She was paid to take our old age from the time we were young. That's why I'm getting younger. I suffer. It's my health that isn't healthy. The fluid . . . '

'What about fluid?'

I held desperately onto this fluid, which was suggesting a delirious field, instead of allowing myself to navigate indeterminately between 'her' and 'me.' OK, she was talking about herself in the third person. But why didn't she stay there? Why didn't she stay at one age instead of constantly changing it? Even if I have the advantage of knowing a little more of the enigma than you do, I was always, and I remain, confused by her linguistic alternatives. They introduced uncertainty and made individuality impossible.

Who was that hospitalized person on the brink of death she mentioned, the one born to die? Do you think it was her or someone else? Who was the subject of the paper illness she demonstrated through her body by turning it into an object?"

Schrödinger didn't seem very surprised by any of this: "You're having difficulty because our language is profoundly impregnated with temporality and thus with causality. It could be that the principle of causality came into being as a way of keeping the dead from coming back. I think Freud said something about this. It's the guarantor of the arrow of time. By sowing uncertainty with her pronouns and her verb forms, she may have found the trick for bringing the dead back to life. . . . Am I wrong?"

"No you're onto something! The trick is what she called the fluid.

'Fluid,' she'd say, 'is what makes us less crazy, less stupid. Fluid is the spirit of the times entering us.' And she recounted, 'It was an evening when I saw the full moon. It gave me fluid. It came into my stomach and that's how I had fluid. I was nine years old. I cried as though it were the end of the world. I can feel in my speech how it's the end of the world. Everybody was transformed into stone, into marble, into statues. All I did was to see it. Day and night, I see it. . . . My brain works. My brain writes.'"

INHERITANCE

"The following week, Elisabeth hailed me: 'Learn to change your writing, put your writing in place. Everything bothers her, Madame V. Madame Mother is nervous. They're living in terrifying fears. How do they want to live? How do you want to live; what life do you want to have? What life would you really desire? That's a question to ask a lady doctor.'

'Are Madame Mother and Madame V the same person?'

'It's the same illness. They want to be spat on. She's low enough as it is. She doesn't want to get old, spend her money. It's so simple as an illness; but she turns it into something huge. She has to talk about it to relax; otherwise we're all going to be nervous in ourselves. I have lots of her nerves. I'm too rich to pay the hospital.'

'Where does all that money come from?'

'From myself. I work by thinking. I have a head to inherit. You have a head to inherit too.'

That remark got to me. I started to blush. Heeding my generation's trend that had condemned inheritance as bourgeois, I'd forgotten about a woods and an orchard that had been handed down to me. I'd completely lost track of them, not even knowing where they were. Her call to order shook me up so much I had difficulty hiding what I was feeling. She was polite enough not to mention anything: 'I only like heads that inherit, that's how it is. I inherit from children.'

'Usually it's the other way around.'

'You'd better inform yourself and then come back. . . . You have to learn to know me. I'm not 'my daughter.' I have to inherit from babies so they can live. That makes my fortune exhausting.'"

Schrödinger dryly remarked: "You're pretty thick, if you can't get this."

"So you understand something here?"

"In this kind of case, you need to conceive of other ways of being—other than in the form of space and time. What about an order of appearance in which time plays no role, where the notion of 'after' is devoid of meaning?"

SHAME

"The next week, she was waiting impatiently for me: 'Here's something I'd like to know. Why do doctors blush when they're available for consultation?'

Of course I didn't see the allusion to the way I'd changed color and I really thought we were talking about other people, those medical doctors I wasn't a part of—as if we were discussing the ethology of a neighboring species. 'Why do you think they blush?'

'I guess it's because of the shame of my being here, the shame of looking at me, of shaking my hand. I'm afraid to contaminate you. You might get my sickness. I'm afraid that you'll die—of never seeing you again, of your becoming someone else.'"

"I see how well you managed to be objective," ironized Schrödinger.

"I would have liked to see you handle it. . . . I assured her that I'd be there the next Monday. But she dismissed me curtly as being part of the healing Saints: 'The goodie-goodie behavior of the nurses drives me nuts. My whole body is dead. My whole head is dead. I'm a living dead. In 1956, I became a statue.'

At this point I must have fled the scene running, because the next notes are already from the following week. She was in her room and she didn't want to see me. I entered anyhow and didn't even knock. Because of my intrusion, she closed her eyes, her mouth, and her ears. I sat down in the chair next to her bed, without asking permission. Opening her eyes, she smiled to see me, and continued out loud her meditation: 'That's what people want to see. No trouble words. No story. I'd like to discover a planet in the sky. A no trouble planet without history. When I was five, I was waiting for real life. My head is too daring. It's folly. I'm crazy. I want the rivers to come back to life. To have real birds that sing, real trees, real houses, real dogs, real cats. It can't snow anymore. It can't rain anymore.'"

Schrödinger interrupted: "I bet you're going to make a big mistake again."

"You win. Instead of recognizing how right her observations were, how carefully she had seen my mood change, how right she was about our inheritances, I stuck her with words without stories or meaning: 'So you'd love the enchantment to stop and life to take over again?'"

"I can't wait to hear how she shut you up after that," smiled Schrödinger, who seemed to be accustomed to this kind of combat.

"With the word 'love.' It's the real word of transference I kept on refusing to use with her. I think I was afraid of the massive psychotic transference older analysts told us to watch out for. She gave me a lesson in transference I wouldn't forget.

'I hate the word "love." Even if my husband said it to me, I'd detest it, I'd strike it away. I can't stand to hear that word. It gets on my nerves; it drives me crazy; it really bothers me. Love, love, love! Even in the dictionary it says: "love, variable word"—that means inexistent. It's a word that doesn't exist. You could even say it's an awful word. Love. What counts is not love.'

'What is it then?'

'I can't tell you. It would cause inhuman jealousies. You have to see my Mother. Give her a call.'"

MADAME MOTHER

"The following week I met with Madame V at the clinic. Known to the staff for years, she'd been presented to me as a paragon of the mother of a psychotic—dismissive and invasive."

"You were still being had by the codes of your fellow health workers," Schrödinger guessed correctly.

"Nervously waiting for her, I saw a lady enter with white hair, a wrinkled face, and a black apron with a purple border. Her lively eyes won me over: 'How's Elisabeth,' she said holding out her hand, as if she'd been waiting for that moment for a long time.

I smiled at her and even felt I knew her: 'She wanted us to meet.'

'It started when she was fifteen. 'You're not my mother.' And to her sister: 'You're not my sister.' The doctor said to leave her in the hospital. She was released after a year and it started up again. She was pretty at her Communion. Now she's dirty.'

'Is cleanliness important to you?'

'It doesn't cost anything to be clean. It's not because you have a lot of kids and not much money that you don't have to be clean. My twelve children were my pride. They weren't just clean. They shone. I never complained. My husband always said he'd rather pity a woman who worked but didn't have children.'

'But Elisabeth says it was hard.'

'Maybe she's the one who best saw a lot of the things the others didn't see. She was the youngest. Maybe that's why she got sick. Say hello from me.'

And so that was the beginning of a strange phenomenon where I felt like I'd become a membrane amplifying the exchanges between a plural body. I've never again had the experience of being a go-between between mother and daughter, which ended, at least that's what I thought then, in failure."

"So if I understand right," Schrödinger commented, "you thought you'd been trapped like the cat in the box, but you see now in opening the box that the cat is still alive."

"I was certainly terrified, like your cat."

"Did you take notes when her mother was there?"

"No, but I often wrote the visit up the same evening."

A DREAM FOR OTHERS

"The next week I greeted Elisabeth with a sentence that became our ritual: 'I saw your Mother, she sends you her hello.'

She'd pick up on her mother's words, without my having said anything else, as if she were in perfect sync: 'I wasn't in her house when I was fifteen. I was suffering because somebody was in the hospital. My mother reassured me with lies. She died. Maybe if I make love to her, she'll come back to life. You're skinny. I would have preferred a lady doctor who was well dressed, with jewelry, with files in her briefcase. Instead of that, those people come see us in the morning to make fun of us.'

'But who died?' I wanted to know, feeling dizzy at the appearance of a third person, dead in the hospital at the age when she'd entered, never to leave again. In fact, I was fighting against that dead person whom she'd hung on my silhouette, like a skinny, even invisible, ghost.

'Her daughter died and I was locked up because I was beautiful. She never worked. It was only a dream. That's not normal for people. For me, I suffered too much because I was locked up. It wasn't me who was locked up. They were dreaming those people.'

'What dream?' I asked, impressed by the dead girl whose place it seemed she'd taken by being locked up.

She quickly handed me a clue, 'That dream about a great queen, that's a dream for others. They want to see me higher than that. If I were higher than that, I wouldn't be in the hospital. She dreamed during the day, my Mama. When I was with her, it was a beautiful life. And then, deva-station. They completely changed me. Nothing's left. By staying an idiot, I don't count anymore.'

I guess I stopped the meeting there. A dream for others. . . . It was impossible for me to understand then that the other to whom the dream was addressed could be me—so I would see her 'higher than that.'"

DEVA-STATION

"I saw that her Mother had made an appointment herself the following week. She began the session with a euphemism families use to speak about delusion: 'With all that nonsense she talked. . . . She asked me to find her a husband. Can you imagine! Impossible with the operation she had! Of course I thought it was stupid. I didn't agree. Nobody asked my opinion—hers neither. All the same, I could have taken care of it. I've always lived in the middle of babies. My mother babysat to earn her living, in addition to all the brothers and sisters I had.'

I realize now that maybe these were the babies from whom Elizabeth had inherited and that such an inheritance had been permanently devastated by her surgery.

As I kept very quiet, Madame V, anxious, asked me: 'Have you seen her? What did she say? She only says nonsense things.'

'The last time we spoke, you said she was the only one to see. What did she see?'

'About my husband. . . . Leave him in peace. He's gone now.' She cried silently and I was ashamed of tormenting her like this. After a minute that seemed like infinity, she looked me straight in the eyes: 'I was never jealous.'

'Did he give you reason?'

'More than once; he never stopped. The children never knew anything about it. What my husband had to tell me, he told me alone. I was never jealous, but how I cried! But they never knew anything about that either.'

'Maybe Elisabeth . . . '

'Certainly not! They couldn't have guessed. I told them nothing so they wouldn't get sick. But there it is: it landed on my last one. She's the one who paid. When I got married, they warned me he chased skirts. I just thought he was a young man living a young man's life. Eight days after our marriage, he'd already started. That wasn't my style. I always stayed clean. Say 'hello' to Elisabeth for me.'

All I had to do was relay this hello to Elisabeth. Connected to her Mother like a spinning wheel, she would spin out the bits of information her mother had shared. So the next week I again fulfilled my mission: 'Your mother sends her hello.'

She didn't hesitate for a second: 'When I was five, I was an old lady of eighty. I'd understood everything about life, all life I understood. Some little girls ask for flowers and no one listens. They mess them up. You look like somebody who asks for everything you want without being paid. You're like me, I look like someone who asks for what I want.'

'And what do you want?'

'You always recognize your Mama. When you only see your Papa fifteen minutes every night, you can't recognize him. When you see your mother cry: 'Where's Papa?' 'He's working.' You see a lot of things when you're a baby. A real Mama knows what her husband is doing. He doesn't need to say he's working. Her husband cheats on her or he doesn't. Mama is a whore. She fucks herself all alone with her pencil sharpener and her pen.'

'Your mother thought she was protecting you.'

'It's a systematic kind of virus that puts our wits outside of us. Can you feel the virus in me? We don't have the right to say what it is. Say it's a cold, a bug, something impure. A seed that has to work. I'm locked up to prove I'm a great queen. If I were a great queen, I'd be outside; I'd have everything I want. But it's just the opposite. I have the opposite of what I want. It's a contradiction.'

So she was locked up not because she was a great queen but in order to prove she was. That's confusing."

Schrödinger seemed to follow: "It's simple, she's challenging the principle of causality."

"The next week her mother came back to the clinic, right on time, and continued for several weeks: 'My legs are old. You might not look your age, but it's all about being old. Anyhow, we're not here to talk about me. Has there been any change in Elisabeth? What do you think about it? It's always the same. . . . And to think I never said anything to them. They never knew anything. I don't have anything to blame myself for . . . ' Her eyes were shining with tears that contradicted her smile.

'Except one time. Elisabeth was five years old. My husband was at work. He'd taken something for his break. We had everything at the house: vegetables, cheese. That day, I'd gone to buy some extra meat, a cutlet to put in his lunch box. Then he left. A little later a guy from his team came looking for him.'

"But he's already left for work." That guy didn't want to believe it and looked around the house. "I told you he's left for work!" "Madame, that's not possible. I've just come from work. The boss needs him to plane a special sheet of wood. He's the only one who knows how."

My husband was a wonderful craftsman, by the way! The other guy left. When my husband came home, maybe I should have kept my mouth shut. But he would've found out the next day. So I said: "They came looking for you."

He said, "Well that's great. Now they're going to razz the hell out of me!" And that's all he said, and he got angry. He left again. I ran after him to tell him to come back inside. The children thought I was arguing with him. But I never held anything against my husband. Anyhow, he made fun of me in front of people. But he's gone now! And now I can say it: it takes two to raise children. He always left me all by myself.'

'Why didn't you talk about it?'

'It wouldn't have made any difference. He was my husband. And if he'd left me, what would I have done with twelve children? And then I did have them, and they were beautiful, you know. They thought their father was the cat's pajamas. They never knew the truth.'

'But why didn't you tell them?'

'They would have thought I was making it up, that I was bad-mouthing their Papa. I only told my oldest daughter. She's gone too. Say hello to Elisabeth.'

From that moment on, truth tried to make itself known as violently as the goddesses of revenge. The play was certainly not being performed before empty seats. But I'd just learned that the Head Doctor was being transferred to a different hospital and I'd have to leave. . . . The following week, Elisabeth took the first step."

INCOMPREHENSIBLE

"'Your mother sends her hello.'

'I'm going to tell you about the incomprehensible. I don't get the incomprehensible. It's the world's terror.'

I realized she was talking about the unnamable, the unimaginable, the 'Real,' according to Lacan. And I wanted to know what that was: 'What's the world's terror?'

'People have sicknesses they don't want to admit to themselves; they land on me. The sun went inside me. I put another one there. You wouldn't think so because it's cold. The sun debased itself in front of me. It liked being inside me. It burned me; it hurt me. You imagine all kinds of things in life, that they are great queens, but they're just assholes. They imagine dreams for everybody, but it's not reality. That's not what you can accept. If only Madame V knew how to pick herself up instead of whimpering like a dog. . . . She never discussed anything with her children. You never talk to me like an adult. It was even less possible with her. I was alive because I was cute, a real little girl. My daughter isn't alive anymore. I wasn't wanting anything anymore. We are in 1966.'

I made a quick calculation. She was fifteen then.

'So what happened?'

'A crime, I have to wear a black dress.'

'Because of the crime?' The word 'because' made her very mad.

'I didn't commit a crime. You just say rubbish, Madame Lady Doctor! You're my older sister. You're not as pretty. I'm going to make you over. I'd like to see your legs. Your legs are horrible.' And then, exasperated, she dismissed me."

Schrödinger was also exasperated: "You need to have your fingers slapped. You just missed the boat again with your causality. You didn't see that as soon as you were in that empty seat watching a dying person, she made you get up on stage and expected you to enter into a dialogue with her. So she put her black dress on. And you kept on watching the scene like an unconcerned observer!"

"Her logic put me off track; it was impossible."

"You should have constructed a fiction, staged the scene she wanted you to perform."

"Lucky man, you seem to have found the solution."

"Not the solution, but a method that would unbridle your imagination. We physicists aren't afraid of sketching to help us think." Quickly sketching a circle on my papers, he named it A, and designated two points situated randomly outside the circle as B and B^1. "Let me explain: when three events A, B, and B^1 are situated in spheres of mutual non-interference, so that A can't present the least trace of B or B^1 and vice versa, it's still possible to construct a spatiotemporal system in which A could potentially be simultaneous with an event in the realm of B or B^1. In fact, this way of reasoning has become a very concrete reality for physicists. We use it very frequently."

"I don't see how I would have been able to construct the least little spatiotemporal system between her sphere and mine. Besides, I refused to consider any simultaneity, even potential, between the events of my life and hers. Yet it's true, her exasperation with me was soon communicated to the outpatient clinic.

'Why doesn't Elisabeth come?' her Mother complained the next time. 'What's keeping her back there?'

I remember thinking that maybe she talked about her husband like that. Without suggesting it, I let her get on with her monologue: 'They don't take care of her over there. They'll never cure her. I'm not going to keep coming if it's like this. We always say the same thing. You can't discuss anything with her. She's always right. She's like her father. He said if I'd worked, we would have had a house. Can you imagine! With that many children! My children never heard us talk about that.'

'How do you know?' I asked a little curtly.

She answered back, upset: 'Elisabeth wasn't even born yet!'

There was no hello to pass on that time. Yet the next week Elisabeth began to sing as if she'd been a little mouse listening in. Paradoxically, the impossible knowledge that preceded her birth perked up her spirits."

A NOMADIC TIME

"'Let's talk about nomadic times. My daughter didn't come. I would have a Mama like I would have wanted a daughter. I have to work some more for that. I think my trousers are prettier than yours and you think yours are prettier than mine. To each their own. Now I am more confident and it came out of the blue. I wonder . . . '

'What are you still wondering about,' I asked, already overwhelmed by what she was going to tell me.

'I wonder why the law exists. Why there isn't real law on earth. There are lots of laws, but the real one, I wonder what it's doing, real law. Does it even exist? Confidence is here. You are my friend, day after day and forever.'

Despite what she was confessing, I must have looked as enticing as a prison door. She added, 'You don't have enough fun. Your mother locks you up. You were in prison.' I didn't answer.

So what do you have to say now?" I jostled Schrödinger. "Why are you looking at me like that? She couldn't have known I was imprisoned by the Germans during the war—in my Mother's belly."

"I didn't say anything. Besides I didn't know anything about it," he muttered, "Then what?"

"Then she went on: 'You have lots of trouble. I'm going to pretend to know how to live in front of you. I'm starting to feel anxious. Now that I'm like that, she's starting to ask for me. You'll see her. Tell her if she has a baby, I'll follow her. I already feel happy about the baby she'll have. I'm the only one who gets younger so my mother doesn't get old. One day she'll understand everything I've done for her. If I stop, the Mamas will yell. I have more than the earth of old age.'"

"Of course you made her anxious," Schrödinger understood immediately. "You didn't know how to respond to her confidence nor how to stand your ground."

"She didn't hold it against me right away. What I was worried about was what I was hearing from her mother at the clinic. She made me worry about persecution when she said, 'I have the feeling that someone back in the hospital is holding her back.'

I finally said to her, after a week of mulling it over: 'You seemed to be thinking that about your husband too.'

'I'm not going to bad-mouth him now that he's gone. Since their father didn't take much care of them, I didn't say anything to my children, so it wouldn't do them any harm. I couldn't say anything to my husband either. Anyway, he always did what he pleased. He accused me of doing what he was doing. But I loved him all the same. He made twelve children with me. Elisabeth is just like her father. What's she doing in there? I'd like to be a little mouse. Tell her I said hello.'

It looked like we were headed into a period of calm. That would've been fine with me, as I didn't want any trouble. But of course trouble in the form of History arrived. If her mother had been a little mouse, she would have heard the change in tone, the voice getting louder."

TRUTH

"'Your mother sends her hello.'

'I can't breathe when I tell the truth. Truth smothers us. Her husband is perverse. He liked to feel up my chest. Everybody would like to feel up my chest. Everybody thinks he's OK in my chest. I don't know why. If I knew why, I'd learn my catechism to find out what the hell he was doing in my chest. This makes me think from far away, far away things. How they all got in my chest. All those sicknesses got into me. They criticized me everywhere. I'll never be her daughter. I could have left. I didn't dare leave. My Mama was thinking about it. If you want to leave, you aren't my daughter anymore.'

'You wanted to leave?'

'I never suffered as much as I suffered. You have to be a monster to do that. Killing us, shaking us up, making us cry. What's wrong with you my daughter? You want to leave? Stay here. Are we living on earth like we expect or like we don't expect? Does a baby think it's alive? You should record a little baby to find out if it thinks it's living or dead. Everything depends on the sound of the voice. If it hears a bad voice, it cries. If it hears a nice voice, it smiles. And if it's aware of itself, if the Mama makes an effort, it cries and laughs but not in an annoying way. If the baby doesn't smile, it's because it's sad. There are some things it doesn't dare do for its Mama. That means she's sick. And the baby isn't happy to be in this world. Babies work. When they sleep, when they suck their thumbs, when they wiggle, when they cry, babies work. React when I cry. You invent impossible things.'

'Which ones?' I protested, as if she'd caught me red-handed making up something.

'We lived in poverty. No family could live as crudely as we did. You can't imagine anything as terrible and as real. I always think about my real Mama who gave birth to me. The way she looked at me the first time. That's what counts in life. When you're a baby, you remember. I respect her and I love her. But I can't love another Mama. If I did, I'd be a whore. . . . You always think about it at the hospital. You're too sad. You did everything to get to the hospital. They throw you out in their thoughts; they spit on you on purpose, they chew you up. . . . I don't know how to tell you . . . and that hurt us.'

Her mother kept up her end at the clinic: 'My son said to me, "You're the one who should be locked up. You're completely crazy. You're like Elizabeth; you only think about money." Of course I've always been careful.

My husband handed his pay over to me. I had to make sure it didn't disappear too quickly. Especially when he changed jobs, he earned less.'

'Why did he change jobs?'

'I don't know. I never asked questions. He said that it was more secure. I was a little dumb. I was like that about children too. Elisabeth was born after I was forty; I didn't know how to stop it. In my mother's day it was worse. She had a lot too.'

'How many?'

'I don't know.'

'How is that possible?'

'It wasn't any of my business. I didn't want to know.'"

DAMNATION

"The week after that Elisabeth did without her Mother's hello and went immediately into a *Theatre of Death*, like the play of Tadeuz Cantor.

'I would ask myself what's the reason for them to believe they're like that, acting like imbeciles, acting like idiots, playing their game. The great queen is serene again; you can speak to her. You can even look at her if you want to. It's pretty overwhelming to see. A kind of damnation. They're the ones who've transformed themselves, with their worn clothes with kilos of dust on them. After, I learned how to be what's on the ground. To be limestone. It's the story of the historical wand: how to become a skeleton. Poor jerk, poor sod, poor fool. He was crazy, sick, enraged. Monsieur V was famous.'

'Are you talking about your father?'

'Her name is Elisabeth V and I am V Elisabeth. You can't put our two lives together. You're jealous of me. I never had such a horrible family. I wonder what you have against her.'

'Against whom?' I echoed, sure of being in that celebrated foreclosure of the Name of the Father that everybody was talking about, and that I recently saw Lacan discuss convincingly at Saint Anne's hospital while he was presenting his cases. I didn't have the time to savor the theoretical moment, because she had begun to rant.

'Just look at that witch, look, look at that, she's showing her tits, her fat ass, her big belly. So many monsters! Be my witness, be a witness! I'm too old for you; I feel myself getting older. . . . Putting yourself in a vision to know is putting yourself in a strictly official position. The mind boggles; you can't believe it! I'm dreaming since this morning. They make me dream and without those dreams, I'm sad. Without them, I don't exist. I wonder if there's a path to take in life by which to become sociable, by which to be true. Don't act so innocent. You're here to treat me, not to criticize. I demand a trial. You have to admit that the present and the past can be written.'

Theory again. 'The Real is what doesn't stop not being written,' I could hear myself 'lacanizing' again. I couldn't foresee that folly was going to rear its head to demand justice for past abuses that had been silenced."

"I fear this is going to degenerate," Schrödinger predicted.

MOTHER FOLLY

"It was inevitable. We were in the Christmas period when I took my usual time off. She greeted my return with: 'You're like someone who pretends to be sick, someone who doesn't want to grow old.'

'Just who's this someone you're talking about?' I said, acting the 'I-am-not-the-person-you-think-I-am.'

'You have a different sweater on. The last time it was an old one. Today I can talk to you. There's a living dead person. I'm not going to die for her all the same.'

'Who is she?' I asked, trying to sound professional.

'Stop this bullshit, stop being such a jerk. You have no sense of style. You shouldn't look so uncomfortable with the patients. Sit up straight. What kind of boots are those? Madame V came to see me. Quite a few Madame Vs. Once a month, they think that Elisabeth V is their daughter. I want to get rid of Madame V. I want to live. What am I doing here? I want a work time and a time to go to the seashore. I want to be respected and not judged.'

'Do you think I judge you?' I whined, guiltily.

'You're even more stupid than I thought. You can't go to the seaside with boots like yours.' (Here I've noted, in the middle of a *lapsus calami* about mothers [*mère*] and the sea [*mer*], that I'd had enough and was thinking about stopping the session.) 'Ask forgiveness. Ask Elisabeth V to forgive you. Excuse yourself!'

'But for what?' I retorted pitifully, making my case that much worse. 'For taking a vacation?'

'No, something else. I won't tell you what. But ask V Elisabeth to forgive you.'

I finally fought back: 'How can I ask forgiveness for something I don't know I've done?'

She welcomed this moment of rebelliousness: 'I can do a lot of things. Sometimes I know how to knit, to sew, the proof that I know how is I'm going to take care of you now. You should get younger.'

'Why?' I asked, getting even more messed up.

'So—you have a mother who drives you nuts?'"

Schrödinger raised his eyes to the heavens: "Of course you were driving her nuts with your whys, your becauses, your hows."

"Please . . .

After a pause, she added: 'I wonder what we do to go from one moment to the next.' Then she turned the radio on. It was a German station. She listened as though I weren't there. I wanted to leave, deaf to the foreign tongue.

'Stay. Why is Lady Doctor L more elegant than you?'

'Are you trying to make me jealous?'

'I'm just wondering what kind of shitty mother you had.'

I wasn't going to tolerate that kind of invasion of my private life and got up for good."

"She really made you furious," smiled Schrödinger, "while wondering where you got the patience to put up with her."

"Maybe she was having as good a time as you are. Accompanying me to the door of her room, she kissed me on both cheeks—before I could say anything.

She ended the session with: 'My body never spoke nonsense.'"

"Your session or hers?" Schrödinger asked.

"I see I noted that the next week I was more careful about what I wore. As if until then I'd thought it was better to dress for the hospital, in hospital drab. She looked me up and down: 'You're a pretty Mama. So it's going to get very complicated. There's a girl who loves you here and that's going to be a problem for her. I have a lot of people to take care of. You, I can handle. But the others, it's a lot of work.'

For once, I was honest: 'It's true, I admit it, you've been taking care of me.'

'Can't we find something to say that will break the deadlock?'

'I'd like to find it too.'

After that moment of understanding, the good humor evaporated. The next time, I found her locked in her room. She had told her roommate she didn't want to see me. The latter opened the door for me all the same. I went in.

'Don't put your fat ass here. You're despicable with your big mouth.'

'With my big mouth and my fat ass . . .' I mimicked her shamelessly, acting the part of a carnival character. So I'd made progress. I'd accepted to wear the mask of Mother Folly. So much the better. In the general hilarity, the roommate collapsed in laughter on the bed. I was pretty proud of myself.

Elisabeth was talking and catching her breath: 'And you even have fake breasts. A Mama believed I was her daughter because I smiled at her. My Mama admired me too much. That made me sick. My blood is too intelligent. I'm way too demanding.'

Her mother had stopped her visits to the clinic after my holiday absence. But she came back that week needing to tell me something urgent: 'Elizabeth didn't want to take a leave to see me, so I went to see her. I took her boots to be re-soled. I have to bring them back to her. But I'm not feeling very well. Something I ate is upsetting me. I threw everything up. And I'm cold too. I keep the heat really low. With my pension, I really have to watch it. My son told me again I was crazy. I could tell you unbelievable things. But what's the use since my husband's gone? I saw more than I should've seen. Anyhow, I didn't really want Elizabeth to come home. It's too cold.'

'Unbelievable things?'

'I've seen too much in my lifetime. I've been really stupid. If I could do it over again, people still wouldn't believe me. My husband used to say I was crazy, that I drank. You see, I lost a daughter when she was twenty-five.'

'Your eldest, the one you told me about?'

'That was the only one I confided in. Had to. One day at school, one of her schoolmates said, "What does your mother look like? My sister, who's sleeping with your father, doesn't even know if she's a brunette or a blond." I said, "Yeah, it's true, but keep it to yourself." And she said, and she was just a kid, "You know Mama, when I'm twenty-one, I'm going to leave home." That's when I should have looked for someone like you, so she could say it to you. But I didn't do it. I'd gone so far, I couldn't turn back. She left when she wasn't a minor anymore. She had a trade. She was a seamstress. When she was twenty-five, a priest called the house. "Come quickly, your daughter is dying." My husband took the news as though it were nothing. She was a strong and hardy girl. Tuberculosis. Elisabeth was fifteen at the time. She didn't know what was going on.'

'Why does she talk about the end of the world when she was fifteen?'

'You know, I'd been very sick. My husband had tried to get rid of me. I didn't dare say anything to the male doctors. And there were other things. I would have told a woman about it.'"

THE TERROR LINK

"Without any greetings, the next week she asked: 'Did you see my Mother?'
    'Yes, and . . . '
    'And you have something special to tell me? I don't want to go home anymore. There's blood there. It's her blood—Elisabeth V. I don't have anything in my head. I'm stupid.'

I noticed she was muttering a bunch of indistinct words. One of them was 'ragamuffin.'
    'What's a "ragamuffin"?'
    She left the session in a fury and ran for shelter to her own room, where I followed.
    'There's a Lady Doctor here who's a lot better dressed than you and who thinks she's the head doctor. It kills me to see you like a "ragamuffin," with no style. I can't live that that. What do you have to say for yourself?'
    'You should have said that to your Mother.'
    'You know when you leave I get normal again. It's only when you're here I say dumb things.'"

There was only one sheet of notes left. Schrödinger asked me, "Is that the end?"

"We're getting there; it's the denouement before my departure.

My notes said that the next time we met she launched into an incomprehensible speech using scientific terms she made up as she went along. I was very careful not to interrupt her, because the sound of my voice seemed to make her suffer. Then she concluded: 'There is a terror link. For the powerful impose on others ideas that drug them and make them think. Elisabeth V was poor. Not a pair of panties, not a single dress to put on. How do you expect her to believe in medicine and that nurses are real nurses? They told her: "You're a big zero." They never stop telling her "You're queer in the head." And when she repeats it, she's ridiculous. There's a "ragamuffin" at the hospital.'
    'Do you mean your elder sister?'
    'She died of T.B. I had T.B. all night long. I have to go to a hospital. This one isn't for tuberculosis.'
    'What hospital did your sister die in?' I remember I asked this as though I were a reporter, not being up to dealing with the tragedy.

'Stop dreaming!' was the last message she sent me. Or maybe it was the next to the last message. I wrote down that from now on 'it's war between us.' I didn't realize then that such a combat was necessary. On the contrary, I seemed to be listening guiltily to opinions about my having gone too far—as her mother might have said—of doing my own analysis at her expense, or of plunging her further into psychosis. Nobody and nothing told me I had to take the war path. Of necessity—because that's where you analyze a Real brought about by transference.

I wrote: 'I have to force myself to go to the hospital, as if I were going into combat with a trench full of mud and blood.' That's when she dismissed me, with the cry that clamored out of that file box where I'd tried to forget her: 'Shit on you Davoine. You're stupid. You're an imbecile. You're hurting me. Help! Help! Mayday! A nurse! Get rid of her! Get out of here! Enough! That's enough!'"

5

The Subject of Coincidence

ON SCIENCE SQUARED

"She was right," Schrödinger said.

"What's your diagnosis?"

"Let's leave these speculations to idle dreamers. Night's flying by, let's get on with it. Concentrate on the theatre she was showing you."

"Who's still interested in that kind of theatre today?"

"If that's what you think, it's not astonishing that you committed colossal errors, and that you believe yourself to be complicit in the failure of the world that she put so much energy into imagining for you."

As he was headed for the door, I yelled out: "Don't leave like that! I promise you'll think the cat got my tongue."

"Really? A cat—he said, backtracking to where I stood. . . . The dead and the living cat, as long as we don't open the box. . . . We can't really say you've opened your box, can we?"

"Up till now, I thought I had registered passively what she'd been dictating. As if my writing had no influence on her speech, as if her world existed in itself, a very objective world, where in her eyes living beings were turned into statues. I thought I was transcribing the apocalypse of a typically schizophrenic universe, without giving a thought that I was there too—that is, until her dead sister, like the statue of the Commander at the end of Molière's *Dom Juan*, struck me down with holy anger."

"I'm sure you believed you could realize this clinical portrait because you—the perfect secretary—kept yourself out of all contact with her delusions, neither refusing nor confirming them, being careful not to let filter in the least little drop of subjectivity."

"I've never been so neutral and benevolent in my life."

"You certainly couldn't have stuck any better to the scientific ideal. So, in your innocence you thought you were recording, without touching it, a world that was already objectivized. . . . It's what we might call science squared."

"Laugh all you'd like. . . . But that's how psychiatry attracts the most objective minds who become champions of the least innovative paradigms. If they sin by an overdose of rationalism, it's because their patients push them in that direction. Sissi's comments on the way I looked, my reactions, my clothes, made me withdraw into myself like an oyster that's been hit by a squirt of lemon juice."

"You were caught in the trap of a strange experiment, weren't you? She noticed accurately your lapses, your differentials, your variations, your bifurcations. She reasoned out your interactions. She saw the wave interferences between you. She turned the course of time upside down. . . . You see, I'm singing the powers of your princess, like the *Minnesänger* I've always dreamed of being."

"So how do you explain that up till the end she kept on conforming to the clinical portrait of a schizophrenic? Acting crazy when she seemed to be doing better?"

"Elementary. She presented you with a depiction of the world that exactly resembled a clinical or scientific depiction—precisely because the subject was excluded."

"Which subject? Be careful not to use that word any which way."

"Good God, the only subject worth anything! The one who surges forth from the question, 'Who are we?'"

"OK. So she presents me a world without a subject, as well as a world without laws. In fact, she doesn't present it. She is that world. Her symptoms of delirium are a method of investigation. And she didn't stop telling me that: she isn't so interested in believing in them as in using them to undercut my lies and false suppositions. What impressed me the most was the way she could concentrate on my least little mood swings and my appearance, without ever seeming to. You're right. She kept asking me the question: Who are we in these interactions? And she was trying to capture a knowledge she thought I had and refused to share, because I had so much trouble accessing it. Since that time, I've started to call those unwitting movements of the analyst—the ones psychotic vigilance keeps such good track of—'cut-out impressions.' In those days, I thought my failure was a result of how difficult anamnesis was. It was impossible to go back farther than her parents' generation."

"Can't you abandon once and for all your quest for causes. Seeking the cause will always mislead you."

"But what can we put in its place?"

"Interaction, you said so yourself, gaps, and blunders."

"Well, when it comes to putting my foot in the gap of my mouth, I really did . . ."

"But it's with those details you unearthed that you were useful to her. You thought you were working in a field of pseudo-archeology. But let us ask if something really exists in a world without a mind and without language to express it?"

"Would you say she was trying to make a world exist by using bits and pieces of my life? That would then be a way of examining the space where her sister was wandering, like the living dead? Like Antigone respecting her bother, she adamantly insisted her sister deserved a decent tomb? Risking her own life. It's too bad I didn't know you then. . . . Without anybody to tell this story to, I wasn't able to stand the cruelty of her attacks, and I left the stage with my tail between my legs."

"You'd better get used to it! Research takes place in nonsense and in cruelty. And don't forget that if our feeling, perceiving, and thinking ego is never encountered in our scientific picture of the world, it may be because that ego has become that very picture."

"I'm not following you. I'm way too tired."

BERLIN 1933

"Hang on, I don't have much more. But I need to tell you that I'm part of the picture you've just presented."

"You're joking!"

"Your patient's story reminded me of a dream. Do you remember? I wanted to tell you about it, but you didn't want to hear it."

"I'm listening now."

"I might as well confess, as I'm eaten up with remorse: a girlfriend of mine. Ithi, had an abortion. It didn't go well."

"When?"

"In 1931. We'd been in Berlin for four years. I'd been honored with the Max Planck Chair for my discovery of wave equations in 1927. I was almost forty years old then. Not very precocious, as you can see, especially when compared to people like Gödel, Dirac, Niels Bohr or Pauli, who all made their discoveries before they were thirty. But you might say in womanizing I caught up with them. I'd never been able to resist the flames of passion, right up to a fairly advanced age—my wife could back me up. Sometimes I even wonder if it wasn't that passion that made me find . . ."

"But that time, with Ithi, I almost asked for a divorce. My wife Anny and I hadn't been able to have children. Neither could Ithi after the abortion. In the end, Ithi got married to an Englishman. Then I became a father, but that's another story, and I don't want to complicate. . . . Your story made me think of the son I never had. He haunted me in a dream, one so precise that I've never been able to forget it. It went like this: I was in bed with Ithi, but there was someone else in the bedroom, who was calling my own mother by her nickname, 'Georgie.' Or more exactly, he lisped like a child: 'Zhorgie' 'Zhorgie.' At the time, my Mother was still in Vienna and was very old. I was her only son. . . . What do you think that was? Oedipus?"

"What do you think?"

"I've always interpreted that voice as my unborn son's. The voice came back to me when your patient talked about the son that was torn from her: 'Maybe he was worth something . . .'"

"You're more gutsy than I am. I've always tried to avoid deepening those coincidences between her story and mine. I was afraid of feeding her delirium with what Freud, in a letter to Jung, called 'the undeniable connivance of chance.' The latter forged from this his theory of synchronicity, I think."

"Let's talk about Jung. I used to know him pretty well. He'd invited me in 1946 to one of his annual meetings in Ascona. The subject was 'Mind and Nature.' My paper was on mind and science. The lectures you've been reading partially come from that meeting. I was able to have great fun citing Indian *Vedas* without fear that some wet blanket would remind me I was supposed to stick to the discipline of my discipline. That's when I borrowed from Jung his phrase on the exile of the subject. He said more or less that the soul is the greatest of all cosmic miracles, the condition sine qua non of the world as object."

"Don't complicate my life with your cosmic soul. All these coincidences are already pretty risky!"

"What's so wrong with that?"

"What about the burning of Freud's works, Göring recognizing Jung's importance? Doesn't that speak to you in any way?"

"That's all in the past. What are you trying to say?"

"In 1933, when the General Medical Society for Psychotherapy was founded in Germany, its President was Mathias Heinrich Göring, a neuro-psychiatrist and cousin to the Army Field Marshall. The President of the International organization was Karl Gustav Jung. Under Göring's direction, Jewish psychoanalysts had to flee and psychoanalysis was marginalized, cut off from mainstream German psychotherapy—which also controlled analytical terminology and analysts' activities. That same year, still in Berlin, the Nazis made a huge bonfire with the books of the Jews and the anti-Nazi non-Jews. When the time came to burn Freud's works, the master of ceremonies proclaimed:

'Against the destructive overestimation of sexual life and in the name of the nobility of the human soul, I offer to the flames the writings of Sigmund Freud.' So when you say 'soul,' you ought to understand . . ."

"What are you accusing me of? I never militated against the overestimation of sexual life, indeed I'd say the contrary. I just proved it to you . . ."

"You're wrong to joke about this subject."

"Oh you know, me and politics . . ."

"Your I-don't-give-a-damn attitude is exactly what posterity reproaches you for. The past gets written, as Sissi would say. You can't get rid of it by a rhetorical flourish!"

"So Madame Virtue, do you think I was among the 960 willing signatories for Hitler on that petition that Heidegger supported? I didn't take you for one of those post-war avengers, distributing as fast as she could labels of good and evil and throwing herself in the arms of the first tyrant to flatter her. *Entschuldigung!* I'm sorry I can't give you that pleasure. No I didn't sign. You can check. I'm allergic to petitions.

I would have liked to see you in Berlin in 1933. You're asking yourself how to place me then: left or right? Left-right, right-left? Schrödinger was unclassifiable! The truth is I've never marched to the beat of any drummer. Neither Hitler nor anyone else. As soon as I saw the turn things were taking in Berlin, I decided to get out. You speak about the book burning of May 10, 1933, about the purging of the press and the publishing world as if I knew nothing about it. But even the months before then. . . . You really had to have lived it. I think I'd better keep my mouth shut . . .

You weren't even born that day in March when they broke all the windows of Jewish stores. I couldn't stop myself from punching one of those uniformed pieces of shit in the face. It looked like I was going to be in very big trouble. Anny and I were on the sidewalk in front of Wertheim's, Berlin's big department store, when the SS arrived. Seeing that I was giving their buddy a rough time, a bunch of them jumped on me. I was only saved by one of my students who happened to be passing by and who was wearing, happily if I must say so, the Nazi insignia.

And then there was all that indignation about Einstein. He was in the United States and refused to return to Germany. When they seized his property and offered a reward for his capture, everybody got in the act to support him. I watched them do it and I knew that all those motions of support would come to nothing. He was right to stay where he was. That day, without saying anything, I left the Academy of Science for good and started preparing my own departure."

"In his autobiography, Heisenberg describes all the incredible research of that period and the sense that the world was ending."

"He was protected by the stature of the Max Planck Institute. Hitler had ordered them to work on an atomic bomb. They almost got there, you know. What a terrible year! Everything began to go faster. We bought a metallic grey BMW and left for Italy. Anny, who really didn't know how to drive, was at the wheel. I was elected to a post at Oxford. Hilde took Ithi's place; Hilde whom I stopped from aborting. Little Ruth was born the next year in Ireland with Anny's benediction and the Nobel Prize as a Christmas present. So you see, in love, in science, or in politics, I act out. Is this worrisome, Madame the psychoanalyst? I see you have nothing to say. Come on, let me give you a hand."

COINCIDENCES

"Before that famous year in which you thought you could entrap me, I published an essay called 'Science and Ethics,' where you can already find the seeds of our discussion. The ethics of science are located in the fact that no one can create a scientific work in complete isolation. Other scientists have to contribute. I asked myself what the status of that otherness was. Were we talking about only a disciplined line-up of the same in a kind of fake brotherhood? Or was it rather something unknown, an X, the 'thing,' as Arab mathematicians used to call it?

In any case it was an otherness tainted by the uncanny, as a three-year old child suggested in a scientific experiment he'd paid me the honor of sharing with me. 'When you pinch yourself, it doesn't do anything to me, but when I pinch myself, it hurts.' It's the 'it,' not the 'you' or the 'me' that matters in this demonstration. You should think about that 'it' with which Lichtenberg rewrote the Cartesian *cogito*: 'It thinks, thus it is.'"

"I'm thinking about your earlier diagram: what 'it' or what coincidences have created a region of potential simultaneity between my giving birth, Sissi's sterilization, and your ghost child? Are you alluding to the inheritance she asked about? A land of springs? Is that it?"

" . . . "

"You're playing the analyst. So be it. What if I went tomorrow, for All Saints' Day, to the country where my woods and orchard are, to the tombs of my ancestors. . . . I haven't been there for ages. Are you listening to me?"

.   .   .

A noise woke me up. I was snoring like a truck driver. Had my nostrils become as huge as my teacher's when I was a child? I was obsessed by examining the holes in the noses of adults who looked down on you, not understanding that your smallness allowed you to observe them from below, and unaware that you pick up their thoughts. In the course of my observations, I had grasped with raised head that the most fantastic and unfettered noses often contradicted the serious and learned words of the mouths underneath them. I discovered this the day the teacher of my one-room schoolhouse called me to the front of the class to stand under her raised platform. (I had been fooling around with the little kids in the first row.) I was at the age where it was fun to stick you fingers up your nose, even though we were told that the effects of such nose-picking would show up one day as huge nostrils in the middle of our faces. But I remained a good girl and stood still, while she articulated with amazing facial gestures a dictation for the older children. It was enough time to observe, from underneath the face of my old maid teacher, the extent of her own forbidden orgies of nose-picking . . .

Schrödinger's book slipped from my hands and fell on the floor. I looked at my watch. It was 6:00 in the morning.

PART III

BIG HISTORY AND LITTLE HISTORY

Which Science Can We Trust?

THE LEGAL CASE

"OK, you're not going to start up again," Monsieur Louis said to me. He was the brother of my teacher with the interesting nose. On that All Saints' morning, we'd set off through the cypress alley of the cemetery. It overlooked the countryside. As I didn't answer, he chided me about my nighttime activities which, according to him, could only bring me trouble.

I protested, "They're completely aboveboard!" I stopped talking for a minute, thinking I saw, hobbling along in her black coat, a friend of my grandmother. Pure fantasy! A contemporary of Schrödinger, Adele would have had to be over one hundred years old. Other similar coats stopped before graves, trying to discern who was in front of which tomb, behaving appropriately for the circumstances. Monsieur Louis dispensed polite greetings between the gravestones, then turned in the direction of his sister's. I went straight to my family's, while looking out over the unchanged horizon—same mountains, same woods, same pastures.

Many of the fields had been left unplowed; fallowing had been declared obligatory from "on high," as everyone around here called the directives raining on them from Paris. It had been a very long time. Since the days, in fact, when I would show up in haste once a year on All Saints' Day until these last years when I stopped coming all together, never thinking about this region, with its harsh character and a climate that pleased only fans of picturesque charm. Having been a land of border crossings and conflicts since the Middle Ages, the region seemed to have preserved, through the acerbic attitude of its inhabitants, the traces of the periodic devastations that had attacked it. They came from every possible direction.

I recited mentally, as a kind of prayer, the litany of the place names familiar to the people resting under the stones. They'd been sung to me in the old days as though lullabies: le Grand Champs, la Croix De Mission, la Paturie, les Lavières, le Sainfoin, Malgovert, Plan Gagnant, le Champ Portant, le Mont Gargan. . . . Saint Gargantua!!! full of grace, keep me from forgetting those magical names so that I may recite them in case of exile. Could I still find those hills, those woods? When she had had to emigrate some 100 kilometers from there, that is to say to the "savages," my grandmother had burned either joyously or out of despair her letters, her photos, her clothes and all her old things, so they didn't fall into the hands of strangers.

Monsieur Louis had done the same thing, setting fire to his old tools, photos and letters, when there were more and more legal investigations casting suspicion on him and making it difficult for him to inherit his family business. It was a gesture of pure folly and I blamed him for it, until I discovered in a history book that this had been the local custom from time immemorial, when faced with invasions. He had trusted in the custom of his forefathers, when the most respected contracts were a matter of giving one's word, without exchanging even a little bit of paper. But for the tax people, that proved to be a hang-up.

I'd visited him in prison in the departmental capital where he'd only been kept two weeks in order to be tried in a case that was designed to take on a lot more than his individual situation. The prosecution was making an example of him in the region, without anyone knowing exactly why. But then the judgment cleared him of any wrongdoing and everything went back to normal, as if there'd been nothing to it. Preventive detention, they told him, wouldn't hurt his reputation. When he tried to get to the bottom of it, the representatives of the law had been reassigned out of the department and his case had vanished as if by magic. His sister had died several months later, and the aunt who lived with them passed the next year at the "specialized" hospital located in the same capital city as the prison.

Behind the rectangular window of the visitation room where I'd gone to help raise his morale, he ended by cheering me up:

"Don't get worked up about this, I'm used to it . . ."

A lieutenant in the Alpine troops in the 1940s, he'd left to go to war in Norway. He'd come back from the Battle of Narvick in the hold of a boat with the remaining one-tenth of his company. Then he'd disembarked at Calais, a bayonet attached to the end of his rifle, and taken up with the French Resistance. Captured, escaped, captured again, deported to Mauthausen, then to the Yugoslavian border—his allusions from behind the prison window were more than veiled. In fact, he never talked about his war experiences. And to the great displeasure of his sister, he had sent back to Paris all his military decorations.

That time I'd asked myself how he was supposed to get out of a situation that had no apparent enemies. He'd explained ironically that for his brief stay in that "luxury hotel," at least compared to the other ones, he'd begun by cleaning his cell with his extra-large handkerchief. Then, after a few mental and physical gymnastics, he'd slept like a baby. In the exercise yard, he'd run into a cheese-maker buddy from the neighboring mountains—as stunned as he was to find himself in a place still marked by the deeds of the militia, to which they associated all the holier-than-thou sorts who liked to right wrongs.

The way the two of them had served in the war had been greeted by a "Nobody forced you to do it," and that from a young, inflexible judge whose father was a known local collaborator with the Germans.

"The poor boy," Monsieur Louis had said, his voice dripping with sarcasm: "it's not his fault; it's become a habit; it's bigger than he is." "Come back again to see me!" he shouted in the visitation room when the guard came to take him away.

His sad smile had haunted me. Yet I didn't go back, not even for his sister's burial nor for his aunt's. I, too, had betrayed him. He'd traveled to Paris three years later to try to get some answers. He'd come back with empty hands, as if his story had never existed, small game in comparison to the scandals in the spotlight then.

BADA

The cemetery held sway over the countryside. Where on earth could a spring-fed plot be? Surveying again the horizon from the heights, I felt like a general in a recognizance operation, scanning territory before entering into battle. But I was a myopic general in front of whom the contours of the land grew fuzzy, losing even their names. Focusing on a point below the walls of the enclosed cemetery, my eyes were attracted to the soldiers' helmets. They were still there, lopsided astride the crosses. "Freedom guides our steps . . ." as *The Marseillaise* jauntily says. I could have sworn to have seen there, long ago, even the pointed helmets of the 1870 Franco-Prussian conflict.

From war to war, my thoughts took me right up to the last one, from a line of peaceful undulations towards the more ragged valley where I'd been born, and whose surrounding peeks appeared in clear weather. Deposited at my grandmother's house far from the bombing, I'd been brought back to the mountains during anticipated lulls in the fighting. During those expeditions, I'd seen whiteness take over, the sides of the roads would rise up covered in snow, the night would fall, and at dusk vertical lights would light up the slopes, moving closer and closer to the stars.

"When do we get there?"

"Soon."

"Where are we?"

"We're in M . . ."

The valley was decked out in flags; they believed in the Liberation. But the ceasefire didn't last long. The defeated came through from Vercors after D-Day and wiped out everything in their path.

M! Em! Love! The name of a city in the valley! What a paradoxical command for someone who learns her mother tongue during a combing operation for Resistance fighters. For a long time I'd had a recurring nightmare in which I was lost and running in front of soldiers in olive green uniforms. Was it a fantasy of desire, I wondered—taking my clue from Freud—or had it been a reality of which I had no memory? Like the time when, two years old, I'd almost gotten the heads of the local Resistance arrested after they'd gathered at our house. Putting my hands on the door of the hot oven, I'd shrieked in pain. They had fled through the cheese cellars, where the mountain cheese was ripened.

Monsieur Louis often brought up the name of the person who'd informed on them. His two sons had been killed by a German shell not long afterwards, both of them in the same field. After or before, here or there, what did it matter? They told the story over and over again, in a time frame that's still in the present to me, as if the repeated conversations night after night around the dinner table, without any concern for tenses or places, made all the stories align with each other. Before or after, that is, now, here and there, they broke windows and store fronts and rounded up men in the barracks of the Alpine troops where Monsieur Louis and his friend, the cheese-maker, had done their military service before the war.

There were the shrieks of the pharmacist whom the Germans had buried alive. . . . Along with another man, Monsieur Louis and his friend had been ordered to seek supplies. They'd escaped from death yet again. That same night, the enemy, with the Resistance on its heels, had had to flee towards the mountain pass with their hostages. The hostages had to dig their own graves over the border in Italy, as a rare survivor had reported. Because of the stench, the mass grave was discovered the next summer, when the snow melted. An arm minus a hand had stuck out from the ground.

Later or maybe earlier there'd been the flight with me in a baby carriage, about which I remembered nothing. Running through streets, mocking the embedded snipers, we'd fled down the valley towards M in order to cross the river. We'd found safety in the Communist mayor's home on the other bank. And then there was the object his wife gave me, a shield against barbarians: a telephone book I wouldn't let go of until the end of the war. In my toddler's language, I named it "Bada," my first transitional object, a name for many books after that. Books that fueled my resistance: *Babar, Don Quixote, Robinson Crusoe.*

WASTE LAND

This cabalistic word brought me back to the "badatorial" misadventures of my article, of which I'd already spoken to my friend Monsieur Louis. The night before, as though in the midst of refugees, I'd hugged to my chest my new "bada," Schrödinger's book, a torn and stained rampart against fate's blows.

"Watch out for words that don't exist!" Monsieur Louis had warned me. "Otherwise your fate is sealed and you'll finish your days in the asylum, like the aunt."

Maybe courting disaster, I felt I absolutely had to see again the places I'd deserted. Finding my old friend towards the top of the cemetery, I asked him if he had time to take me to the vineyard where the grape vines had been pulled out. I knew of it because I'd heard my grandmother speaking about it loudly to herself—unless she'd been addressing her invisible husband, returned to demand vengeance for his disappeared vine stock.

The wine-fleshed peaches had also disappeared and the vat where the men, their pants rolled up, crushed the grapes. I'd flown through it in their arms, just the time to step lightly and to land on the other side, my feet pricked and stained. The giant vat was surely languishing in some cellar; I wanted to see it. Monsieur Louis dissuaded me, leading me up a sloping path.

Without being able to explain it, I knew that the vineyard had been there. Its dry stonewall was crumbling in places. Apparently the village had once been a city around the remaining chateau. I could imagine the games of *fin amor* in the enclosed garden before me, where people still used to get together before the war on Sundays for conversation, their hands busy with work of some kind. Never doing nothing. And now, look at what had happened: an unrecognizable place, invaded by brambles, wild roses, blackthorn bushes. The wild vines were taking advantage of the situation to act like virgins, climbing up the disheveled trees like Virginia creepers.

I walked along the low wall, saddened by so much love taking the shape of a wasteland. A wildfowl path suggested an opening into which I disappeared. When I was able to stand up straight again, I saw plums I'd seen grafted, before ending up in a fruity brandy, and I saw, too, crimson-colored apples, the kind that had disappeared from Parisian fruit stands. My pockets full, I returned to the sloping path and handed Monsieur Louis the fruit I'd harvested. He offered in turn to help me one day clean up the place. I asked him first to help me sort out the conversation of the previous night.

"You already drove me to distraction with your Wittgenstein ten years ago when I went to Paris. Is this your new boyfriend?"

"You be quiet! He's a great scientist, a pioneer of the new physics. He had something to say to me, personally."

"I knew it. There you go, invested with a mission, just like the aunt."

"Where are we going now?"

"We're going to see if you recognize it."

MADAME LA FRANCE

The path led away from civilization and began to climb, becoming harder under our feet. Nothing grew on those stones. From time to time, the sun made the grass shine, brought out the mauve in the sloe as well as the garnet of the rosehips and crab apples that had survived the frost.

"So, where are we?"

"Well, I bet that according to you these fallow fields exist all by themselves. My guy Schrödinger says that without our minds, this world would only be a play performed before empty seats, not existing for anyone, and thus not really existing at all."

"If that's what your great scientist is discovering . . ."

"He says that science has banished the mind with its dreams and its follies, so the mind is bound to come back like a ghost."

"You better keep an eye on your tendency to see phantoms everywhere."

"I couldn't have invented him. He also says that after such a long exile, the return of the outlawed subject surely means a form of retaliation. It causes panic, then goes on to head a brand new scientific field."

"In my days, they talked about brain accidents. . . . My sister died of one after our legal troubles. May she rest in peace! If she were with us now, she'd tell you you're getting edgy . . ."

"You don't have to believe me. Besides, it seems that scientists hate each other—just like psychoanalysts. From one school to the next, they take each other for . . ."

"Really?"

"Indeed. Schrödinger confided to me that the Copenhagen School actually disgusted him, as if their equations smelled like cheap wine or overripe cheese. Heisenberg, his German rival, reciprocated the repulsion. A whiff of madness is wafting out of our authentic quantum physicists. They're tempted by all kinds of excesses: parapsychological, orientalist, materialist, even spiritualist forms. . . . But the mind, he suggested to me, is really the business of psychoanalysts. We might well have something to say in all this scientific havoc."

"That fellow is complicating his life. The scientific heroes of my day, Pasteur, Marie Curie, didn't make so much fuss. He doesn't want to start science over again from scratch, does he?"

"He says not. But he also says the mind can't be a stranger to its own construction. More concretely, he spoke to me about the sharp minds of researchers, often wounded by their heroic quest to go beyond what is nameable. To put it succinctly, they sometimes fear they're going crazy. One of the most famous stayed sane to the detriment of his own son, who was sent to the Burghölzi asylum in Zurich."

"If you're speaking in this roundabout way about Einstein's son, let me stop you right now. To be frank, I really don't like all this blah blah about the private lives of people, whether they're famous or not."

After those words, I shut up, regretting having embarrassed him. Monsieur Louis had had a schizophrenic aunt. Local gossip had propagated the rumor—as usual stigmatizing old maids and old bachelors, that neither he nor his sister had gotten married because of her. And yet when I was a child, she wasn't so scary. When she had an episode, she took off into the streets, tri-color cockades pinned on her hat and her blouse. She carried a heavy shopping bag, probably full of pebbles. Everybody called her Madame La France. The kids followed her in the street and we used to ask her why her bag was so heavy. We giggled when we heard her invariable answer: "Little ones, I'm carrying the sins of France."

The rest of the time she was confined to the house, a little too quiet in her wicker chair, a little too pale. When I went to visit the teacher, she frequently offered me a piece of candy that got sticky in my hand while I waited as a good girl should.

That same kind of candy, lifted out of the porcelain candy dish bought for special occasions, was meant to keep me quiet on vaccination day—in the great mayoral waiting room, full of kids—a kind of massacre of the innocents. I don't know what the others were thinking, but I was terrorized by those little saws meant to cut off the top of the glass phials. I was sure they'd be used to cut me up alive, like during the Festival of the Pig. And then there was that piggish doctor who stuck us without talking to us, as though we were part of an assembly line . . .

"You're unfair about those men of science. Doctor Thévenin came to see the aunt every week. She liked him a lot."

"You don't say!"

Those vaccination candies brought back the unforgettable taste of the ones I'd stuff down my throat during mass. They had a hole in the middle, like the coin for the collection plate I held in my other hand. I kept watch for the tall paunchy figure of the beadle coming down the aisle, draped in a sky-blue uniform, coiffed by a bicorn, punctuating his steps with his staff. His arrival was enough to make me freeze, almost in the image of saintliness. His magical powers were much more effective than the priest's—so far away at the other end of the church. I could only see him on tiptoes from my chair. Balancing like that, what I really wanted to watch were the choir kids in red at the back of the choir stalls. I thought they were angels, dear to my heart. My faith and my hope were in them, with all due respect to the fat man.

"And the beadle of the church, is he dead too?"

"For a long time. . . . You should visit the chateau's museum. He's the one who created it by asking everybody to empty their attics. You'll see he has some of your grandfather's tools. I gave him some things too, before the trial. They even came from Paris to study us and take our picture. What an honor—becoming a museum piece!"

I stole a glance at him. My companion was smiling while climbing the hill and seemed to be absorbed by the rhythm of the slight rocking movement that propelled him forwards.

"Where are we going?"

"Just wait a minute. We're nearly there. . . . So, just like that you've heard a call?"

"He's the one who appealed to psychoanalysis."

"What a strange idea."

"He takes seriously the work-related accidents of researchers set off to climb the slopes of vertiginous sciences. It's a high-risk profession, and sometimes they fall."

"But what does psychoanalysis have to do with it?"

"It can help tie us together because it understands the slippage of time."

"The aunt also lived the past in the present. Even a slight mention of De Gaulle's call on June 18, 1940, was enough to bring that whole period back to her—and she mixed it up with the previous war. She swore she saw her grandfather deported to Germany, to a concentration camp, during World War I. But you know, according to my sister, she was the smartest of all the girls when they were in boarding school together."

THE APIARY

"She was a friend of your sister's? I always thought she was your aunt. . . . Nobody knew her age."

"She didn't have one. The name, 'Aunt' stuck to her after one of her nieces died. She, too, was from a village near Verdun. Both of them came during the war to take refuge near here, where my sister met her at boarding school."

"I never even knew a niece existed."

"One day she disappeared. It was a mystery! Nobody talked about it in the region. As a consequence of that misfortune, the aunt became apathetic."

"There's just been another misfortune: the day before yesterday a patient at my hospital died. He, too, spoke about the 1914 deportations into concentration camps. Another patient from the outpatient clinic has the same kind of delusion. It's a disturbing coincidence, isn't it? Does the name Holtzminden mean anything to you?"

"Not that I can think of. . . . Leave the past where it is. Tell me more about the call of your man of science. It's my sister who would've loved talking to you about this, like in the good old days when the aunt would ramble. Even I'm getting a little lost these days. Imagine this: last summer I received a book from Norway, from a war buddy. We've stayed in touch, a Christmas card from time to time. . . . His son, in Oslo, is in the same profession as you. He wrote something in the book he sent me. In English.

. . . You'll tell me what it's all about. Here we are. Do you recognize something? No? Too bad for you."

The spot didn't remind me of anything. We were at the edge of a wood overlooking a fallow field scattered with shriveled bushes. I plopped down on the grass. The abandoned field inspired me to take it easy . . .

"Too bad for me! You know, for some time now I've not wanted to be a psychoanalyst. I've had enough . . ."

"What?" he said, more absorbed in finding wild fruit trees than in my whining. His pruning knife in hand, he was walking towards the chosen subject. "What's eating you?" In one swift gesture, he cut off a few grafting branches, took some string out of his pocket, and tied them quickly together. "It's what you wanted to do; what are you complaining about?"

"About not knowing how to proceed, especially when the patients have to go back to the hospital from time to time."

"That's how it was with the aunt. You end up accepting it."

"Not me."

"Think about something else. . . . You didn't even notice that this woods is bordered by acacia flowers. What do they teach you in Paris? I planted them with your grandfather for his bees. His apiary was right there where you're seated."

"Really? For years I've been passing by the apiary school in the Luxembourg Garden without daring to enroll."

HOLTZMINDEN

"I'll build you a hive, in case you decide to sign up. Promise to ask me?"

"Promise."

I'd agreed, my curiosity peeked to discover at last what was hiding behind the veils. We were in the kitchen, seated in front of a glass jar full of cherries soaked in eau-de-vie. Monsieur Louis broke the silence again in which I'd been enveloped, lulled by its warmth.

"I've been thinking about your patients from Lorraine. I think I have a book about civilians during the First World War, written by an historian from the Verdun region. I don't even know where I've put it. Maybe it's with my sister's books. I'll go look."

He disappeared for a long moment, during which I concentrated on the design of the floor tiles and the waxed tablecloth. My legs were relaxing.

"Here's that Norwegian book!" he announced proudly, as if the friend's book were worth all his military decorations.

He dumped three books on the table. One was pretty worn, covered with the blue paper of school books, a souvenir of his sister he wanted to give me. The second was in English, published in Oslo, entitled *Pain and Survival*, that I put aside in order to take a better look at the third one: *A Portrait of Occupied Lorraine*. I leafed through it while he busied himself with filling his pipe.

After a few minutes of looking, I found a full-page photo of barracks and barbed wire in the snow, and the caption: "The Holtzminden Camp." It proved that the ghostly place had really existed, where the families of the aunt, Aristaeus, and Séraphine had suffered. I couldn't control my emotions.

"Listen to this, it's written right here: entire populations of civilians, from babies to old people were deported there, supposedly for their own good, to distance them from the hell of Verdun. Some of them came back through Switzerland with the Red Cross, after an exhausting journey. But the others? Maybe their descendants had to become delusional in order to bear witness to their agony? Were they worth less than the soldiers in the trenches?"

"If you go down that path," objected Monsieur Louis, annoyed because I wasn't interested in his friend's book, "there's no end to it. France also had its shameful camps."

"So you want us all to be guilty of France's sins, just like the aunt?"

It seemed I'd just blasphemed. Monsieur Louis's blood was boiling.

"Who do you take me for? Here, you can have it, just take it with you."

I took the book he was holding out to me and gathered up my things: "I guess it's time I left for Paris. I have an appointment tonight."

"You can't leave without eating something."

He'd grown calmer and left the room to find me something more substantial to eat. Regretting what I'd said, I glanced at the Norwegian book. It was the product of a collective of people working at a refugee center in Oslo, directed by Svere Vervin, the psychoanalyst son of Monsieur Louis's friend. The various chapters focused on normal madness, deliberately inflicted by domestic and political "organized violence," techniques that Argentines had dubbed *el proceso*.

ORGANIZED VIOLENCE

The afternoon had begun. Refusing to believe any of my reasons for being in a hurry, Monsieur Louis announced our menu of sausages and polenta. He turned his back to me to peel the onions.

"Look at that book, take your time. Can you understand what they're saying?"

"Nobody could say you spoke a lot about that period of your life. Your sister certainly complained enough about how much you'd changed. After you got back, you became taciturn."

"What should I have talked about? Go see the Norwegian film, *The Battle of Heavy Water*, read Lacaze's *The Tunnel*. He's a friend of mine. I'll lend it to you another time. . . . But take your time with what's in front of you. I'm going to take a stroll in the garden while everything is cooking."

Our conversation at the lunch table was about how thin the onion skins were, a sure sign of an easy winter, and about the damage done by the exploding wild boar population.

"They raise them in special pens in order to release them. . . . Pigs that eat out of your hand," he grumbled, evoking the solitary and savage Black Beast, a totemic animal, whose matriarchal social ties he admired. Our own society should take its inspiration from them. No, he would not participate in those sacrificial hunts. His father's gun would stay affixed to the wall over the fireplace.

After coffee, the old man sat down in his armchair in order to hear what I had to say about the book. I glanced over at him. Hands crossed over his stomach, pipe in his mouth, eyes half-closed, maybe he was already taking his nap . . .

"Let's hear it. I'm listening. Don't pay any mind to me."

"To summarize, this book exposes how organized violence can turn to terror under the effect of a crazy hyper-rationality. Guilt spreads like a forest fire, and nobody is responsible but everyone is guilty. Blame extends to dear ones, parents, and children; families explode, everybody informs on everybody else. The analysts of the refugee center believe their patients' symptoms are in fact salutary madness, survival techniques. In order to face the wordless collapse of reality, these analysts refuse to remain neutral, because that would risk re-actualizing an outrageous, almost pornographic, silence."

THE TORTURE CHAMBER AS LABORATORY

Monsieur Louis emerged from his half sleep.

"Madness in order to survive madness. . . . A little dose of folly saved me. When I arrived at Mauthausen, I felt I was entering an asylum where the nurses were the crazy ones. Apparently, we were in an ideal laboratory where they could verify experimentally techniques for conditioning social life. You know, what really gets to me is the continuation of this kind of thing in descendants. The children of my friends who got out didn't always have it very easy. Myself, coming back from there—I certainly wasn't the hero your thirst for idealism would like to change me into. That's why I never wrote anything about it. I would have been forced to lie too much to prettify reality. How do you talk about it, when you're no longer sure of your own feelings, when everybody else looks like a puppet to you?"

"In that kind of violent climate, Sissi, a patient at my hospital, could only see in her home imitations of a father, a mother and brothers. She said she should have killed all of them . . ."

"Being capable of killing your father and your mother, taking the food of a friend who's dying while he watches you do it . . ." Monsieur Louis's voice was trembling. I wanted to kick myself for bringing up what he'd sworn he'd never talk about. He continued, staring into the distance: "I started to think they were right, we were shits, and their order was the right one. In my cell, I saw again my buddies from Narvik, not the living ones. So you see I wasn't far from the aunt's visions. The worst was the good Samaritan, the guy who held out a cigarette by compassion, who made you crack before it all started up again. I saw it: nice guys becoming monsters and ne'er-do-wells giving their lives. It's not what you think. When I got back, I found I was scary."

"Sissi said what you're saying: 'I've seen so much of people becoming monsters. Be my witness! I demand a trial . . . ' That's what the Norwegians want: to establish witnessing like that . . ."

"So much has been said. . . . If you really want to know. . . . If I'm still here, it's just a matter of luck."

I plunged back into the book, skimming as fast as I could the description of nightmares, the constant surveillance, the fear of speaking during sleep, the apathy, the agitation that I heard his sister complain of to my grandparents. He'd been so weird. . . . A child, I hadn't understood it—or perhaps I had.

Techniques of manipulating masses, the book went on, but I didn't dare translate anymore. Paradoxical messages: you're free to choose so choose us! Cognitive dissonance: it's impossible that such a democratic State would torture and kill in the name of humanity. Incitement to denounce: your father's a communist, your mother's a fascist, or vice versa. Normalized pedophilia, wiretaps on telephones, impossible intimacy, forbidden mourning other than at national funerals of the heads of the party. The past no longer has any importance: act as though everything is as normal as possible, ignore the mental wounds, despise subjectivity, but if you do accuse the regime, then it's your family's fault, or your sexuality, or your Oedipal complex; psychoanalysis is there to collaborate.

In the silence that surrounded me, I heard Monsieur Louis hum "Le roi des cons." To that tune by Brassens about the king of fools, a black cat entered the room.

WOMEN'S PRISONS

"He's still alive!"

Monsieur Louis looked at me strangely: "It's not my sister's. It's one of his grandchildren."

The cat sniffed the air in my direction then left by the cat door.

"It's not that I'm bored . . ."

I was about to close the book, but a last title of a chapter stopped me from doing so.

"What's the matter?"

"Nothing. . . . It's the testimony of an Iranian woman, a mother, pregnant, locked up in her pee and her shit with a dozen others in a cell meant for two for forty days. Beaten in the next-door cell by mothers who'd learned how to hit, because only married women were allowed to torture. One woman's child was killed, another's husband. They didn't know where the graves were to go cry over them. Common graves were called places of shame. Nobody dared go for fear of being caught. She's speaking for the forgotten victims, those ignored by public opinion and whose situation wasn't interesting in the great scheme of international politics. Mothers . . ."

"Are you thinking of yours?"

Monsieur Louis was serving us coffee in small red bowls with yellow dots.

I'd always thought that my mother's stay in prison had been normal in war time. I'd only learned recently about how thin she'd been, how she stank, about how numbed she was when they opened the door—her with her big belly. Wearing the same lightweight clothes, worn to a frazzle, in which she'd been caught one fine autumn day.

And yet she'd described it to me, with no emotion, as though it were an everyday occurrence. A slight grimace, nothing more. The overcrowded cell, the canned food, the slop pail, the sound of machine guns in the early morning for the cell selected as hostage the night before, the torture chamber next door and the chocolate bar given one day by the Bishop of Autun to each prisoner, of which she'd wanted, impossibly, to keep a piece for the next day.

"If I believed the U.S. diagnostic manual, that DSM, I should be a schizophrenic given what happened." I was acting out so as not to show how disturbed the Iranian's text had made me.

"You're supposed to speak about it, everybody says so," murmured Monsieur Louis, "not to forget, but it's impossible to forget. That's why it gets repeated. . . . Speaking is all well and good, but to whom?"

"To you, for example . . ."

I gulped down the rest of my coffee and stood up to go.

"Wait, don't leave like that."

Lifting a trap door in the flooring, he climbed down to the cellar where I heard him rummaging. I looked quickly at the last page. This book called for a judgment, regretting that most often the trials of torturers ended up as farces. . . . A farce where "the clown doesn't laugh," as David Rousset would entitle his post–World War II book on Nazi thuggery.

But what if a farce were exactly what was needed? I remembered the stinging souvenir of my own farcical trial. The truth was I wasn't at all in a hurry to get back to Paris. The Norwegians' book was challenging analysts, and I was backing away from it. Lacan said the psychoanalyst loathed his act. . . . That enigmatic sentence corresponded perfectly to my mood.

Monsieur Louis's head reappeared with several bottles.

"Keep my sister's book. You'll tell me what it's about when you come back. It's in old French; she loved that book."

On the sticker on the upper right side, he read: "*Discourse on Voluntary Servitude, or the Anti-Dictator*. By La Boétie, Montaigne's friend, do you know him . . ."

"I even think I've met him already."

2

The Anti-dictator, One for All, and All Are Rotten

I came back to Paris with a bottle of Mirabelle plum brandy, another of sloe gin, some dried mushrooms, raw honey and the promise of a hive in case I decided to take a course in apiculture in the Luxembourg Garden. I regretted a little my exorbitant enthusiasm inspired by one last nightcap. "Good-bye. See you soon, I promise." Was I really capable of keeping my promises, when even that visit, I knew, was going to be like ink on a blotter as soon as I got wrapped up in Paris again.

So to resist being absorbed by the *zeitgeist* of the city, as one always is once past the Porte d'Orléans, I started to work when I got home on deciphering my teacher's magical text. She had annotated and underlined it, scribbled notes in the margins. The text confirmed my recent experience that chaos was the norm, uncertainty a constant, and honesty an exception.

La Boétie described one kind of a social link as a strange attraction: *a great thing and yet so common, to see a million men serve miserably, having their necks in the yoke, not by the force of a greater power, but enchanted and charmed by the name of one man.*

The link was less connected to a person than to his name. That's why combatting one tyrant didn't necessarily vaccinate against the charms of another's name. The "anti-dictator" would attempt to eradicate the enchantment without strengthening it by so-called subversive discourses: *I do not ask that you place hands upon the tyrant to topple him over, but simply that you support him no longer.* Despite my slow progress through the teacher's graffiti scribbles, what I was reading made me feel better. I slept like a rock. No one came to visit me: The Festival of Samhain was over and Schrödinger was fading from memory.

Dear Erwin, who hadn't ceded a whit of scientific collaboration to those disciplines the Nazi regime exalted, and who'd exiled himself to Ireland without saying a word, while Nazism plowed over towns, cities, nations in an ever-increasing number, such as described in La Boétie's text citing *the justly famous battles of two thousand years ago, still fresh today in recorded history and in the minds of men as if they had occurred but yesterday.* My teacher had especially marked up this passage with an angry pencil and commented next to it: "like the last three wars!"

Maybe she'd been thinking about those people who'd informed on her brother when she'd underlined *those monsters of vice, for whom no term can be found vile enough, which our tongues refuse to name? But O Good Lord! What strange phenomenon is this? What name shall we give to it? What vice is it, or, rather, what degradation? To see an endless multitude of people not merely obeying but driven to servility? Not ruled, but tyrannized over? These wretches have no wealth, no kin, nor wife, nor children, not even life itself they can call their own.*

I thought I recognized there the "real other," who fears neither God nor man, the hidden Unnamable that madness seeks to hunt down. To my astonishment, I found threaded throughout those pages all the ingredients necessary for analyzing such a Real.

LA BOÉTIE'S APPEAL

I was beginning to like this book. It was describing psychotic transference in the Sixteenth Century, with its properties of atemporality, de-subjectification, and contagion. At that moment, I wasn't really bothered about the differences between the tyrannies of the past, recent totalitarianisms, or the fundamentalisms so in vogue today. Carried along by La Boétie's words, I saw thanks to his text what was invariable in an analytic discourse: looking for the seed of a subject when it seemed to be caught up in zones of death, as active then as they are now.

From an obstacle, the scribbling of my teacher turned into a guide, as I grew accustomed to her slanted writing. She had highlighted: *When not a hundred, not a thousand men, but a hundred provinces, a thousand cities, a million men, refuse to assail a single man from whom the kindest treatment received is the infliction of serfdom and slavery, what shall we call that? Is it cowardice?* And she'd added at the bottom of the page a note of her own:

"Like an ice crystal that spreads to cover the surface of a lake, thus freedom can also spread out."

But her optimism didn't last long. "Consensus!!!" she'd marked indignantly with three exclamation points after this warning: *Obviously there is no need of fighting to overcome a single tyrant, for he is automatically defeated if the country refuses consent to its own enslavement: it is not necessary to deprive him of anything, but simply to give him nothing. There is no need for the country to make an effort to do anything for itself, provided it does nothing against itself.* What is this "self" of a people, I wondered then, a people that subjugates itself and cuts its own throat? She'd answered in the margin: "Collective suicide!!!"

For a moment, all those exclamation points made me wonder about my very reasonable teacher's reason. With her brother in prison and the aunt in an asylum, did she lose her way? Judging by the date when the book was reprinted, this text could have been her last interlocutor in her reclusive phase, when she wouldn't let anybody in, even the neighbors. And hadn't I allowed this isolation, hadn't I joined the consensus, as if she and her brother had lived on another planet, situated light-years away from my Parisian obligations.

THE PEOPLE'S "SELF"

My worries didn't last long. The grammar teacher in her had taken over and she'd noted approvingly the plethora of reflexive verbs, just the opposite of today's abusive use of the passive voice when talking precisely about abuses. La Boétie would never write that "we are subjugated by all kinds of evils" but, rather, *We allow ourselves to be subjugated, to be seduced by others, tricked by ourselves, we become accustomed to it and to forgetting our former freedom.*

Thus the "self" of the people had regained a good deal of strength in his text. "That's it," I exclaimed. His syntax foregrounds the subject. La Boétie makes it burst forth with every line, flushes it out, takes it to task, awakens it to its apathy. I would have liked to tell Schrödinger about La Boétie's response—a long time before his own appeal.

No one should be surprised that this text has been re-published throughout history, at every moment when the people's self has been threatened. I remembered that Freud, fleeing a similar devastation by going to London, had already baptized that "self" the "subject of historical truth," a subject of the unconscious, not so much repressed as cut off, abused, wiped out.

To define the people's "self," La Boétie spurned such modern dichotomies as the individual verses the collective. Rather, in his writing, the self is
more like the average fellow of the farces, like you and me, not easy to classify, not really an alter ego, numbered in order to take stock of the limbs of
the wounded body of the world that's going from bad to worse.

One of the self's attributes that the tyrant wants to control and crush
more than any other is the sense of "worth." No crime merits death as much
as the idea of pride in one's own. I heard Aristaeus's favorite expression resonating in La Boétie's text. If the self of the people was, then, made up of
the idea of its "own," what was this "own" made up of? The response wasn't
long in coming, in a whole series of La Boétie's reflexive verbs: the "own"
permitted one to say the "self" that one was—to oneself.

Was that the spring-fed plot Aristaeus had ordered me to find? Sissi's
legacy as well? Maybe it was things or goods, but surely it was transmitting
and exchanging one's own, that which guaranteed one's word, that which
honors one's debt to the dead and to descendants. Without it, the seeds
of freedom could never last and be handed down through generations.
The people could never say of its self that it was theirs, because their children and their dreams would be stolen from them by slogans that enclosed
them in the "right way" to think.

Faced with the people understood as subject, La Boétie hadn't hesitated
to get up on stage and say "I." Transference to a people who is also himself. To dissuade it from its self-annihilating, destructive love, La Boétie reminded the people that it, too, was a desiring subject: *What then? In order
to have freedom nothing more is needed than to desire it; only a simple act of
the will is necessary. . . . But men seem not to desire freedom; for surely if they
really wanted it, they would get it.*

PLUNDER

Had Monsieur Louis given up his desire for freedom, handed over his legacy to the highest bidder? The business he'd received from his family had
gradually disappeared, with all the tools, techniques, and ancestral know-
how. . . . *You let yourselves be deprived before your own eyes of the best part
of your revenues,* the next page scolded, and then, *Your fields are plundered,
your homes robbed, your family heirlooms removed. You live in such a way that
you cannot claim a single thing as your own.*

It seemed like the maiden lady-teacher's furious comments in the margin of that page were aimed at her brother. I was stricken with remorse for

having given in to the consensus that found his loss quite normal—to hell with a land of springs, with fields, woods, promises, etc. As if Monsieur Louis's house were a little bit mine; I burned with shame for not having stopped any of it.

In this context of predation, a contagious hate is unstoppable. There the page was marked by a chocolate wrapper. The taste of the traditional 4:00 P.M. treat melting on fingers mixed itself with La Boétie's metaphor: *Everyone knows that the fire from a little spark will increase and blaze ever higher as long as it finds wood to burn. Similarly, the more tyrants pillage, the more they crave, the more they ruin and destroy, the more one yields to them, and obeys them, by that much do they become mightier and more formidable, the readier to annihilate and destroy. But if not one thing is yielded to them, if, without any violence they are simply not obeyed, they become naked and undone and as nothing, just as, when the root receives no nourishment, the branch withers and dies.*

And here my old teacher roared again in the margin: "Sacrifice!!!" Perhaps at the last phase of her life, she'd regretted her own sacrifice to her pupils, to the aunt, to her brother, or else she'd been revolted by the massive transfer of their possessions, and especially of their business, to an anonymous, sterile office, in an absurd potlatch, one with no ritual meaning, insane.

By that unspoken takeover, the body of the people became the body of the tyrant, collaborating more each day in its own de-possession. I recognized in La Boétie's text the words of the man in black, whose bursting into the hospital honor court had cast a chill over the joyous mood of the jesters: *The one who rules you has only two eyes, two hands, one body. Who gave him so many more eyes to spy on you, if it was not you, yourselves? Where did he get so many arts to beat you, if not from you? Did not the feet he uses to trample your towns come from you as well? You sow your crops in order that he may ravage them; you furnish your homes to give him goods to pillage; you rear your daughters that he may gratify his lust; you bring up your children in order that he may deliver them to butchery; you yield your bodies unto hard labor in order that he may indulge in his delights and wallow in his filthy pleasures. You weaken yourselves in order to make him the stronger and the mightier to hold you in check.*

STUPIDITY

I felt targeted. Had I, without realizing it, led Aristaeus to the slaughter in order to please the charming political monsters he was always talking about? By failing to identify the "The Name of One," that is, the Tyrant to whom his family had sacrificed, I found myself accused of that stupidity for which Sissi always blamed me. As La Boétie remarked: *Stupidity in a tyrant always renders him incapable of benevolent action; but in some mysterious way by dint of acting cruelly even towards those who are his closest associates, the tyrant seems to manifest what little intelligence he may have.*

Stupid bastards, whose cruelty comes from not knowing how to love themselves. So says la Boétie, the Renaissance analyst. He interprets the enigma of voluntary servitude as an impulse of the collective body trying to help its weakest member. The people, the tyrant's therapist, give their everything to nourish the monster they engendered, that *naked and defeated shrimp*, already rotten while alive.

To help the people locate a sense of pride, La Boétie suggests animals as masters: *I shall have to do people the honor that is properly theirs, and place, so to speak, brute beasts in the pulpit to throw light on their nature and condition. God help me! The very beasts, if men are not too deaf to hear, cry out to them "Long live freedom!"* My teacher had starred that passage.

"All my relatives," I concluded, Indian style. In Sioux ceremonies, these words spoken in turn by all present signal our debt towards other living beings, including plants, animals, and minerals, without which we couldn't survive—whereas they could manage just fine without us.

But I had been deaf to Aristaeus's silent appeal when he opened the bird cage. . . . What ill luck had made me forget the price of freedom? *What ill luck*, comments La Boétie, *has so denatured man that he, the only creature really born to be free, lacks the memory of his original condition and the desire to return to it?*

IN THE HABIT

I had resigned myself to the fact that I'd done what I was supposed to do and that ill luck came from this act, from *that habit that nourishment brings.* My maiden teacher explained on the bottom of the page that "nourishment should be understood at that time as education." And then she commented, "Today children have lost, along with the verb *to nourish*, the ground soil that really nourishes them. Now they're only educated."

No doubt in honor of her brother she'd turned down the corner of the page where the metaphor of the garden is developed: *Men are such as nourishment makes them, and good seed depends on the grafting, the soil, the frost, and the gardener's hand.* There follows a striking example from antiquity, a dialogue between a Greek and a Persian who are not on the same wavelength: *Both of them spoke as he had been nourished. It was impossible for the Persian to regret freedom as he had never known it, nor for the Greek to support subjection having known freedom.*

The difficulty for analysis, and this is still true today, comes from the confusion between three registers of otherness that La Boétie details with a Lacanian kind of rigor. There's the little imaginary other of the mirror: *We're all brothers of the same image and each one of us can behold ourselves in one another.* There's the other of the spoken word: *Nature has bestowed upon us the great gift of speech to get to know each other and have fraternal relationships.* Finally, there's the real other who fears neither God nor man, the "name of one," supported by the air-tight discourse of totalitarian ideology: *The worst tyrants are the ones that get themselves elected, for to consolidate their power they remove their subjects so far from any notion of freedom that they eradicate memory.* Habit sets in and puts servitude in place.

At the bottom of the page, the teacher had connected this passage to Chapter V of *The Prince.* I took a look at it and was astonished to see under Machiavelli's hand an analysis of repetition compulsion meant to be applied on a large scale. In Machiavelli's thinking, republics got into the habit of serving or of rebelling, according to whether they preserved the memory of a former state of subjection or of the name of freedom—as if the death instinct could more easily take over and spread like fire in societies that had been accustomed for a long time to the torpor of terror.

THE SEED

Halfway through the text, I'd lost all distance from it and become jittery: when you're tested, what makes you resilient? Nerves? An unmovable ideal? Monsieur Louis had said it was a matter of luck. La Boétie said it was a matter of memory. Whose memory?

I belonged to a time in which we were told to speak, to not forget. But experience has shown that the memory of yesterday's massacres, an abundance of archives, books, and films, unanimous appeals to transmit and to witness, didn't stop the same atrocities from happening all over again.

On a smaller scale, in the work of analysis, I had to admit it was useless to speak of the past when nothing was inscribed, when every symbolic trace had been wiped away. Facts recorded in History might not find a place in an individual's own history. Then, just like in the theatre of fools, Everybody lost face, his tongue tied by Fear and Absence of Words.

Reading more closely, I saw that La Boétie insisted less on the memory of disasters than on the germination of freedom. In the same way, Monsieur Louis didn't give much credit to media spectacles of atrocities but, rather, made sure to cultivate the seeds of honesty that, just like his grafts, he'd protected from frost during killing seasons. For him, speaking was less a question of expressing a core belief than of trust: you should choose when and to whom to speak, and speak to those who could hear you—not just anywhere, or at any time.

The enigma of the unconquered was solved by the stroke of La Boétie's pen: *There are always a few, better endowed than others, who feel the weight of the yoke and cannot restrain themselves from attempting to shake it off: these are the men who never become tamed under subjection and who cannot prevent themselves from peering about for their natural privileges and from remembering their ancestors and their former ways. These are in fact the men who are possessed of clear minds and far-sighted spirit.*

I winced when I read this. Wasn't that clear-sightedness often at the price of folly? Sissi remembered too well the baby she'd been, before even her birth, before the voluntary servitude of her mother. She shared her understanding with her hospital companions, whose excellent memories scorned the arrangements of normal social interactions. Our amnesties had no power against the core of historical truths of which these madmen were the guardians. Hence their problems with sleeping and their reluctance to mix with our society.

Like them, La Boétie was frankly elitist; my teacher too. She had circled the paragraph concerning: *Those who are not satisfied, like the brutish mass, to see only what is at their feet, but rather look about them, behind and before, and even recall the things of the past in order to judge those of the future, and compare both with their present condition. Even if freedom had entirely perished from the earth, such men would imagine it.*

Fearing not to be part of the latter, I decided that the brutish mass was not really me either. From the depths of their provincial France, La Boétie and my teacher suddenly appeared reactionary, even anti-humanitarian, like Hippocrates, cited by La Boétie who *found it weighed on his conscience to cure the barbarians and who refused to make use of his science to treat the Persians who were trying to enslave his fellow Greeks.*

The recipe was too easy: take as your whipping boy the Grand Turk whose empire at the time extended as far as Algiers, *using techniques of mass manipulation and other such opiates, as well as sweetly poisoned words about the public good, in order to lull his subjects into sloppiness and mindlessness.*

And talking about the opium of the people, La Boétie then took aim at fools and jesters. That was enough of that! The guy had become frankly disagreeable to me, just like I'd first seen him when he showed up to read the riot act to the jokesters and buffoons in the honor court. I started identifying with his *brutish mass, fascinated by the pastimes and vain pleasures flashing before their eyes, amusing themselves as naively but not as well as little children.* That was really too much!

I turned the page automatically to glance at the rest. Bad idea! The little devil had more than one trick up his sleeve. Like Socrates with his palinodes, he was contradicting the thesis he'd just put forth.

He'd sacrilegiously attacked the genius of the French language. Now he was backtracking so as not to besmirch our verse. He praised *our French poetry, now not merely honored but, it seems to me, reborn through our Ronsard, our Baïf, our Du Bellay.* Look at that, here was La Boétie upholding *The Defense and Illustration of the French Language* and even vaunting the beautiful tales of King Clovis.

I'd had enough of those chimeras! To tell the truth, I was starting to find him a bit archaic and, in the final analysis, old hat.

The room had started to grow dark, and I suddenly felt like going for a walk and getting some air, when the doorbell rang. I wasn't expecting anyone. Who could have known I was in Paris at that hour?

3

The Erl King

HERLA, KING OF THE DEAD

Book in hand, I got up. The unknown silhouette framed by the open door made me realize I'd completely forgotten the appointment I'd given— against my better judgment—two nights ago, to the friend of the resident at the outpatient clinic. All of that now seemed to belong to another time.

He doesn't look like himself, I said under my breath, as if I'd expected to see the young man from the street who'd helped me with my things. Yet this one, too, looked like he was from nowhere.

"What brings you here?"

"Well—nothing. . . . My buddy, the resident, knows you. I've been on the streets for about a month. He thinks I ought to speak to somebody."

"What do you mean, on the streets?"

"Homeless, I guess, but not unemployed. I even have something to pay you with. That's not the problem. The fact is I'm not keen on opening my box, so to speak, on telling you my life story. I don't like to make a spectacle of myself. I'm here to make him happy."

"Your friend?"

"We studied math together. He went into medicine. I stayed in science. I'm working in a lab not far from here."

"Are you a physicist?"

"No, I'm kind of the reason for your colleague's fascination with math, if you know what I mean."

"He only swears by René Thom these days! So you're working on catastrophe theory?"

"No, on chance. But as I don't intend to give you lessons, or speak about my past, or gab about politics, or even confide in you where I live, our subjects of conversation are pretty limited."

Taken aback, I tried: "Speaking of chance, your call came at a good time. I've just met someone who seems, like you, to be on the streets."

"That's a pretty thin coincidence, but maybe it'll work to get things started. I'll think about it. Give me another appointment. Maybe I'll call you to cancel."

I opened my appointment book; he was already changing his mind: "Do you really think it will help?"

"What's your name?"

"Erlat."

And he was gone, enigmatic, carrying his secret with him. I was sorry I'd insisted on seeing him again. Unable to concentrate, I stopped reading La Boétie's *Anti-Dictator* to go to bed.

CATASTROPHE

When I woke up, I was trying to push back a dream that was heroically resisting my attempt at repressing it into the unconscious it should never have left. "Dream," I scolded, "don't you know that your work is all about censorship? Why give me so baldly what I should have only been able to decipher of your condensations and displacements at the end of the analysis? You're too clumsy for me to be interested in you. Have you forgotten that for some time now I've preferred the charms of daydreaming?"

Quite decided to pay no more attention to it, I stuck my nose in my fragrant hot chocolate in order to draw courage for the day ahead. Having drunk half of it, the perfect contour of the foam on the red-brick color of the bowl seemed to capture for a moment my entire universe. I told myself that to be happy all I had to do was self-hypnotize with the scent of honey, wax, and toast. Outside, day was breaking. I finished my bowl in one gulp, and from its compelling damp and blotchy bottom the Other from my dream reappeared to taunt me. I was forced to admit I'd been dreaming in German: "Wer reitet so spät durch Nacht und Wind?" (Who rides so late through the endless wild?), he asked me, not realizing I was awake.

And I answered: "Es ist der Vater mit seinem Kind" (It's the father with his infant child) . . .

These two verses summed up my entire knowledge of German. Even before the great Other asked me, I had—well-trained as I was—associated "Erlkönig," Goethe's Erl-King, with Erlat, the name of the young vagabond. Goethe's poem spoke about a dead child carried off by that king, no doubt the Herla of the wild hunt that Antonin had called on to terrify me. My unconscious had apparently patched together a meaningful bridge between the homeless man and the theatre of fools of two days ago.

Nevertheless, I couldn't get rid of a nagging sensation I wanted to clarify, still hidden from me by the blotches on the bottom of the bowl. It stemmed from a trace on the ground in the dream, where a living thing was dissolving as though it were a silent bubble. Buried alive, the creature couldn't cry out for help. What the devil could it be?

A chimera! The beginning of the dream came back to me: there was a terrible battle between a chimera and a griffon, each of them positioned as though on a heraldic blazon. But instead of standing there with dignity, face to face, they attacked each other brutally. The griffon was the winner and he disappeared, while the chimera agonized pitifully, quickly reduced to a pool of liquid, growing smaller and smaller, literally shrinking. "Without even a cadaver for its tomb," as Niels Bohr had said, according to Schrödinger.

Another anxious thought: as a witness to this carnage, I had to save my own skin. And I'd been the only one to hear the absence of the cry of that trace on the ground. Little by little, the chimera took shape again, and I threw myself on its neck. To hug it or choke it? No, the chimera wasn't the young man, not at all. I couldn't accept that this dream represented the simplistic and explicit image of potentially repressed desires.

"I should never have agreed to see him," I said to my bowl of hot chocolate.

"I was too upset when he called."

"Still throwing yourself at people," the bowl freely associated. "Forget about your attempt to seduce Schrödinger without even working on his equations. He's dead anyhow. But what are you doing with a young mathematician who's alive?"

I rinsed out the bowl to make it shut up.

"Anyway, he won't come back, I'm sure of it," I answered, opening the cupboard.

Perfectly dried off thanks to me, the bowl found its place with the others and didn't say another thing.

AUXILIARY SPACE

In what was left of my vacation days, I found myself leafing through René Thom. I thought I'd try *Parabolas and Catastrophes*, by way of being on top of things.

The introduction wasn't completely unknown to me. It discussed *recognizing and giving spatial form to accidents of defined forms in a given space called the substrate space of a common morphology.* Carrying no negative connotation, the word "catastrophe," indicated *the set of points in the substrate space where things change.* In fact, the arrival of the young man the other night had indeed caused a rupture in a space of well-earned calm, and my dreams seemed to want to give spatial form to that discontinuity.

To know more, I plunged into a text that was really quite welcoming. The author was inviting disciplines that didn't function through experimentation to make themselves worthy of science *provided that the morphologies they study enjoy a certain stability.* I liked that word "morphology"; it evoked for me the urgent situation in which one had to give shape to the shapeless, or else analysis couldn't go forward.

But soon I was disillusioned. The author, generous in spirit, nevertheless found psychoanalysis unworthy of his theory, because of its concern with results. On the other hand, he criticized it because it was so inefficient when dealing with the mentally ill. This contradiction pleased me.

Like Schrödinger, he affirmed the importance of the psyche in scientific research and the possibility of "entities more fundamental than space-time, in a sense more psychic, more connected to the psyche of the observer."

But then, he asked himself *if phenomena appear in a break of intersubjectivity, how does one synthesize the different visions of the observers, how does one circulate the different visions in the scientific community, one founded on the equality of peers in the acquisition and interpretation of knowledge.*

Once again shaken by the pull of analogy, I stopped to think about that intersubjective break. I couldn't resist it. Paying no attention to the gap between my experience and his, between his intellectual level and mine, I situated myself without problem among his peers.

Isn't the difficulty of psychoanalysis that it rests entirely on that break of intersubjectivity? Those who'd tried out any number of analysts' couches would confirm that every analyst has not only his or her own style and theory, but also his or her own pet ideas. Especially in the case of folly, where the space-time of the session would always be broken by disturbing morphologies, due to the clairvoyance of the patient, a kind of impenitent observer. As if the observer were a master from early childhood on of the art of deciphering the unconscious of those on whom he or she depends.

I stopped the analogy there, for no one had ever seen a particle take up the language used to describe it in order to give its own perspective on the scientist's psyche.

Besides which, Thom's text took up the nature of verbal matter to ground the dogma of the irreversibility of time. The sequence of subject, verb, object (for example, the cat eats the mouse) was to him fundamentally irreversible. And, indeed, Tom was never eaten by Jerry, nor were analysts consumed by their patients. That was reassuring. My dream of being a predator in which I threw myself at the neck of the chimera went along with that notion. And yet I felt so much more chimera than griffon, torn between two poles of attraction, fear and seduction. The buzzing of "I should have" started up again in my head.

It would have been better if I'd given the young man the address of someone more competent than I, I worried, while noticing that Thom carried on with his remake of the myth of the Platonic cave: *The theory of catastrophes assumes that the things we see are only reflections, and that to arrive at being itself, one must multiply the substrate space by an auxiliary space and define in this produced space the most simple being that, by projection, gives the observed morphology its origin.* Thom summed this all up by citing the physicist Francis Perrin: *One must substitute a simple invisible for a complicated visible.*

This sentence captured precisely the impasse where I found myself. I could think of my dream as the production of a simple invisible, substituting for a complicated visible which was the young man's non-request for analysis. Maybe, like me, he was already deploying an auxiliary dream space to give form to the chance of our meeting, a meeting that resembled nothing else.

I remembered the lesson I'd given to the bee about the Greek *therapon*: the ritual double, I'd explained, an auxiliary offering its services to an equal, a second for battlefield combat. Prevaricating no longer, I finally decided to offer Erlat the auxiliary or *therapon* space that came open during the night.

INANIMATE OBJECTS

The next time, he kept his mouth shut, looking me straight in the eyes, apparently expecting nothing. After it was over, I felt I'd been aggressive, assailing him with an avalanche of questions to which he answered politely after a few moments of silence.

"You see, I don't have a lot to say to you."

"Don't you have a home?"

"I purposely shut myself out of my house."

"Why?"

"No reason. . . . Not to give a sign of life."

"And now?"

"My boss wants to put me in the hospital so I can be treated. He thinks I've got a screw lose. But he can't complain about my work; my brain is still more or less pretty effective. Besides, so as not to scramble what's still working, I stopped taking the pills my friend prescribed for me."

"We could all the same try to see more clearly into this."

"It's all clear to me. Don't take it wrong. But this conversation is absurd. I feel like I'm on stage, in a world of make-believe where I see the performance space and back stage at the same time. But I have no role to play and I have no intention of playing."

Seeing his determination, I thought I also saw a slight movement to get up, leave, finish with all of this, and on his features a silent threat that must have alarmed the head of his lab.

"Try to describe the last moments you spent in your house."

"Totally normal, I welcomed a friend who was passing through and needed a place to stay."

"What's his name?"

"Gilles. All you need are interrogation lights and a typewriter . . ."

Assigned to the role of the person who wrings out confessions, I could see that not opening "his box" was usual. Clearly something he'd hardened himself against for a very long time. But I didn't have the choice or probably the talent to try anything else. Without thinking about my dream, I went after him again, not really expecting an answer.

"Have you ever gone through catastrophic times, you or your family?" (In the realm of nonsense, at least this question connected him to his favorite author.)

"Of course. And yet my childhood in a country at war didn't traumatize me in the least. I have pretty good memories."

There was a long silence after that. And to my surprise he was the one who broke it: "I don't want to give you the impression I'm making fun of your work. Since childhood, I've kept a few strange things, without any importance. Three objects in pitiful shape. It seems like they can't disappear. Whatever happens, they're always with me. They're the only things I took from the house."

"And they are?"

"Insignificant. An old scarf, a pair of broken glasses, and a pen that doesn't work anymore."

Grabbing hold of this godsend, I asked him to free associate, as is customary in our business. When I saw how he looked at me, I realized how much it had cost him to talk to me. Indeed his look said he needed a break. The session had obviously worn him out.

PROGRESS

Contrary to what I'd expected, he came in for session after session and, I have to say, they were very psychoanalytical ones at that. Little by little he agreed to open "his box" and was astonished to hear himself speak and take up the threads of his past. He became a productive researcher again, stopped worrying his boss, and rented a room half-way between his work and my office. Sometimes I ran into him on the street, and I always had the impression of some kind of uncanny familiarity.

We didn't solve the enigma of his friend Gilles, whose simple presence was enough to chase him out of the house, and who finished by joining the three strange objects. We didn't pay them any mind, as if the importance given to them during our second session had faded away again.

As we went on, I became more and more interested in René Thom's auxiliary space. *The surprising character of facts,* he wrote, *only appears if one has a theory that makes us really look at them.* My enthusiasm was all the more hyperbolic in that I was incapable of recognizing in practice what had so thrilled me in theory. And since neither Erlat nor I had any theory about his three strange objects, they stayed politely in that nowhere where they'd been, while I encouraged him to revisit the better marked paths of his past.

He often complained of having no ego. That the boundaries between him and other people were so fragile he was incapable of making a decision. Yet, even according to him, he was regaining a taste for life.

One day he had to choose between two fantastic jobs, each one available to him at the end of his post-doc. It produced a crisis. He was invaded by indecision, emptiness, apathy. He kept on courageously coming to our sessions, without believing in them, and our conversations got stuck in a deadly torpor, without a future, without a past.

SINGULARITY

From the beginning I knew, without wanting to admit it, that we were headed towards this risky moment. René Thom, in whom I had more and more confidence, spoke of it: *That fascination exerted over the psyche by catastrophes, for example, in the form of predator/prey, when they can't be named.* He added that man has been able to depend on the mediation of language to unhook him from this form of alienation.

That was precisely the situation: a paralysis in the face of mortal danger that we had all the trouble in the world to name. Silence took over, words were smothered, as if all the air of the session had been sucked out of the room. I saw Aristaeus again bracing himself against the closed door. Should I have spoken of my dream to escape the torpor? The chimera attacked by the griffon—a fine example of predation! Stuck in suspended time, I was a thousand miles from remembering what I'd dreamed.

We got in the habit of those silences, as if in voluntary servitude. But who was the tyrant subjecting us? René Thom had also given the name of "habit" or "pleat" or "crease"—*pli* in French has these two meanings—to one of his elementary catastrophes: *When one projects a space onto something which is smaller than that thing's own dimensions, it* (the crease, the pleat) *accepts the constraint, except on a certain number of points in which it concentrates its primary individuality. It is in the presence of this singularity that resistance occurs.* I grabbed on to this singularity, to this pleat or crease, in our tissue of silence.

Everything occurred, indeed, as though Erlat and I were huddled in a pleat of time, each of us in our own way, accepting that constraint. Talk about resisting: we resisted. But instead of deploying the auxiliary space that could have constructed a safe form that was also in the guise of a source of danger, we stared at each other like figurines on a mantelpiece.

Now that auxiliary space had from the outset been offered in my dream. I had it in hand, but I continued not to use it—so true it is that our dreams dream of being forgotten. That one came back once in a while, erratic, and unconnected to the time of our sessions, and I regularly chased it away.

I was mad at the resident for getting me into this mess. I would have done better to recall what he had cited in the clinic: "The edges of a table conserve the memory of the saw that cut the original tree." In the same way, the sharp edges of my dream kept the traces of my patient's arrival, and this at the time when the head of an editorial committee had cut her way into the life of my article. . . . But I wasn't thinking about it anymore, no more than about the edges of the table where her letter had remained, since I'd received it.

DAIMON

One day, without warning, the "morphology" in question landed in the "substrate space" of a session. On the appointed hour, I saw a weird character when I opened the door. The young man had donned an old faded pink scarf and broken glasses. I imagined he had in his pocket a Waterman pen that didn't work anymore. Instead of waiting for him to explain his disguise, I threw myself at him again, as if to conjure away the apparition.

"What's that scarf for?"

He didn't lose a beat: "To attach my head to my neck."

I stood there, flabbergasted.

He came closer: "Sometimes I feel I've got a girl's head on a boy's body."

I felt stupid. "What girl?"

He answered as normally as possible, as if that were, in fact, the real question: "The one whose photo I found when I was twelve years old, when I was checking out the drawers of my grandparents. The photo of a baby. I asked if it was me. They said: 'No, it's a photo of your sister who died before you were born. She had a malformation of the spinal column.' Then I learned that a boy had also died of the same condition—after I'd been born."

"What was his name?"

"Gilles."

"Like the boy you hosted?"

"A pure coincidence."

"How terrible for your parents!"

"Cut the melodrama. They never spoke about it. There's the proof."

"Maybe they split up because of that?"

"We, too. This is the last time you'll see me. I'm planning on killing myself. Don't worry. It will look like an accident. It's not your fault. I've signed a paper that gives my body to science."

I stammered: "It's the babies who should die, for once and for all."

"I don't understand what you're saying."

As if I were responding to the silent appeal of the chimera of my dream, I heard myself affirm forcefully: "I feel responsible for what happens to you, because of the simple fact that you came to speak to me. You're undoubtedly right. Something has to be killed. But not you. You must bring it here."

What was I saying? He looked at me without understanding, got up, and thanked me for doing everything I could.

There followed a horrible moment of suspense where the folly of the projected sacrifice, instead of acting like an *engin* to appease his little ghosts, risked becoming his *destin*, his fate—sealed and delivered.

My dread came from his threat but also from the strange appearance of that outlandish character, dressed in attributes contemporaneous with the catastrophe in question. And there I was, unable to hold onto this witness of a world without a subject, this effigy of a time frozen by words with no history. And yet, despite their silence of worn-out things, those three objects had succeeded in signaling to me the traces of disaster. But I was at a loss. I should have found the words . . .

The time had come for the "Tote Kinder" to return: the dead children carried off by the Erl King who was threatening this stunned witness with his invisible horde. To think that I'd not been able to make the first move and welcome on the stage of my chimera dream the death zone of that wild hunt. . . . The lessons of the Festival of Samhain had served no purpose. Worse than that, I didn't even have the presence of mind to suggest hospitalization, like his boss had done.

A DREAM SIGNATURE

When he rang on time for his session, I remained impassive. I could just as well have thrown my arms around him. He opened his "box" himself to tell me he was alive, and no longer among the living dead. Even better than Schrödinger's cat, he would be able to tell me about the forms of witnessing in that no man's land.

As in legends, the three old and discarded things he'd kept through any and all circumstances had demonstrated the powers with which they'd been endowed: the scarf in order not to lose his head, the broken glasses to see what others don't want to see; and, finally, the pen to write the story and then be able to forget it.

He'd practically become talkative: in the mythology of his Celtic ancestors, the souls of dead children became birds. By his magic name, Gilles, the visitor, had served as decoy to these souls. So Erlat had had to venture into the streets as a knight errant in quest of a place where they could finally rest in peace.

When he got back to his place, after our last session, he'd remembered what I'd said to him in the beginning: if he couldn't speak, he could always draw. At the time he'd found the idea childish. But then he picked up a pen that worked and let his hand draw what it wanted without guiding it. He couldn't imagine anything anyway. The drawing was ridiculous. He hadn't brought it to me. It looked like someone flayed whose skull had been sawed horizontally in half. That gave him the odd idea of exchanging brains to give the girl back hers and to recuperate his own. That idea of exchanging standard parts made him laugh, so he decided to wait until the next day to kill himself. And he slept like a baby. He had a dream that he'd wanted to tell to me while he slept.

"We're in a school yard. You're the schoolteacher who's responsible for the children's play time. You put me at the head of a column of girls, knowing full well that I'm a boy. And you put a girl at the head of a column of boys. And just like that the fatal spinal column becomes a child's game.

And that's not all. You make us return to the classroom, all lined up in rows. We're doing a dictation. I start to write in a school notebook the verb *proferam*, a Latin word which means nothing to me.

"Make an effort . . ."

"To proffer? Do you have a dictionary?

I handed him my good old Latin-French *Gaffiot* and he read the translation: "to expose, to reveal openly, publicly, overtly," but also "to bring forward, to put into motion . . ."

"Now I remember: I proffer, I will proffer, I wish I would proffer . . ."

I hailed the return of his "I."

"Look at what awaits you. Not bad for a subject who didn't want to open his 'box'!"

MA, AIDA, IN-BETWEEN

After that session the course of his analysis changed. We talked about the direction his life should take, about what he wanted to devote himself to.

The banished subject of his story had, through a pretty terrifying assault, first taken the form of a demanding ghost, but appearing in my doorway had to come back into language. Alive or dead—be it only a name on a tombstone. By claiming my own responsibility, I'd shown him that he wasn't alone in doing his work. It wasn't necessary to sacrifice his self, a piece of paper would do the trick, as long as it could circulate, as long as it would be significant for someone else.

His dream had been the grammatical operator of the language game that transformed the killing spinal column into a column of girls that he led. In Thom's vocabulary, into which he'd initiated me without realizing it, and that I used in all kinds of good and bad ways, his dream had proceeded to *exfoliate* a space that had been frozen by a fascination with danger. The dream language space of the Latin verb *proferam* brought on movement, desire, a future.

Now I was fond of this word "exfoliation," which in Thom's writing introduced both foliage and folly into his mathematical formulas. Other words of his, like "fluid," which designated the propagation of long-lasting forms under the effect of vivid terror, for example, reminded me of Sissi's theories. And I could imagine Gilles, Erlat's friend, whose stay had provoked his crisis, in the features of Watteau's painted character "Gilles," to whom I likened Pierrot of the Carnival of Fools.

I still hadn't taken on the exfoliation of my own dream. Should I have spoken to Erlat about it? What a sacrilege in terms of psychoanalytic rules! And yet I couldn't stop thinking that the subject of *proferam* was born first in the empty bubble of my inaugural dream. My immediate response to the chimera's silent cry—throwing myself at its neck—had been very ambiguous indeed, and it still bothered me.

"I embrace my rival, but I do so to better suffocate him," confessed Nero before killing Britannicus, his brother, in Racine's play. Yet that young man wasn't a rival, even less a brother, I contended—in denial and without delving further.

For the hour was one of triumph. *Proferam*—I proffer—had just inscribed its signature in the space between the silent bubble of my dream and Erlat's writing of his own. A dream signature, it attested to the return from exile of the subject—a subject that had first sheltered the secrets of childhood in the theatre of my dream.

Erlat was free to pursue his path of secrets. What was left for me were the outlines of the opening dream, one I could remember as clearly as though I'd dreamed it the night before. It had appeared through the door half opened by Erlat, between the figure of my chimera and his experience of an unspeakable real.

To whom could I speak of it? To Schrödinger? He'd become again a name on a book. As a souvenir of that strange period in my life, I was keeping on a shelf near me an ideogram meaning "the in-between," the *ma* or the *aida*. The ideogram represented the day, or the sun, in a doorway. It had been introduced in the halls of a Parisian exhibition on Japanese art that materialized the concept of the "in between" in various forms, including through the small stage of a Nô theatre. The *ma* is, then, among other things, the bridge between the here and the beyond, a space on which a masked character, returned from the very ancient past, advances to dance, for instance, her death, a death that official history has falsified. The action takes place, it seems, at the crossroads of dreams, *yume no shimata* in Japanese, as the museum's program explained.

All that is lovely enough, I said to myself one morning, but this dream of the chimera is reoccurring. How will I get rid of it?

Considering the model of predator and prey, I had only two solutions to deal with the intruder. One was egotistical: play dead and let it go, but really the dream refused to go away. The other was altruistic: set off an alarm, but then, which of my fellows should I warn?

As I was digging into the jar of honey Monsieur Louis had given me, I thought again about the visit of the messenger bee. She must be sleeping like an angel, considering the time of year, her season of hibernation. I remembered I'd proposed to her a visit to Gaetano Benedetti in Basel. He'd know, if anyone would, how to fulfill his role of Elder.

It was February; Carnival was right around the corner. It was time to send off to the moon the souls that had been wandering since Samhain. I picked up the phone. Benedetti would be waiting for me next Sunday afternoon, just before the famous Morgestraich night began.

4 ▨

Gaetano Benedetti

NEGATIVE EXISTENCE

On the highway between Beaune and Besançon, I turned off at Seurre. A small city on the banks of the Saône, Seurre was the home of André de la Vigne, the author of farces. The square in front of the church is where his theatre was performed. The departmental road winds around the Abbey of Citeaux where I was looking forward to another appointment. For as long as I can remember, when I took this route, a monk on the side of the road would wave a wooden dove that he had made himself. That fleeting apparition made drivers honk their horns out of friendship as they came out of the turn: Brother Philibert was well-known here as well as outside of the immediate region.

I slowed down to get a better look at him. He wasn't there. Fearing the worst, I turned around and entered the narrow lane that led to the Abbey. I wanted to find out about him from the monk who sold cheese, their delicious citeaux, a kind of *reblochon*: Brother Philibert, I was told, had left for a retirement home far from there.

Relieved and disappointed, I got back on the highway towards Basel. Three hours later, I crossed the medieval doors to the city and traversed the Rhine to head towards the neighboring hills. Gaetano Benedetti was waiting for me with his wife, on the threshold of their house. They invited me to taste the lacey puff pastries prepared in honor of Carnival.

I told them the story of Erlat and of the chimera reduced to a puddle in my dream, all of it mixed in with the story of Sissi. She was now an integral part of the repertory of my wondrous tales. After letting me speak as much as

I wanted, Benedetti thought for a while, then asked his wife to help translate so as to answer me in my own language, while I ate incomparable beignets.

"That young man transferred to you a horror that he couldn't experience himself, having been cut off from information otherwise essential to his life. That kind of transference is inevitable, because, in this sort of case, a neutral observation cannot possibly exist. You see, there is a lot more than technique in the psychotherapeutic position. It's a way of being with the patient, the only way that allows you to apprehend what I call a negative existence. What I mean by that is an experience at the limits of human existence; it appears through traces—in your life as well as in mine."

I agreed, thinking about how I'd collapsed on the sidewalk. "Did the puddle of my dream hold traces of that particular meltdown?"

"Most certainly. That's a way to realize a possible contact with the strange worlds of our patients—within the framework of the fragile human dimension that nowadays has taken the shape of psychotherapy. In the transference, the analyst resonates from analogous traces in his own story."

Suddenly the mute cries of the chimera made me think about the cries of the pharmacist in Monsieur Louis's story who had been buried alive before the men were massacred on the Petit Saint Bernard Pass between Savoie and Italy.

"But how does this contact end up touching on the most intimate details of our lives?"

"Because our patients never had the information they needed on a conscious level, they have learned to read the unconscious and to understand it lucidly. But in their own way. Your patient Sissi is a good example. She lived her perceptions of you like a transformation of her own being or like bizarre personifications. As strange as it may seem, it's really a phenomenon based on a high-level of communication in a sophisticated language expressed by concrete images. Outside of psychotherapy, such intensity is not acceptable."

"But, then, why did she kick me out with such ferocity?"

"To understand what happened, you have to conceive of what a death zone might be, an *area di morte*. In some families, there are zones of interaction where certain information essential to living is missing. Not because of repression—censorship implies language. It's really a question of silent zones, devoid of any trace of language. That's where the tragic lies. Mind you this could be overcome if these zones were defined, but they are constantly trivialized, made unreal by unconscious manipulations."

"So you agree? There are, then, two types of unconscious: one which is the domain of the repressed, implying a language that is already in place, the other that comes from a cutting off of all language. Freud explains this in his essays written between the two wars: 'Moses and Monotheism,' and before that in 'The Uncanny,' and 'Gradiva.'"

"Exactly, and in the second case of an unconscious which is not a matter of repression, he doubts that transference can take place, and thus even the possibility of analysis is called into question, for no language, therefore no otherness, is available. That deserves to be explored. He's wrong and right at the same time. When knowledge about vital situations is refused, the result is a feeling of not existing, of dissolving once in contact with the Other, of becoming the thing thought by the Other. From that perspective, Freud is right: to talk about analysis in any normal sense is a nonsense, for any spoken interpretation is a threat. It's useless, too, to try to overcome anxiety, because even anxiety is preferable to nothingness. Here, the old saying that psychoanalysis is counter-indicated is really right on the mark.

That's why your patient chased you away. Your nearness endangered her existence. She preferred to see you reduced to a machine, to dehumanize you."

THE THERAPEUTIC UNCONSCIOUS

"I see! Does this mean that you, too, favor the new electrical and chemical panaceas?"

"I believe that the publicity surrounding all of this today is a sign of cowardice on the part of society in order to reduce delusions and squash any revolt. Those shocks produce states of sub-depression and thus apparent submission. They immolate innocent people on the altar of social aggressiveness. Indeed, this monstrous abuse of aggressiveness can intervene at the expense of political minorities, in fact of everyone, without our even noticing it.

And I haven't finished yet. I didn't say that psychoanalysis was impossible. It's what I do after all. But it's only possible if we are prepared to analyze ourselves continuously and to endure situations of partial dehumanization where we are, also, deprived of speech, of thought, of freedom. From that perspective, analysis consists in weaving a dialogic fabric at the site of the death zone—owing to the powerful effect the sensation of psychic death for others has on our own unconscious."

"So that dream where I must save someone from being swallowed up . . ."

". . . was the beginning of a dialogue without which nothing was possible. The mirror of the therapeutic unconscious is indispensable for giving, in a certain way, the patient back to himself. Otherwise, he lives through our words and loses himself. Any kind of creativity is welcome, whether it be through dreams or fiction, without aiming for mastery, without manipulation. By dint of fleeting impressions, conscious and unconscious associations, we demonstrate that the irrational can be approached and spoken of.

You should also know that the swallowing represented in your dream might also be something the patient was looking for. The self-hate and hating others that kept him going give him a form of omnipotence. It's a bitter alternative to negative existence! But becoming a monster is preferable to nothing."

"The analyst you're describing has to be a saint."

"Or have a bad temper. It's not a good thing to be taken advantage of. The most talented therapists always seem to me to be those who are in contact with their aggressiveness. Thanks to the capacity not to deceive oneself and a solid dose of patience, the magnifying glass of our countless hours of listening permits us to enter a world that's not accessible to scientific impartiality.

It's true that sometimes symptoms can so transform the identity of the subject that a careless approach confuses them with a deterioration in the nervous system. But that kind of interpretation gives way as soon as the observer allows himself to be affected. He discovers very quickly that even the most aberrant transformations are always a function of the interaction between himself and his patient.

You, yourself, saw this very quickly with your patient Sissi. Paradoxically, the fact that reality had lost all credibility made her a lot closer to your own truth. Your patient lived in herself what you couldn't accept of yourself. That kind of lucidity can't be analyzed. It's experienced. In that light, it's impossible to say, as Freud did, that there's no transference in psychosis. Nobody, no serious researcher, would confirm that."

COGNITIVE SOLIDARITY

"You're right. I always had the impression of being on the hot seat, of being judged."

"For our psychotic patients, the dangerousness of existence is a constant. It's there even under the most apathetic appearance, like a cat who's dozing . . ."

"So you have a cat too?"

"No. Why?"

"I'm sorry. . . . You were speaking about danger . . ."

"To deny the real dimensions of the catastrophes they've gone through would be on our part a sort of negative hallucination, a denial of scientific clues, analogous to the Inquisition's condemnation of Galileo! As my friend Otto Will said, it's aberrant to deny the patient's interpretations, especially when he himself uncovers his analyst's weaknesses. You see, our work is shared research between two equal beings on the level of the unconscious.

You experienced it yourself. Your patient became anxious every time she saw you were anxious. That's how it always is. After all these years, delusions seem to me to rigorously describe concrete reality in its irrational guise."

"So, then, you go in the direction of the delusion?"

"But without encouraging it. Nothing is more therapeutically absurd than to want to suppress a delusional masterpiece. The person who is delusional has the courage to accept the role of the divine lamb, or of the only guinea pig capable of making it possible to progress in the scientific vivisection of the species. It's easy to notice that one's mental clarity remains intact in such a delusional quest. In fact, in being so aggressive through her delirium, your patient Sissi tried to enter into your reality."

"What should I have done?"

"Not run away and refrained from negative judgments. This kind of work requires respect."

"That's exactly what she was asking for—to be respected and not judged. But respect isn't enough . . ."

"There has to be intelligence as well. The more contact I have with these patients, the more I have the impression of not understanding well enough their misfortune. It's something that can't be compared to any other thing, like the sounds that nothing can represent to a non-hearing, non-speaking person. But once one gets there, the terrible normality of indefinite catastrophe rushes in, and can be felt in the insignificant creaking of a door, opening up to infinite possibility. That's why the analyst's intelligence depends on her abilities to identify."

"The word is so misused. How do you understand it?"

"As an act of cognitive solidarity with our patients, knowing that human psychobiology takes shape from the beginning in a history, and that it's never accessible outside of that history. That kind of intelligence is more than ever relevant at a time in which we are discussing whether or not it's possible to conceive of the ultimate structure of matter in other than positivist terms. One might say that the old question of soma and psyche can be looked at today at the point where the previous aporia of the problem may suggest new premises for new solutions."

His allusion to this century's scientific revolutions nearly prompted me to speak to him of Schrödinger's visit. I just managed to keep my mouth shut, fearing that he'd see all of that, too, as a delusional masterpiece.

Madame Benedetti served me some more tea. The conversation turned to the preparations for Carnival, in which one of their children was participating with a group of friends. While his wife got up to look for photos of last year's festival, Benedetti asked me abruptly: "Why do you think psychoanalysis is losing ground on every front?"

CAUSALITY

Surprised, I struggled to answer: "A *zeitgeist*—that favors drugs of oblivion."

"Maybe . . . but also because we're under the awful pressure of an outsized demand for certainty, rooted in a conception of causality fundamental to the natural sciences. Under the pretense of scientific rigor, psychological factors are subsumed under biological considerations and the patient is condemned to solitude.

There is, however, another way of thinking about causality, born of a refusal to make the patient a scientific object. Believe me, a statistical examination of the schizogenic, rejecting, mother would never allow the least breakthrough. On the other hand, causality lies in the therapeutic encounter where analysis becomes a joint research project . . ."

"But that's another kettle of fish."

"Do you understand Italian?"

"A few words, especially since I was kidnapped. . . . I'll tell you about it some time."

Without his wife there, Benedetti expressed himself slowly, in a French mixed with Italian that his very careful pronunciation made understandable to me: "The most difficult thing for the analyst is to know how to stay precariously balanced on the fugitive moment. Some patients can't be themselves unless they don't have a past.

Like poets, they're close to those zones of creativity at the margins of existence. But they don't have access to the safety of self where analysts, and also artists, can take refuge in case of danger. Because of this, a patient's description is always better than a theoretical concept. One of them said to me: 'I'm not nothing, because nothing is still too precise. In me, there is absolute indetermination.'"

"Did he know he was schizophrenic?"

"Don't ever give preference to research that concludes that patients are mad. As if believing one is crazy could help. . . . One becomes even more crazy with anxiety and despair."

"And yet, research into 'psychotic structure' is everywhere. There isn't a single conference that doesn't advertise it on their programs . . ."

"I look askance at those armchair theoretical constructions they're drowning us in. Lacking examples taken from experience, far from any kind of deep appreciation of our patients, they seem to me like sophisticated recipes that decorate a plate but don't nourish anyone. Their greatest error is to want to refer only to the observer who then takes on excessive importance. They neglect, with their chatter, the need for survival of the 'case,' who stands like an immutable ghost in a field of cadavers."

"You're pretty tough . . ."

"When it comes to psychosis, psychoanalysis often has the tendency to jump into bed with psychiatry. It gives too much importance to diagnosis, or worse, it tries to correct the symptoms by prescribing drugs. Yet we mustn't think of these symptoms as defense mechanisms to conquer, but rather like clues to welcome in our research, listening and participating, as long as it's necessary."

"Analysts are probably tired of having to be so patient. . . . In the United States, the country of your friends Otto Will and Harold Searles, once home to the Palo Alto Mental Research Institute, the pioneering discoveries in the analysis of psychosis have almost been forgotten."

"Medicating patients is everywhere; but symptoms are an expression of survival and not of illness."

MIRROR OF TRANSFERENCE

"What you're saying is by no means obvious. You have to admit it. It seems like we have to keep on rediscovering it."

"Because if neurosis represses the negative, in madness it's the positive that's cut off. In fact, psychotic processes always revolve around a de-realized Real, an erased outline. That's where the concrete force of metaphors comes from: words taken for things, images understood literally. Language is concretized to give all of its weight to a Real that's been conjured away from speech. For example, the experience of 'losing face' translates exactly as the physical loss of a face, or not being able to recognize oneself in a mirror."

"Sissi was afraid that my face would disappear."

"Because the analyst becomes the mirror in which to find one's own face. Of course we're tempted to protect ourselves by adopting a detached attitude and interpreting, for example, the hate thrown at us as a projection of the patient's aggressive impulses."

"You don't agree with that interpretation?"

"In this case, explanation by projection has nothing to do with the situation. In order to project, the inside and the outside have to exist, be built up. And in the death zones we're talking about, there isn't any more of a 'self' than a 'non-self.' What the analyst feels is the authentic violence she's reflecting. Why doesn't she allow herself to assume it, in order to confirm its existence, instead of sending it back as if she weren't involved?"

"She prefers staying to the side. You can understand it."

"In truth, she needs courage to transform these situations, these hopeless experiences, and she must have confidence in the hidden potential of the patient. Why should we always see the patient as victim? After all, the psychotic experience can be considered the patient's achievement. One can harness her responsibility in what has happened to her, and especially her intelligence."

"Where does an analyst get such courage from? I have to admit lacking it more often than not."

"From your own depths. Certainly not from the objective tableau of a reassuring psychogenesis. Without your own experience as guide, the same proposition suggested to the patient will appear as though learned, gratuitous, predictable, remotely controlled."

POTENTIAL SUBJECT

"'My own depths,' as Wittgenstein would say. . . . So there we are. What exactly does that mean?"

"Make sure you see that the only factor that cures is the therapeutic unconscious. It goes back and forth between the analyst and the patient. I call the subject of that unconscious a 'potential subject.' It's activated by channels that are certainly not verbal but which constitute nonetheless a language. The dreams and daydreaming of the therapist are a powerful amplification and a verbal transcription that allow her to enter into the other's hell, dressed like a demon."

"And these dreams, these reveries, should they be spoken about or not?"

"It's up to you. You could just as easily have told your dream of the chimera to the young man at the very beginning of your work. Everyone acts according to his or her own style. But silencing your dream didn't stop its chattiness from weaving throughout your sessions, despite your precautions. In fact, these kinds of dreams are pretty frequent when you pay attention to them. They mark the entrance of the therapist into the patient's world and always produce a transformation, like fermentation. Such a yeast effect always brings about for the analyst some strange perceptions that she must formulate and communicate. They're the echo of the psychotic pain that, even if not felt, is always more intense than one imagines."

"I can't see myself communicating to the patient that in my dream I was throwing my arms around his neck."

"But without saying it, you did so. *A contrario,* I remember in the hospital how certain colleagues allowed their fear and rejection to show. They communicated in their skeptical silence the sense that they didn't believe one iota of what they were hearing from their patients. Yet the therapist is credited with being able to accommodate the most bewildering forms. She interacts with them and must give them the right to exist, like those grotesque figures that will invade the streets of Basel tonight. Moreover, when the analyst is talented . . ."

FICTIONS

All this talk of such a competent analyst started to depress me. Happily, Madame Benedetti came back with some photos of maskers dressed in strips of green cloth, fifes in hands, under a snowy sky.

Maybe Benedetti noticed my discouragement? Ignoring the entertaining pictures, he started up again: "The analyst I'm talking about is not an ideal. Sometimes a therapist even doubts her own reality."

"And what do you do when that happens?"

"Try to get over the feeling of being a thing, of reification. Sometimes we can even enjoy the relationship, have fun without any purpose."

"Have fun! Just listen to you! Although . . . in the common room of the hospital, I've already experienced allowing myself just to be present, nothing more, and to feel good about it. I was able to see and hear differently. . . . It's difficult to explain."

"So invent a story! In order to validate your experience to your colleagues, it's the only solution."

"Fiction doesn't have a very good reputation in the human sciences."

"Your patients will prompt you about what to say. But don't fool yourself. Your creation will always be incomplete, unsatisfying. And so much the better! That's how you'll escape the current delusion of exhaustiveness."

"Are the analyst's dreams part of that fiction?"

"Of course. By the creation of dream images, between sleeping and wakefulness, we establish virtually an objective reality that permits the patient to forge our reality as much as we forge his.

To enter into contact with a zone where all logic has been abolished, it's useless to attempt interpretation. Whether they're attempts at explanation or just signifiers, they won't have any effect. The patient can't receive them, even if she understands them intellectually. You have to leave that which is inaccessible to meaning, even to signifiers, and find a place of otherness. What alone will be received are the messages sent through your responses by the therapeutic unconscious, because they don't try to interpret anything."

"So the fiction is a shared one."

"Indeed. You can't imagine the force of a psychotic's desire to communicate. Even in autism, even in the prison of negativity, she never ceases to try."

As I was telling him about Viviane's quacking and our mutual coming together, he confirmed: "That communication is what patients want and are afraid of the most, both at the same time. Their tragic impasse comes from this paradox: they're thrown back on their solitude at the point where they're trying the hardest to express themselves, but in bizarre and crazy ways. Don't ever forget—and I can't repeat this enough—that the symptom is always and before being anything else a statement that can't be expressed otherwise. Only the therapeutic unconscious is capable of registering that incomprehensibility, in order to understand it later on—on the cognitive level."

THE FUTURE PAST

Madame Benedetti lit the light. I launched into a thank you in order to take my leave. Benedetti paid no attention to any of it.

"Now listen well to what I'm going to tell you: even when the images concern the therapist's life, they've been solicited by psychotic perspicacity as a tool, and are part of the shared production. There should be no fear in restoring them to the patient, as long as it's in the perspective of life and living.

Inversely to working with neurosis, where the analyst waits for the patient's request, there, in the death zones, she must open the analysis by a liminal statement of some kind, and show that she's entered into the dilemma that's been brought to her. But such a declaration—and I'm repeating myself—has to emerge impromptu from the unconscious. If it's planned, or if it's an imitation, everything takes place as though doing dance steps in the other's hell. The essential thing is the right wave length."

"I get it. But what if I had talked to Erlat right away about my original dream; would that have gotten us sooner to his past, which he didn't want to speak about?"

"For once and for all, you have to get rid of the illusion of a reference to the past. This kind of interpretation is sterile, and your patient was a lot more conscious than you were of the role you wanted him to play. Moreover, your insistence could only have comforted him with the feeling that he was captured by your omnipotence, and thus that he only existed in relation to you."

"But the past certainly played a role."

"Certainly. But remember his reticence to speak to you about it. When he allowed the past to filter in through his objects, or his drawings, the aim wasn't to give you the pleasure of lifting the repression, but a second chance to try the impossible with you: to get out of phony situations where everybody was being tricked. Through a different present established with you, he got hold of a truth, and put stopped time in motion."

"I have to say that I felt I was living with him the last days of a man on death row."

DREAMS OF AN ANALYST

"Now you've touched on one of the most critical aspects of what we do. The temptation of self-destruction is huge, in order to exit the death zone."

"They say that suicides often happen when everything seems to be going better."

"In the moment of revival, the impossibility of existing translates by an irresistible need to destroy everything, as if to dramatize *in extremis* the infinite misery of non-existence. It's a way of trying to control it. Faced with that kind of rage, we're not all-powerful."

"That's what the head doctor said when one of my patients died of an overdose a few months ago. In fact, that's when I first had the idea of coming to see you."

"I, too, have had moments like that. I'm not ashamed to say so. But fortunately those ephemeral moments come back, so difficult to talk about, where the fleeting form of what is happening reveals itself. Self-destruction is an active non-existence, and thus animated by a breath of existence: the two opposite streams of a therapeutic embrace. . . . Both streams are, of course, present in your dream, when you throw yourself at the chimera's throat to hug it and to strangle it.

You took the risk of responding to its silent cry, for the one who chooses to be the spectator of the psychic death of another—of he who is dissolving inexorably under the impetuosity of the external world—is also witnessing her own death. That ridiculed, exiled subject rises out of the battle that's raging to pull the other out of the death zone with the help of language. I've called this the 'transitional subject' to describe the genesis of a subject that circulates between characters on the analytical stage. Because in decisive moments, one can't say that there is, on the one hand, a damned, and on the other a savior, a *salvator mundi*."

"Is it possible that this transitional subject was a rival, a brother, between Erlat and me?"

"Why not? What counts is taking a stand. Whatever you develop, nothing is more important than indicating your position and opening a dialogue with the unconscious."

Just about ready to leave, I hesitated a moment: "I'm afraid to explain the reason for my position. . . . Erlat succeeded on a scientific path, while I gave up when I was younger. But I never really accepted it. And another thing, the dead children in his story brought up the story of a very sick baby close to me who, be assured, did get better. I know these are small, ridiculous details, not admissible, scientifically speaking . . ."

"It all depends on which science we're talking about, the one that adapts itself to the politics of health, or the one that can't stop uncovering society's hypocrisy, as well as the unbearable attitude of healthy people when confronted with their so-called mentally ill fellow creatures."

I got up once and for all.

"You should get a little rest," Madame Benedetti advised me, while she accompanied me to the door. "You'll have to be ready to go at 4:00 in the morning. . . . Come back to see us next Carnival."

From the street in front of their garden, I waved goodbye.

5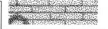

Morgestraich

The road wound down directly towards the city. Before crossing the bridge over the Rhine, I had to slow down behind a group of fife players that had taken over the whole street. They were walking slowly in time to the music, behind an immense veiled figure they accompanied in a procession.

Wherever I turned to find that famous bridge, I ran into groups of all sizes who walked on, their faces uncovered, in fur coats or nylon parkas. I took the time to look at the faces that would soon be covered by masks. Men and women of a certain age, others, younger, with their children, adolescents. I saw again all those "Folks," they, the People, I'd met in the courtyard of the hospital. Behind their veiled idol, their faces were serious, concentrated on the strange but familiar music that I'd never forgotten, ever since my first visit.

Suddenly, without quite knowing how, I found myself above the Rhine and turned left after the bridge, towards an open alley that led up to the Cathedral. I approached the façade of red sandstone, wanting to pay my respects to Erasmus's tomb. The door was closed. In front of the foolish virgins of the tympanum, surmounted by a Saint Martin brandishing the lance of a gallant knight, I promised to come back the next day.

To get back down, I had to heed again the fifers walking behind veiled gods and goddesses. Having learned from my previous visit, I knew that those white sheets hid immense painted lanterns, covered with caricatures and vengeful inscriptions, mocking the abuses of the powerful.

And then it was silent. Each shape was parked at the place from which it would start out a few hours later. It was already 8:00 in the evening. The hotelkeeper promised to wake me in time.

At 3:00 in the morning, there was already a crowd on the Marktplatz. I'd forgotten how cold it could get. My hands in my pockets, I had to defend my piece of sidewalk against a well-insulated human tide. While I was trying to warm up by taking in the red-colored Mayor's Palace lit up with warm colors, I attempted to remember where the devil I'd read how this Catholic Carnival, in a city won over early to the Reformation, was so atypical. It starts on Monday after Ash Wednesday, to commemorate a sixteenth-century massacre whose ghosts come back right up to today to haunt the city. . . . Impossible to find the source of that information, and all the more so because the citizens of Basel don't like to share the secrets of their Carnival.

I was about ready to concede that maybe I'd dreamed all of this when suddenly all the lights of the city went out. The crowd froze. A great red devil surged forth a few centimeters from where I stood. A drum major with an enormous head surrounded by tiny arms, he brandished his cane in a strange flip of the wrist. Thousands of drums and fifes resonated from the four corners of the city, behind the parade lanterns flaming with radiant colors. Emerging from everywhere, they floated over the crowd of phantom figures, the "larva," who followed them.

Indeed, the maskers here were called *larvae,* from the Latin, as Madame Benedetti has taught me. Each one carried on his head a small lantern recalling the master lantern. They might have been taken for the illuminated souls of Mother Folly's henchmen, come for a few days to occupy the city. Most of the masks' faces were white, with enormous lowered eyelids— heavy, perhaps, with the sadness of several centuries.

The force of the music was such that I was pulled in to follow the slow and swaying rhythm of one of the cliques that climbed up to the front of the cathedral. From there, I could see that the parade lanterns had taken possession of the bridges over the Rhine. They, too, were marching to the rhythm of their brightly lit escorts.

What, I asked, were the lanterns saying with their startling acrylic designs? The one that accompanied me had a baby, some lollypops, a few condoms, a bishop. . . . Ah yes, I got it: that year the very Catholic bishop, whose crozier appeared on the city's coat of arms had had a baby. "The Sex Bishop." His "baby" wiggled like the infant Jesus among baby bottles and condoms on the she-devil of a parade lantern above my head.

I left my clique to follow another one and then another one. Tired from the up and down of all the alleys of the old city, drunk from the vision of these faces so much more real than our faded ones, I followed a group of larva who'd taken off their masks and stopped drumming to enter a café. Just like those big-bellied men, dressed up as enormous women, I ordered onion tart and flour soup.

Seated next to me, an old woman, dressed in a multi-colored costume made of thousands of strips of superimposed felt, whispered in my ear, with a gleam in her eye, that our food was made for farting. "And for sending the dead to the moon?" I asked. She didn't know and even if she had, in the commotion of the unmasked maskers who came and went, I wouldn't have heard a thing.

When the grey dawn broke, I went back to the hotel to a soft sleep, a sleep rocked by the stifled sound of the music. In isolated groups, some of the maskers continued to wander across the city—resolutely, not in any hurry.

Monday morning the stores were open and I stocked up on cheese. Fife and drum players were mixed in with everybody else in the most natural way possible. There wasn't an inch of space that didn't at one moment or the other include some larva, a lone fifer, or a fifer with a drummer—or a fifer and drummer with others, in formation behind their giant drum major. In daylight, the larva confirmed my impression of the night before: they were undoubtedly more real than reality. Living portraits of our souls whose characteristics they emphasized, they poured out of every crossroads, from the slightest recesses, like the subjects we don't dare to be, that we've banished from ourselves.

Around one o'clock, I finally went to honor the tomb of Erasmus, and then had lunch in the facing café, Zum Isaac, while waiting for the afternoon parade. I was eating dessert when a drum roll of fantastic virtuosity made me get up and rush to the window.

Two apocalyptic demons strutted back and forth in front of the Cathedral. Frightful, determined, they drummed as though it were the end of the world. I paid my bill hastily in order to see them close up. Both of them were dressed in leaves. They had the heads of fishes—emotionless, implacable. I understood right away that they were "wild men," and followed them as if I'd known them forever.

They advanced in the middle of the street, sometimes together, sometimes marching to alternate rhythms, changing cadence seemingly without checking with each other, and never repeating the same thing. They were as if possessed with a sacred rage, only mastered by the rhythms exploding outwards from an inexhaustible source. We were already at the ramparts of the old town. They stopped in front of a porch-way and on its threshold drummed one last time. Then they took off their masks and disappeared from sight.

I had had the time to see there was a young man and another one, a little older. Aristaeus? Schrödinger? The *dervé*? His father? I said good-bye to them in my thoughts and hastened to turn back towards the city center from where I could hear the high-pitched voices of the fifes and the pulse of the drums. The parade should have begun by now.

Deer-men were parading in serried formation, followed by witches with string hair and wooden faces, their fingers in their enormous nostrils. Then the two-faced masks of the Folk, on backwards, were lugging a washing machine to wash the dirty money that Switzerland had accumulated. They were followed by very sexy mad cows, and by lewd nuns, wriggling to a frenzied tempo, quite excited by the misdeeds of their bishop. Other religious figures, more contemplative, staring wide-eyed, brandished condoms in the form of miters.

From the top of their floats, the *Waggis* showered me with confetti. Those pseudo-Alsatian farmers, with enormous heads, red hair, blue smocks, white scarves, phallic noses, and buckteeth, distributed satirical couplets in the local dialect on narrow pieces of paper. I soon had quite a collection of multicolored sheets, with most verses written in decasyllables—just like *The Ship of Fools* by Erasmus's friend Sebastian Brandt, a poem which Dürer had illustrated right there in Basel.

Already 4:00 in the afternoon! It was time to be reasonable and leave these wonders if I wanted to get to Paris by early evening. Reluctantly, headed toward the highway, my car forged a path among the crowd, against the current and against my will.

Passing the train station at Montbéliard, I thought about René Thom, whose mathematical curves strangely resembled the shape of the railroad switches that had fascinated him when he was a child, there in his birthplace.

The shoulders of the highway rose up as I approached the Jura Mountains. On the slope of the mountain, there was a group of beehives, snug for the winter with their store of sealing propolis. Soon the bees would attempt their first excursion out of the hives. And I would call—the next day—the apiary at the Luxembourg Garden.

All of a sudden, from the top of a bridge over the highway, a familiar

figure made me slow down. Braking almost to a stop and at the risk of provoking an accident, I recognized without the shadow of a doubt Brother
Philibert, quite alive, waving his dove at the travelers, as he'd always done
since the dawn of time. Maybe he'd escaped from the retirement home? I
greeted him with a hoot of my horn.

Bibliography

Note: The translator has used parts of the translation of La Boétie (*Anti-dictator*) and Wittgenstein (*Philosophical Investigations*) cited in the bibliography. However, most translations of cited texts and intertextual references are her own.

Adam de la Halle. *Le jeu de la feuillée.* 1276. Reprint, Paris: Flammarion, 1989.

Arras, Jean d'. *Mélusine.* 1392. Reprint, Paris: Stock, 1991.

Artaud, Antonin. *Selected Writings.* Edited by Susan Sontag. Translated by Helen Weaver. Berkeley: University of California Press, 1988.

———. *Le théâtre et son double.* Paris: Gallimard, 1964.

Aubailly, Jean-Claude. *Le monologue, le dialogue et la sottie: Essai sur quelques genres dramatiques de la fin du Moyen Age et du début du XVIème siècle.* Paris: Librairie Honoré Champion, 1976.

    Among the sotties referenced:

    "De la Dame Ecouillée"

    "Fabliau du Berangier au long cul"

    "Farce nouvelle de Mestier, Marchandise, Pou d'acquest, le Temps-qui-court et Grosse Despense"

    "Farce nouvelle de Tout, Rien Chacun"

    "La morale de Tout le Monde"

    "La moralité de Chascun, Plusieurs, le Temps-qui-court, le Monde" "La sottie de Science et d'Asnerie"

    "La sottie des sots nouveaux"

    "La sottie des Sots qui remettent en point Bon Temps"

    "Le rêve du moine"

    "Le souhait réprimé"

    "Les vigiles de Triboulet"

Bazin, René. *Balthus le Lorrain.* Paris: Calmann Lévy, 1926.

Benedetti, Gaetano. *Alienazione e personazione nella psicoterapia della malattia mentale.* Torino: Gulio Einaudi, 1980.

Brant, Sebastian. *The Ship of Fools.* 1494. Reprint, New York: Dover, 1994.

Changeux, Jean-Pierre. *L'homme neuronal.* Paris: Fayard, 1983.

Delmas, Luc. *Visage d'une terre Lorraine occupée: Le Jarnisy, 1914–1918.* Conflans-Jarny: Centre d'études historiques, 1988.

Descartes, René. *Discourse de la méthode/Discourse on the Method: A Bilingual Edition*. 1637. Translated by George Heffernan. Reprint, Saint Paul: Notre Dame University Press, 1994.

———. *Méditations métaphysiques*. 1641. Reprint, Paris: Presses Universitaires de France, 1956.

———. *Meditations on First Philosophy/Meditationes de prima philosophia: A Bilingual Edition*. 1641. Translated by George Heffernan. Reprint, Saint Paul: Notre Dame University Press, 1990.

———. "Olympiques." *Œuvres philosophiques*. Edited by Ferdinand Alquié. Paris: Garnier, 1963–67.

Dodds, E. R. *The Greeks and the Irrational*. Berkeley: University of California Press, 1951.

Drury, Maurice O'Connor. *The Danger of Words*. London: Routledge & Kegan Paul, 1973.

———. *Recollections of Wittgenstein*. Oxford: Oxford University Press, 1984.

Eliot, T. S. "Dante." 1932. In *Selected Essays*, 199–237. Reprint, New York: Harcourt, Brace, 1950.

———. *Old Possum's Book of Practical Cats*. 1939. Reprint, London: Faber and Faber, 1986.

Erasmus, Desiderius. *Praise of Folly*. 1509. Edited by A.H.T. Levi. Translated by Betty Radice. Reprint, New York: Penguin Classics, 1994.

Fenton, William N. *The False Faces of the Iroquois*. Norman: University of Oklahoma Press, 1986.

Foucault, Michel. *Madness and Civilization: A History of Insanity in the Age of Reason*. Translated by Richard Howard. New York: Random House, 1965.

Freud, Sigmund. "Delusions and Dreams in Jensen's 'Gradiva.'" 1907. Vol. 9. In *The Standard Edition of the Complete Psychological Works of Sigmund Freud*, 7–93. Edited by James Strachey. London: Hogarth Press and the Institute of Psychoanalysis, 1964.

———. *The Interpretation of Dreams*. 1900. Vols. 4 and 5. In *The Standard Edition of the Complete Psychological Works of Sigmund Freud*, 1–628 . Edited by James Strachey. London: Hogarth Press and the Institute of Psychoanalysis, 1964.

———. *Moses and Monotheism*. 1939. Vol. 23. In *The Standard Edition of the Complete Psychological Works of Sigmund Freud*, 1–137. Edited by James Strachey. London: Hogarth Press and the Institute of Psychoanalysis, 1964.

———. "The Uncanny." 1919. Vol. 12. In *The Standard Edition of the Complete Psychological Works of Sigmund Freud*, 217–52. Edited by James Strachey. London: Hogarth Press and the Institute of Psychoanalysis, 1964.

Fritz, Jean-Marie. *Le Discours du fou au Moyen Âge, XII–XIII siècles: Etude comparée des discours littéraire, médical, juridique et théologique de la folie*. Paris: Presses Universitaires de France, 1992.

La Boétie, Etienne de. *Anti-dictator: Discourse on Voluntary Servitude*. 1548. Translated by Harry Kurz. Reprint, New York: Columbia University Press, 1942.

Lacan, Jacques. *Autres écrits*. Paris: Seuil, 2001.

———. *Ecrits: A Selection*. Translated by Alan Sheridan. New York: W. W. Norton, 1977.

———. *Ecrits I*. 1966. Reprint, Paris: Seuil, 1998.

Lacaze, André. *Le tunnel*. Paris: Julliard, 1978.

Lavik, Nils Johan, et al. *Pain and Survival: Human Rights Violations and Mental Health*. Oslo: Scandinavian University Press, 1994.

Le Goff, Jacques. *The Birth of Purgatory*. Translated by Arthur Goldhammer. Aldershot: Scholar Press, 1990.

Lévi-Strauss, Claude. *The Jealous Potter*. Translated by Bénédicte Chorier. Chicago: University of Chicago Press, 1996.

Lin-Tsi. *Les entretiens de Lin-Tsi*. Translated by Pierre Demiéville. Paris: Fayard, 1972.

Mauss, Marcel. *The Gift: The Form and Reason for Exchange in Archaic Societies*. 1925. Translated by W. D. Halls. Reprint, New York: W. W. Norton, 2000.

Mohatt, Gerald, and Joseph Eagle Elk. *The Price of a Gift: A Lakota Healer's Story*. Lincoln: University of Nebraska Press, 2000.

Monk, Ray. *Ludwig Wittgenstein: The Duty of Genius*. New York: Penguin, 1991.

Moore, Walter. *Schrödinger: Life and Thought*. Cambridge: Cambridge University Press, 1992.

Plato. *Phaedrus*. Translated by Alexander Nehamas and Paul Woodruff. New York: Hackett, 1995.

Rabelais, François. *Gargantua et Pantagruel*. Paris: Editions G. Crès et Cie, 1922.

Ridington, Robin. "Telling Secrets: Stories of the Vision Quest." *Canadian Journal of Native Studies* 2 (1982): 213–19.

Rouget, Gilbert. *Music and Trance: A Theory of the Relations between Music and Possession*. Chicago: University of Chicago Press, 1985.

Rutebeuf. "Le dit de l'herberie." In *Œuvres complètes de Rutebeuf*, 51–62. Paris: Paul Daffis, 1874.

Schmitt, Jean-Claude. *La raison des gestes dans l'Occident médiéval*. Paris: Gallimard, 1990.

———. *Les revenants: Les vivants et les morts dans la société médiévale*. Paris: Gallimard, 1994.

———. *Le Saint Lévrier, Guinefort guérisseur d'enfants depuis le XIII siècle*. Paris: Flammarion, 1979.

Schrödinger, Erwin. *Mind and Matter: The Tarner Lectures Delivered at Trinity College, Cambridge, in October 1956*. Cambridge: Cambridge University Press, 1958.

———. *Nature and the Greeks and Science and Humanism*. Cambridge: Cambridge University Press, 1996.

Schur, Max. *Freud: Living and Dying*. Madison: International Universities Press, 1972.

Searles, Harold. *Collected Papers on Schizophrenia and Related Subjects*. Madison: International Universities Press, 1965.

Sullivan, Harry Stack. *Schizophrenia as a Human Process*. New York: W. W. Norton, 1974.

Thom, René. *Paraboles et catastrophes: Entretiens sur les mathématiques, la science et la philosophie*. Paris: Flammarion, 1983.

Wang, Hao. *Reflections on Kurt Gödel*. Cambridge: MIT Press, 1987.

Winnicott, Donald. *Playing and Reality*. New York: Penguin, 1971.

Wittgenstein, Ludwig. "A Lecture on Ethics." *Philosophical Review* 74, no. 1 (1965): 3–12.

———. "Notes for Lectures on Private Experience and Sense Data." *Philosophical Review* 77, no. 3 (1968): 275–320. doi: 10.2307/2183568.

———. *Philosophical Investigations*, 3rd ed. 1953. Translated by G.E.M. Anscombe, P.M.S. Hacker, and J. Schulte. London: Basil Blackwell, 2001.

———. *Remarks on Frazer's Golden Bough/Bemerkungen über Frazers Golden Bough*. Edited by Rush Rhees. Translated by A. C. Miles. Retford: Brynmill Press, 1987.

Zumthor, Paul. *Le masque et la lumière. La poétique des grands rhétoriqueurs*. Paris: Seuil, 1978.

Cultural Memory in the Present

Stéphane Mosès, *The Angel of History: Rosenzweig, Benjamin, Scholem*

Pierre Hadot, *The Present Alone Is Our Happiness: Conversations with Jeannie Carlier and Arnold I. Davidson*

Alexandre Lefebvre, *The Image of the Law: Deleuze, Bergson, Spinoza*

Samira Haj, *Reconfiguring Islamic Tradition: Reform, Rationality, and Modernity*

Diane Perpich, *The Ethics of Emmanuel Levinas*

Marcel Detienne, *Comparing the Incomparable*

François Delaporte, *Anatomy of the Passions*

René Girard, *Mimesis and Theory: Essays on Literature and Criticism, 1959-2005*

Richard Baxstrom, *Houses in Motion: The Experience of Place and the Problem of Belief in Urban Malaysia*

Jennifer L. Culbert, *Dead Certainty: The Death Penalty and the Problem of Judgment*

Samantha Frost, *Lessons from a Materialist Thinker: Hobbesian Reflections on Ethics and Politics*

Regina Mara Schwartz, *Sacramental Poetics at the Dawn of Secularism: When God Left the World*

Gil Anidjar, *Semites: Race, Religion, Literature*

Ranjana Khanna, *Algeria Cuts: Women and Representation, 1830 to the Present*

Esther Peeren, *Intersubjectivities and Popular Culture: Bakhtin and Beyond*

Eyal Peretz, *Becoming Visionary: Brian De Palma's Cinematic Education of the Senses*

Diana Sorensen, *A Turbulent Decade Remembered: Scenes from the Latin American Sixties*

Hubert Damisch, *A Childhood Memory by Piero della Francesca*

José van Dijck, *Mediated Memories in the Digital Age*

Dana Hollander, *Exemplarity and Chosenness: Rosenzweig and Derrida on the Nation of Philosophy*

Asja Szafraniec, *Beckett, Derrida, and the Event of Literature*

Sara Guyer, *Romanticism After Auschwitz*

Alison Ross, *The Aesthetic Paths of Philosophy: Presentation in Kant, Heidegger, Lacoue-Labarthe, and Nancy*

Gerhard Richter, *Thought-Images: Frankfurt School Writers' Reflections from Damaged Life*

Bella Brodzki, *Can These Bones Live? Translation, Survival, and Cultural Memory*

Rodolphe Gasché, *The Honor of Thinking: Critique, Theory, Philosophy*

Brigitte Peucker, *The Material Image: Art and the Real in Film*

Jacques Derrida and Catherine Malabou, *Counterpath: Traveling with Jacques Derrida*

Martin Seel, *Aesthetics of Appearing*

Nanette Salomon, *Shifting Priorities: Gender and Genre in Seventeenth-Century Dutch Painting*

Jacob Taubes, *The Political Theology of Paul*

Jean-Luc Marion, *The Crossing of the Visible*

Eric Michaud, *The Cult of Art in Nazi Germany*

Anne Freadman, *The Machinery of Talk: Charles Peirce and the Sign Hypothesis*

Stanley Cavell, *Emerson's Transcendental Etudes*

Stuart McLean, *The Event and Its Terrors: Ireland, Famine, Modernity*

Beate Rössler, ed., *Privacies: Philosophical Evaluations*

Bernard Faure, *Double Exposure: Cutting Across Buddhist and Western Discourses*

Alessia Ricciardi, *The Ends of Mourning: Psychoanalysis, Literature, Film*

Alain Badiou, *Saint Paul: The Foundation of Universalism*

Gil Anidjar, *The Jew, the Arab: A History of the Enemy*

Jonathan Culler and Kevin Lamb, eds., *Just Being Difficult? Academic Writing in the Public Arena*

Jean-Luc Nancy, *A Finite Thinking*, edited by Simon Sparks

Theodor W. Adorno, *Can One Live after Auschwitz? A Philosophical Reader*, edited by Rolf Tiedemann

Patricia Pisters, *The Matrix of Visual Culture: Working with Deleuze in Film Theory*

Andreas Huyssen, *Present Pasts: Urban Palimpsests and the Politics of Memory*

Talal Asad, *Formations of the Secular: Christianity, Islam, Modernity*

Dorothea von Mücke, *The Rise of the Fantastic Tale*

Marc Redfield, *The Politics of Aesthetics: Nationalism, Gender, Romanticism*

Emmanuel Levinas, *On Escape*

Dan Zahavi, *Husserl's Phenomenology*

Rodolphe Gasché, *The Idea of Form: Rethinking Kant's Aesthetics*

Michael Naas, *Taking on the Tradition: Jacques Derrida and the Legacies of Deconstruction*

Herlinde Pauer-Studer, ed., *Constructions of Practical Reason: Interviews on Moral and Political Philosophy*

Jean-Luc Marion, *Being Given That: Toward a Phenomenology of Givenness*

Theodor W. Adorno and Max Horkheimer, *Dialectic of Enlightenment*

Ian Balfour, *The Rhetoric of Romantic Prophecy*

Martin Stokhof, *World and Life as One: Ethics and Ontology in Wittgenstein's Early Thought*

Gianni Vattimo, *Nietzsche: An Introduction*

Jacques Derrida, *Negotiations: Interventions and Interviews, 1971-1998*, ed. Elizabeth Rottenberg

Brett Levinson, *The Ends of Literature: The Latin American "Boom" in the Neoliberal Marketplace*

Timothy J. Reiss, *Against Autonomy: Cultural Instruments, Mutualities, and the Fictive Imagination*

Hent de Vries and Samuel Weber, eds., *Religion and Media*

Niklas Luhmann, *Theories of Distinction: Re-Describing the Descriptions of Modernity*, ed. and introd. William Rasch

Johannes Fabian, *Anthropology with an Attitude: Critical Essays*

Michel Henry, *I Am the Truth: Toward a Philosophy of Christianity*

Gil Anidjar, *"Our Place in Al-Andalus": Kabbalah, Philosophy, Literature in Arab-Jewish Letters*

Hélène Cixous and Jacques Derrida, *Veils*

F. R. Ankersmit, *Historical Representation*

F. R. Ankersmit, *Political Representation*

Elissa Marder, *Dead Time: Temporal Disorders in the Wake of Modernity (Baudelaire and Flaubert)*

Reinhart Koselleck, *The Practice of Conceptual History: Timing History, Spacing Concepts*

Niklas Luhmann, *The Reality of the Mass Media*

Hubert Damisch, *A Theory of /Cloud/: Toward a History of Painting*

Jean-Luc Nancy, *The Speculative Remark: (One of Hegel's bon mots)*

Jean-François Lyotard, *Soundproof Room: Malraux's Anti-Aesthetics*

Jan Patočka, *Plato and Europe*

Hubert Damisch, *Skyline: The Narcissistic City*

Isabel Hoving, *In Praise of New Travelers: Reading Caribbean Migrant Women Writers*

Richard Rand, ed., *Futures: Of Jacques Derrida*

William Rasch, *Niklas Luhmann's Modernity: The Paradoxes of Differentiation*

Jacques Derrida and Anne Dufourmantelle, *Of Hospitality*

Jean-François Lyotard, *The Confession of Augustine*

Kaja Silverman, *World Spectators*

Samuel Weber, *Institution and Interpretation: Expanded Edition*

Jeffrey S. Librett, *The Rhetoric of Cultural Dialogue: Jews and Germans in the Epoch of Emancipation*

Ulrich Baer, *Remnants of Song: Trauma and the Experience of Modernity in Charles Baudelaire and Paul Celan*

Samuel C. Wheeler III, *Deconstruction as Analytic Philosophy*

David S. Ferris, *Silent Urns: Romanticism, Hellenism, Modernity*

Rodolphe Gasché, *Of Minimal Things: Studies on the Notion of Relation*

Sarah Winter, *Freud and the Institution of Psychoanalytic Knowledge*

Samuel Weber, *The Legend of Freud: Expanded Edition*

Aris Fioretos, ed., *The Solid Letter: Readings of Friedrich Hölderlin*

J. Hillis Miller / Manuel Asensi, *Black Holes / J. Hillis Miller; or, Boustrophedonic Reading*

Miryam Sas, *Fault Lines: Cultural Memory and Japanese Surrealism*

Peter Schwenger, *Fantasm and Fiction: On Textual Envisioning*

Didier Maleuvre, *Museum Memories: History, Technology, Art*

Jacques Derrida, *Monolingualism of the Other; or, The Prosthesis of Origin*

Andrew Baruch Wachtel, *Making a Nation, Breaking a Nation: Literature and Cultural Politics in Yugoslavia*

Niklas Luhmann, *Love as Passion: The Codification of Intimacy*

Mieke Bal, ed., *The Practice of Cultural Analysis: Exposing Interdisciplinary Interpretation*

Jacques Derrida and Gianni Vattimo, eds., *Religion*